St. Mother Cabrini

Philippians 4:6,13

"Have no anxiety at all, but in everything,
by prayer and petition, with thanksgiving,
make your requests known to God.

I have the strength for everything
through Him who empowers me."

Dedications

To St. Frances Xavier Cabrini and The Missionary Sisters of the Sacred Heart of Jesus.

SAINT FRANCES XAVIER CABRINI

Photo Courtesy of The Missionary Sisters of the Sacred Heart of Jesus
and the St. Frances Cabrini Collection, Holy Spirit Library,
Cabrini University, Radnor, PA 19087

Contents

Acknowledgements

To my beautiful wife and best friend for all her support, love, and dedication to our family. I could not have done this without her being my reliable mentor and soundboard throughout this process.

Thanks to my faithful sister for all her prayers, spiritual example, and support which is never ending.

To my mom who has always been my spiritual leader and who has dedicated a lifetime of prayer for our family's wellbeing.

In special memory of my late dad. He set a positive example for our family to follow through his hard work and simple, polite, and humble personality.

To My late grandpa and grandma for their generosity and Christian example and for teaching me how to pray.

My late uncle Bill who served the poor most of his life as a Brother for The Missionaries of Charity Sisters, St. Mother Teresa's ministry.

My son Noah for setting the example for me to reach out beyond my comfort zone by his creativity and hard work ethic to pursue his goals and dreams and most importantly, for his passion to help others realize their dreams.

My brother for always keeping me up to date on things that matter, especially those concerning my faith.

Our Lady for saving me and helping me stay on the straight and narrow path towards her Son.

Special thanks to:

The Mother Cabrini Shrine and all the staff, especially Sister Alice Zanon, MSC, JoAnn Seaman, Tommy Francis, John McEncroe, Fr. John Lager, OFM Cap, and Brother Jude Emmanuel Quinto, OFM Cap, for their help making this possible and providing a beautiful place for a spiritual retreat.

The Missionary Sisters of the Sacred Heart of Jesus, their Communications Director, and the St. Frances Cabrini Collection, Holy Spirit Library, Cabrini University, Radnor, PA 19087.

All the priests and deacons who have provided spiritual support — Monsignor Jim, my confessor and friend. Father Kevin and Father John for their enlightening homilies. Father Rob for his ongoing spiritual direction and support. Father Michael Gaitley, for helping to lead me to Jesus through Mary through his book, *33 Days to Morning Glory,* and the time spent with him and two of his seminarians hiking in the San Juan Mountains in prayer for those in need. Father Donald Calloway (who I named, "The Captain") for teaching me about Saint Joseph through his book, *Consecration to St. Joseph,* and for being there for me in time of need providing humorous messages when I needed to laugh. . . . Father Svets from Medjugorje whose calm words of encouragement to get out into nature and "Let God lead you," was life changing.

All Scripture (unless noted otherwise) was quoted from the *New American Bible*: http://www.usccb.org/bible/books-of-the-bible/index.cfm.

Note — St. Mother Cabrini is available in eBook format and in three print editions: black and white, standard color, and premium color. All pictures in the book can be viewed on the website gallery tab which is password protected (found in book). https://stmothercabrini.com/

Introduction

Mother Cabrini's good works and presence continue to this day. My family has been firsthand witnesses to her fruits. She has helped us out through her presence and intercession, especially with our difficulties, on so many occasions.

On August 31, 2023, early morning around 6 a.m., I was lying in bed awake not feeling well, praying to God our Father, when suddenly I heard an interior voice loud and clear:

"I want you to write a book about Mother Cabrini."

At first I was shocked, not expecting that. I never planned to write a book about Mother Cabrini even though she has been such a wonderful saint for me personally and our family. I have spent many hours up at the Mother Cabrini Shrine in Golden, Colorado where she has blessed me with healings, spiritual renewal, and especially amazing wonders of God's beautiful creation. Not being able to return over four years at the time of this writing, I have missed this Shrine and Mother Cabrini's presence terribly. . . .

Nevertheless, I did not want to write a book again, especially since I was suffering from a long-term illness that had mostly brought my life to a standstill. In my mind and heart, I replied back to God, "I feel too terrible to write a book, but I will do my best." The inner voice was so clear I knew for sure it was from our Lord so I had to obey Him, but how was the question?

I have already published two books so I know how hard and exhausting it can become. Authoring a book is not for the faint of heart even in the best of health. I got up from bed and started to research the Internet intently, which only made my condition worse.

In October of 2021, I started to experience heavy neck and head tension along with whole body weakness. After my doctor finally prescribed a heavy metal blood test per my request, I found out I was flagged high with double-digit mercury and arsenic. This was in addition to a lessor condition I was experiencing making matters even worse. Come to find out I had been eating too much wild caught cod from Alaska.

Unfortunately, one of the symptoms from mercury exposure, at least for me, is intense head pressure and body fatigue at times and using my computer, cell phone, or other electronic device only intensifies it. I have read where the electronic magnetic field (EMF) can potentially mobilize the mercury trapped in my brain exacerbating the effects along with my bad posture aggregating an already severe condition. Regardless, working on the computer writing a book for many hours has proved to be very challenging. There have been times when my prayer for the day was, "Lord Jesus, please let me live long enough to finish this book." But if this was from God, and I believe it was, I had to obey Him, no matter the consequences. I consider this an honor and thank our Lord for the opportunity to serve Him and all of you.

I wasn't given specifics on how to write this story so I decided to include Mother Cabrini's life foremost, and how me and my family have been touched by her grace. I began by researching long and hard, as much as I could tolerate and then some. Within the first couple of days, I had already amassed a large volume of information that made me realize how little I knew about her amazing life. Some of the material online was contradictory so I knew I had to get ahold of more reliable books written about her. I was blessed to get help from various people that are part of Mother Cabrini's thriving ministry and organization. I found that some of the best books written about her, in the early to mid-1900s, are no longer in print.

I did not think I could do this on my own so I reached out to family members and even on Facebook to ask if anyone would be willing to help. Most everyone was too busy, but I didn't give up hope and kept reminding myself that **if God wills it, He will find a way. . . .**

A kind lady from Iceland volunteered to help who is not Catholic but is a wonderful prayer warrior and has a special devotion to the Virgin Mary and other saints. She offered ongoing special prayers to help this book reach people all over the world to come closer to Jesus. A faithful Catholic and good friend from England also offered to pray for this project. Another woman from my hometown of Durango, Colorado offered to help if needed. Many others from around the world offered their prayers. I really appreciate all their kindness and have felt the good fruits of their prayers on many occasions. As far as the main workload, no matter how hard I have tried to delegate some of this out, God has entrusted this to me and has provided the strength to do this. There are days in which I cannot believe how much I was able to accomplish, even with my condition. I can feel His power working within me. Apart from the formatting, I am doing almost everything including most of the editing, front and back cover design, website, book trailer, and other promotions. It has been a bit overwhelming and apologize for the mistakes that will be found no matter how hard I try to purge them.

Who Was Mother Cabrini?

Saint Frances Xavier Cabrini – Beloved Missionary Sister of the Sacred Heart of Jesus who just happened to be a remarkable teacher, humanitarian, caregiver, nurse, healer, mystic, prophetess, miracle worker, businesswoman, administrator, entrepreneur, writer, orator, explorer, traveler, frontierswoman, naturalist, gold prospector, storyteller, communicator, adventurer, dreamer, mentor, friend, companion, and confidant among many other attributes.

Mother Cabrini was a Catholic missionary first with the evangelization of souls her main priority. What set Mother Cabrini apart was her obedience and steadfast faith to the Sacred Heart of Jesus.

She believed with all her heart and soul that Jesus was with her in all things, especially in her sufferings, which were many. She completely surrendered herself to God's Divine will. Mother Cabrini gave everything she had to serve Jesus to help bring others closer to Him and she thoroughly enjoyed doing it.

On her way to Panama departing from New Orleans – May 1895, Mother Cabrini expressed these words:

> . . . What have we to fear if the most Sacred Heart protects us? And what may we not hope for, if we confide in the Heart of such a compassionate and powerful Father? Let us fix our gaze on the Wound of the Sacred Heart of Jesus. We shall read in characters of blood the height and depth of the love that He bears us, and we shall always feel, wherever we are, comforted in hoping for everything from His infinite goodness. Very often our prayers are imperfect and deserve to be rejected by God; but the loving Heart of Jesus sanctifies them. He Himself asks for us that which He sees will be for our greater good, and compassionately covers our unworthiness with His merits.[3]

Mother Cabrini also had a passion for God's beautiful creation in nature and often expressed how it surrounds and sustains us in all our needs. As a professional landscape photographer and lover of the outdoors and nature, and especially our shared Catholic faith, this is where Mother Cabrini and I really connect. Through her intercession she helped extend my time up in the high alpine photographing God's beautiful creation. Many pictures posted on my website, under the most recent photos menu tab, were possible in part due to her healing intercession for me while at her Shrine. I am forever grateful.[4]

https://patrickdillonphoto.com/

Genoa to New York – September 1894 she wrote:

> We have entered the Gulf Stream where everyone says the sea is very rough, but up to now we have enjoyed wonderfully fine weather. Everyone is astonished. So, we have reason to praise and thank God for His goodness in commanding the elements to adapt themselves to our comfort and convenience.

Love the good God, for the sky, earth and sea tell us to love Him! The immense ocean, set with wonderful gems, clearly reveals the ineffable solicitude (with graces and blessings) with which our loving Creator surrounds us. We look at the sea, the earth with its inexhaustible fecundity, the firmament with its stars, and the whole Universe reflects God's attributes. His power. His wisdom and goodness, and we cannot but exclaim with admiration, "How wonderful is God in His works! . . ." [5]

The front cover picture is a painting of Mount of the Holy Cross and is a perfect example of Mother Cabrini's reliance and love of God's creation. She owned a portion of this beautiful mountain located in the beautiful Rocky Mountains of Colorado. She established three mining claims there and used this property as her place of healing. Spending time in her small cabin at the base of this mountain, with its fresh air and beautiful landscapes, she restored her deteriorating health on several occasions.

In fact, when she was searching for properties for her ministry, beautiful views and peaceful settings were her utmost priority and God blessed her with many such properties throughout the world.

Mother Cabrini is needed just as much now or even more than when she was still on Earth. Our problems today have intensified with an unprecedented moral crisis at hand. We are under a spiritual attack like never before, our families, our marriages, our youth, the unborn, the elderly, and the very core of our Catholic Christian doctrine and faith. Learning about Mother Cabrini's life and reading her spiritual journals can really help us get through these trying times. Her words are full of hope, wisdom, and joy even in times of suffering and sorrow. I know she has really helped me and my family, and it is my heartfelt prayer that this book will help you and yours as well.

Mother Cabrini offered up her body as a living sacrifice so others might have some joy in this sometimes-cruel world. Her battered shoes tell her story better than any words can.

With that in mind, let us begin this incredible journey of faith, courage, perseverance, and love serving our Lord and His people throughout the deepest reaches of our world.

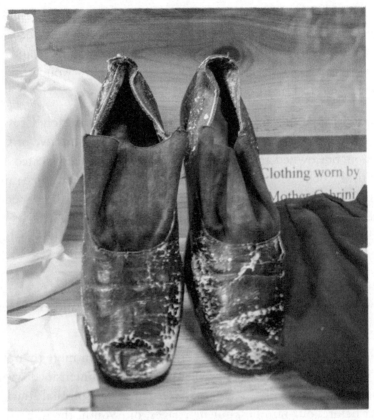

Mother Cabrini's Shoes –
Courtesy of the Mother Cabrini Museum, Golden, Colorado

Chapter 1

Mother Cabrini Shrine – The Storm

With great anticipation as we began our climb up the 373 steps to pray the Rosary, claps of thunder could be heard off in the distance with dark ominous clouds. A major summer storm was looming, but it was still calm in our location.

My wife and I had traveled seven hours across the Rocky Mountains to get to the Shrine to meet and pray the Rosary with Robert, who is a longtime participant and supporter of the Shrine, and my sister. We planned to hike up to Jesus who was awaiting us at the summit and our desire to pray the Rosary powered us forward.

By the time we approached the giant statue of the Sacred Heart of Jesus, the storm had unexpectedly intensified as lightning bolts were striking off in the distance. I have a high level of respect for lightning as I was once caught in a major thunderstorm at 12,000 feet in the high alpine of the San Juan Mountains. I was hiking with my uncle and his wife with nowhere to hide. The small hail stones were pounding the back of our heads and backpacks as we hunkered down helplessly, completely at the mercy of the elements. Lightning was striking all around us hitting the ground with large chunks of tundra and other debris exploding into the air. It was a terrifying experience and one I did not want to relive again. This type of weather in Colorado during the summer months is something we have to deal with on a daily basis.

Back at the Shrine, the best thing we could do at that point was to seek shelter, hunker down, and pray. Fortunately, the lightning was still off in the distance and located at the top of Jesus's head, a lightning rod was attached to help safely ground strikes near us. The wind picked up considerably as the ominous storm clouds were now upon us with sudden bursts of rain pouring down. After a few minutes, the distant lightning and heavy rain suddenly stopped to our relief as it headed towards Denver. A light rain continued with heavy wind gusts allowing us to feel the power of God in motion.

After the lightning threat subsided, I found myself running all over taking pictures and videoing the glorious surroundings as Jesus stood tall with no need to worry about anything. I was caught up in all the action as it was intense, exciting, and beautiful out in God's creation; everything a landscape photographer loves. The others remained sheltered from the rain at one of the mysteries of the Rosary stations covered by some low hanging tree branches. I soon joined them in praying the Rosary and invited some Facebook friends to join in via live video.

As we prayed with people all over the world, the light rain stopped, and to the south, I could see a rainbow starting to form! I ran back out taking multiple pictures of this wonderful sign from God. If that wasn't enough, the sun suddenly broke out into a beam of heavenly light that bathed the Sacred Heart of Jesus and the Blessed Virgin Mary statue with a beautiful glow accentuated by the ominous dark sky in the background. It was as if Heaven itself was descending upon us showing us that no matter how terrible the storm, Jesus will always be with us when we focus on His light.

Little did I know that in the coming months our world would be put to the test like no other, including our own personal lives.

After all the action, I rejoined my prayer partners who stood steadfast, praying the Rosary through it all. I felt guilty not praying it all the way through with them but as an avid photographer and lover of God's creation, I was temporarily sidetracked capturing His creation which became my prayer, at least for the moment.

The wind calmed down and the loud claps of thunder in the distance were no more but what remained looked like something out of a scene from *The Lord of the Rings*. Dark mystical-like clouds that took on the shape of angel wings appeared in the heavens above. It was so beautiful to behold with Jesus's statue standing tall and strong as our protector through it all.

As we were standing there looking up towards the heavens, the sun broke free under the heavy dark clouds lighting up the statue of Jesus and all of us with a heavenly golden glow. God was surely with us on this special afternoon of prayer as the dark clouds turned into beautiful shades of golden reds near the western horizon.

It was all too much to process at the moment, something that would have to sink in. We started back down the long staircase giving us time to reflect . . . this experience will never be forgotten and remains ever-present in my mind.

None of this would have been possible without the strong faith of Saint Frances Xavier Cabrini who steadfastly followed the will of our Lord overcoming impossible odds to bring hope, faith, charity, kindness, and love to those suffering in the new world of the Americas and beyond.

Mother Cabrini

Mother Cabrini truly believed that everything she encountered in her life was the divine intervention of her beloved Christ, whether it was a flock of birds flying overhead, a person who came up and talked to her, the weather, a breeze, the water spraying off the ocean, rough seas, calm seas, nice people, difficult people, whatever she encountered she felt confident and inspired by our Lord.

Jesus's presence gave her unbreakable confidence, allowing her to go forward in life no matter how challenging the situation and she did this without fear knowing that God willed it. If her plan did not work

13

out, she knew God had another option because she understood that our Lord was in complete control where all things were possible through her beloved Jesus. Everything in her life was a spiritual exercise that helped bring her closer to God.

October 1895, on her journey from Panama across the Andes to Buenos Aires she writes:

> Heart of Jesus I go to fulfill my mission. Holy obedience and the blessing of the Holy Father accompany me and remove all fears. I fear nothing, repeating continually my motto, 'Omnia possum in Eo qui me confortat!'

> The wind roars, the heavens darken, the treacherous waves arise and beat against the steamer, everything turns topsy-turvy. We are threatened with a terrible tempest. All this matters nothing; I have given my trust, I must keep my word of honour, and with faith and confidence, I hope, with God's grace, to go on repeating, "Omnia possum in Eo qui me confortat!" We are Missionaries, oh, daughters, and the Missionary should never shrink from difficulties and dangers, but, rather, confiding in Jesus and resting on Mary, she will overcome all difficulties and escape dangers.[6]

The Early Days of Francesca Cabrini

So how did this Saint of God become so dedicated to our Lord that she was not afraid of anything, even death? When Francesca was a young girl, she often played along the swift waters of the Venera River Canal launching her little paper boat filled with violets, each representing her make-believe missionaries sailing off to China. Her father would often tell her stories of missionaries which young Francesca took to heart. [7]

Francesca was known to act out this dream of hers on many occasions while visiting her Uncle Don Luigi Oldini who was the local parish priest of the town of Livagra, Italy. This was close to her hometown village of Sant' Angelo. She loved to visit her uncle who was truly kind and generous often donating essentials to the poor.[8]

On one particular visit when she was around eight years old, Francesca became so carried away with her fantasy that she fell into the fast-flowing canal which quickly swept her downstream. Nearing a tunnel gasping for air with her body twisting and turning held under by the frothy undertow, the end of her life was quickly approaching, but Francesca was suddenly snatched out of the Venera River where she found herself lying on the bank. [9]

A little boy found her soaked with water lying along the river and quickly went to her uncle who ran down to her aid. Bending down looking upon her, Francesca opened her eyes and He replied, "Thank God you are all right! But who pulled you out of the water?" She replied, "I don't know, Uncle. I just found myself lying here." After a thoughtful pause he said, "Are you sure you don't know who pulled you out, Cecchina (her childhood family name)?" Francesca again said no, and her uncle exclaimed, "Then I know, it must have been your guardian angel." [10]

Her uncle then carried her to his home where his housekeeper placed her in bed where he started to gently lecture Francesca telling her to never play with her boats again. He told her, "What would your mother have said had anything happened to you while you were staying with me." "Don't tell Mother she begged. Say you won't tell Mother Uncle."[11] Her uncle was hesitant to grant her request and told her he did not think he could keep this from her mother. Francesca was more concerned about her sister and told him not to tell Rose because she was always getting on her for her fantasy trips about missionary work. Her uncle understood why she made this request and granted it.[12]

After nearly drowning, Francesca developed a great fear of water, yet she ended up steaming across the Atlantic Ocean 23 times along with many other adventures, but once again, she did not let her fear control her but rather, she relied completely on her beloved Jesus to overcome her fears.

On July 15, 1850, Francesca Cabrini was born and because she was the last of thirteen children, Francesca's mother relied on her sister Rose to help raise her which she did in the strictest manner.[13]

Francesca was born two months prematurely with her mother being 52 years of age. Little Francesca was not expected to live very long due to her frail body. Despite her shortcomings she was considered a special child. On the day of her birth a flock of white doves flew down upon their farm while her father was outside threshing grain. Naturally, he tried to scare them away with his fleshing tool but they kept returning with one getting entangled in his blade. Her father, Agostino Cabrini, brought the unhurt dove indoors to show the children. They all wanted to keep it but he said, "No, no, let it join the others."[14]

He carried the frightened dove to an open window where it flew off to freedom. Many people, including their family, took this as a sign from God of just how special Francesca really was.

Both her parents were devout Catholic Christians who offered up many hours of prayer at the crack of dawn and before going to bed. This event was surely an answer to their prayers that little Francesca, despite being so early in the pregnancy, would be all right.[15]

Francesca's father would have certainly been worried about the safety of his wife as well, especially considering her advanced age, and would have been in deep prayer for her as well.

Young Francesca was very small and sickly growing up, but her frail condition didn't stop her from living her life to the fullest, even at an early age.

She was confirmed July 1, 1857, before she made her first Holy Communion which was one of the great experiences of her childhood and a turning point in her life. Francesca was quoted later in life as saying, "The moment I was being anointed with the sacred chrism I felt I shall never be able to express... I seem no longer on earth. My heart was replete with the most pure joy. I cannot say what I felt, but I know it was the Holy Ghost."[16]

Una futura santa

Chi avrebbe pensato, vedendo la fotografia di questa fanciulla che essa, un giorno, sarebbe diventata santa? La foto, fatta verso il 1860, ritrae Francesca Saverio Cabrini.

Francesca Cabrini petting her dog at an early age.

Courtesy of The Missionary Sisters of the Sacred Heart of Jesus and the St. Frances Cabrini Collection, Holy Spirit Library, Cabrini University, Radnor, PA 19087

Heavenly Protection

Francesca had special protection from heaven as one day while off praying by herself as she often would, this time near a pile of wood, it fell down the moment she left it. Another time when she went to the church, she found the door open for her when it was usually locked. On another occasion during an earthquake, which shook the village, panicked neighbors ran to the house to save her, but we're shocked to see her in a corner calmly saying her prayers.[17]

Because of her delicate health, she was often left out of special celebrations and fiestas, but she did not feel sorry for herself; rather, she showed self-control far above her years. Her first spiritual director was Don Melchisedecco Abrami, the parish curator who used to call Francesca his "little child" [18] due to her frail body. At the age of eleven he allowed her to take a private vow of chastity but through his wisdom, just for one year. At the age of 19 she was able to make her vow permanent. Many years later he wrote that he always considered Francesca to be a saint.[19]

Francesca Cabrini at the age of 13 was sent to a private school conducted by the Daughters of the Sacred Heart at nearby Arluno. She remained there for five years taking the courses that would lead to her teacher certificate. In 1868 she returned home and made no effort to obtain a teaching position but rather, returned to her regular duties in her family and fervent prayer life. Her dream to become a missionary remained strong in her heart.[20]

Death of Her Parents

At the age of fifteen Francesca confided to her second spiritual advisor, Don Pisano Dede, her small problems. After deep thought the pastor of the parish would wisely say, "Go and tell that to Jesus."[21]

This helped Francesca to learn at an early age to always trust in the divine promptings and providence of God which would greatly help her later in life where it would be impossible to have regular spiritual direction due to all her travels.

This all changed abruptly after her dad, Agostino, had a stroke which caused him to suffer for about a year. Before he died, he told his wife that they would soon be reunited in heaven. Less than a year's time his wife, Stella, suddenly became ill before Mass and died later that evening. At this time, only four out of 13 children remained with one girl who was severely crippled.[22]

Francesca, her sister Rose, and her brother, Giovanna Baptista were now responsible for taking care of the family farm.[23]

Prior to her parents passing away Francesca's older sister Rose, was overly harsh with her at times often ridiculing her for her dream to become a missionary as she took on the role of educating Francesca and helping her mother out with many other duties. As a child, Francesca's hair was beautiful with natural curls and for whatever reason, her sister Rose did everything she could to crush her vanity. To try and eliminate Francesca's curls, Rose would use a stiff bristle brush and press down hard enough to bring young Francesca to tears. "There, that's better. I'm not going to have you looking like a silly simpering doll." [24]

On another occasion, Francesca opened her heart to Rose and told her, "One day I'm going to be a missionary." Rose replied, "You a missionary! One so small and ignorant as you a missionary!"[25]

This wasn't the first time Rose had ridiculed her over her dreams. Despite the severe harshness of her sister's words and actions, this only strengthened Francesca's resolve to become a missionary. Anyone else may have been crushed by these disheartening words but they proved to only strengthen her like a grindstone sharpening the edge of a sword. Francesca was known to speak highly of her sister Rose regardless. After the death of their parents, Rose became gentler and more compassionate towards Francesca. When their mother was still alive, she would often temper Rose telling her to not be so harsh which would work for a time. After her mom's death, Rose was on her own with no one to help guide her, so she took on the responsibility herself to become more gentle and kind because of it.[26]

Smallpox Epidemic and Teaching

Not long after, in their newfound role without parents, the smallpox epidemic came upon them. Francesca became ill nursing those infected by it. She was comfortable being around those with this type of illness; the smells of the open sores didn't bother her. She showed great works of charity and sacrifice for those she cared for. Although Francesca ended up catching it herself, her sister Rose lovingly nursed her back to complete health with such devotion and care that Francesca had no pockmark scars disfiguring her beautiful appearance.[27]

This reminded me of the story of St. Kateri Tekakwitha who had the same outcome of not showing any pockmark scars after recovering from smallpox.

When Francesca was at the initial stages of recovery from smallpox, local priest, Don Bassono Dede, asked Francesca if she would be willing to be a substitute teacher for a couple weeks for a teacher who became ill at a public school in Vidardo, about a mile and a half away. He explained to her that the teacher might lose her job if she would not take on this role making it hard for Francesca to decline his offer.[28]

She accepted and found her role as the newfound teacher difficult, as Francesca felt shy and lacked experience. At first, she fashioned her teaching skills after her sister Rose being sterner but was later criticized for this. She ended up taking on this role for two years.

It was here at her first teaching job that she learned how to manage the classroom with all its challenges, joys, and difficulties. Being over a mile away from the classroom each day, her walks to and from school provided her the opportunity to witness God's beautiful creation as she walked down the narrow tree shaded road with beautiful green fields and even snow on a winter day. She was often found kneeling under a tree, praying to her beloved Jesus.

The town of Vidardo where she taught had a mayor named Carlo Zanardi whom Francesca was able to soften up in his antagonistic views where he granted her to teach Christian doctrine, and even allowed her to have special devotions to Mary during the month of May.[29]

Towards the end of her tenure teaching, the parish priest of Vidardo, Monsignor Antonio Serrati, became her long lasting spiritual director. He was a very loyal priest but would often let his self-interest dictate his spiritual guidance for Francesca. About that time, Francesca let him know that she wanted to reapply at the Daughters of the Sacred Heart where she had been rejected once before. The Monsignor had another plan for her. Behind Francesca's back, he privately told the superior at the Daughters of the Sacred Heart that Francesca's health was too compromised, so the superior declined her request. She then went to the Canossian Sisters located at Crema because they had a mission in China. They too denied her because Monsignor once again recommended against her.[30]

House of Providence

Francesca soon found out his motives, as the Monsignor would soon be transferred to Codogno where he would be elevated in dignity and stature. Monsignor Serrati finally divulged his ulterior motive to Francesca where he asked her to run a very troubled orphanage called the House of Providence. At first Francesca wanted nothing to do with it. At the time there were three women who wore a simple black gown without a nun's veil, and they took their vows, but they did not live like nuns.[31]

Francesca told Monsignor there was no part in missionary work there which was her life's dream and desire. But the monsignor was persistent and finally won her over. She agreed to work there for two weeks while on summer break from teaching school. During those two weeks she became attached to the girls in the orphanage who were in much need of her help. Francesca did not return to teaching as it was the difficulties she found at this orphanage that kept her there instead. She found herself in one of the most challenging environments she had ever been in. She was under the authority of Sister Antonio who resented her presence. She felt intimidated by Francesca as she could see that Francesca had a natural gift relating to the orphan girls and the ability to help manage the situation. Sister Antonia would often criticize her, yell out insults towards her, and remind her who the boss was. Regardless of her trials working at the orphanage, her planned two weeks turned into six years.[32]

It was there that Francesca was put to the test, a spiritual exercise, a difficult situation, where she learned how to be tolerant with even those who despised her, in an environment where she only had a simple black habit with no authority. She had not taken her vows the first three years, technically a novice. Yet, she would often gather the girls she worked with in spiritual conferences telling them that one day they would all become missionaries.

Francesca's work at this orphanage was the training ground for her future life as a saint in the missionary field. Monsignor Serrati was not aware of all the tension between Francesca and Sister Antonia as Francesca never complained to him; but the Monsignor was fully aware that Sister Antonia was difficult. In fact, on the eve of Francesca taking her vows, he was quoted as saying:

> Tomorrow, Francesca, you are going to take your vows. You know that woman is insane. Yet you were about to promise her obedience. What will you do if she orders you to throw yourself down the well?" Francesca replied, "She is my superior and I will obey her.[33]

"Mother Cabrini"

But the monsignor would have nothing to do with this scenario and directly after Francesca had taken her vows, he announced to her that she would now become the new head superior. It was with tears in her eyes that she obeyed him as difficult as it was. Sister Antonia was so distraught that she even resorted to violence and some of the other sisters had to stand around now, "Mother Cabrini," to protect her. Because of her great suffering, Mother Cabrini found herself weeping when alone in her room away from the others. Mother Cabrini was later quoted with the following:

> I wept a great deal, and a missionary must never weep. Not to complain when I had to suffer and to bear it all with patience and fortitude would have been a virtue... But at that time I did not understand the value of the Cross and of suffering. [34]

Because of her great difficulty, Mother Cabrini had to reach deep into her faith where she had a long devotion to the Sacred Heart of Jesus. It was there her devotion deepened and became the foundation of her spirituality. It was there that she would be able to have complete confidence in God, trusting Him in all things, no matter the difficulty at hand. It was also during this time that Mother Cabrini began her in-depth spiritual exercises during retreats at the House of Providence.

St. Francis Xavier

In 1877 at the age of 27, Francesca Cabrini took her profession of religious vows along with her companions where she added "Xavier" to her name in honor of St. Francis Xavier, whom she admired for his missionary work in China and other areas of Asia.[35]

https://www.mothercabrini.org/who-we-are/our-history/the-founding-of-the-institute/

October 22, 1878 – House of Providence in Codogno – Mother Cabrini's spiritual retreat journal notes:

> The soul will never find rest if it is not intimately united with Jesus because, no matter how good and dear a person is, he or she it's always fragile and prone to fall. Therefore, this person must not be surprised if some good-intentioned person approves of her today, but tomorrow contradicts her. We creatures can be like breezes – blowing here and there. Only Jesus Christ will never go back on His word – therefore we must put all our trust Him alone, fear Him alone, and love Him alone.
>
> **The earth is not our place of rest – our dwelling place will be in heaven.** Therefore, we must regard all the things of earth in the same way a passing pilgrim does. No fleeting thing should capture our hearts, because it would be adulterating the sweet bond which unites us with our loving Jesus, the only being worth our aspirations. . . .[36]

. . . Even in things that are good, it is not advisable to be either overly troubled or overcome with melancholy when they do not turn out well, beautiful and holy according to our way of thinking. From the moment that we were created, we deserve nothing so we cannot expect anything. Therefore, in all things, whether holy, sweet or bitter, we must always bless God with all our whole hearts and repeat: **"Lord, it is good when you permit things to happen that will help us to exercise the virtues that you are asking of us."**[37]

The remaining three years as superior of this orphanage were even more difficult than before. Sister Antonia became even more troublesome even after the Bishop of Lodi tried to talk her into retiring with a nice pension. In the end, the Church excommunicated Sister Antonia after she filed civil action against the Bishop.[38] Under legal proceedings against him, the Bishop was compelled to dissolve the House of Providence at the end of 1880. This must have been another heavy cross for Mother Cabrini and her seven sisters running the now dissolved orphanage.[39]

Bishop Gelmimi of Lodi did not forget about Mother Cabrini. He told her, "I know that you want to be a missionary. I know of no ministry order of women. Why not found one yourself?"[40] Mother Cabrini became silent in utter surprise! At last, her lifetime dream had come. She was overflowing with gratitude and thanksgiving to God. Mother Cabrini simply replied, "I will look for a house."[41]

Monsignor Serrati remained loyal to Mother Cabrini by helping her establish their own motherhouse, a mostly abandoned friary in the town of Codogno. It needed repairs, but it was a well-built structure that would suit Mother Cabrini's needs.[42]

The Missionary Salesians of the Sacred Heart

With help primarily from the local Bishop and Monsignor Serrati, and a lot of demanding work on their part, and by the grace of God through the Sacred Heart of Jesus, the Missionary Salesians of the Sacred Heart was born on November 14, 1880. It was not until October 10, 1899, in America that their name was finally changed to the Missionary Sisters of the Sacred Heart.[43]

Mother Cabrini's Life Onward – "*. . . With God all Things are Possible.*"

Wow, a lot was going on in Mother Cabrini's early life. It's time to take a breather for a moment to reflect on how God was continuously leading her towards her ministry, sometimes in the most indirect manner. Yes, it is true that she was persistent, a diligent worker, a good negotiator, and had a gift working around other people, but it was her devotion and love of the Sacred Heart of Jesus, through her many hours of dedicated prayer, which made all of this possible. Mother Cabrini was the first to admit this truth, but this was just the beginning. She would go on to accomplish so much more, and again, not through her strength and wisdom, but through her beloved Lord's.

Mother Cabrini didn't waste any time basking in her accomplishments; rather, she got right to work with her sisters in their humble beginnings with hardly enough cutlery for all of them to eat their dinner, but they had God, and their beloved Jesus, and the blessed virgin Mary, and all the saints working on their behalf, and this is what strengthen them, and they were fully aware of it.

The following Holy Scriptures became the foundation of her ministry and life's work:

"Jesus looked at them and said, "For human beings this is impossible, but with God all things are possible." (Matthew 19:26).

"I have the strength for everything through him who empowers me." (Philippians 4:13)

Because of this supernatural power and grace instilled upon her from above, she quickly garnered an exceptional reputation that reached all the way to the Vatican. Mother Cabrini was highly recommended by the Bishop which gave her the opportunity to go directly to the Pope with the request to begin missionary work in China which was her lifelong dream; however, God uses our ambitions and dreams sometimes in ways beyond our understanding, not in the way we had intended it.

First Audience with Pope Leo XIII

When Bishop Scalabrini of Piacenza first suggested she work with the poor Italian immigrants of New York, Mother Cabrini replied, "But New York is too small a place for me." Monsignor replied, "Well, what about the United States, Mother Cabrini? You ought to find it large enough." She smiled, "No, Monsignor. **For me the whole world is too small.**"[44]

Mother Cabrini was getting pressured from all sides before her first meeting with Pope Leo XIII. She soon obtained an audience with the aging pontiff where she humbly shared the projects, plans, and aspirations of her missionary ministry. Pope Leo listened intently and was very kind to her. However, not once did Mother Cabrini mention her dilemma with New York.[45]

Shortly thereafter, Mother Cabrini had a dream where she was shown an immense stretch of land as a voice declared to her, "Look, all this land is entrusted to you; you must cultivate it and look after it with great care so that it may produce good and abundant fruits."[46]

Only Two Years to Live

When Mother Cabrini started to seriously consider going to New York after her dream, she consulted her doctor who said she only had about two years to live. This made those around her wonder if it was realistic for her to go. Pressured by some of her sisters, Mother Cabrini went back to her doctor to get his opinion on whether she was well enough to travel. He replied, ". . . If you stay in Italy you will die of a broken heart. Your ailments can't be cured except by God. Go to America – then perhaps you'll get better."[47]

Second Audience with Pope Leo XIII

After Mother Cabrini had another opportunity to have an audience with the Pope, she fully opened her heart to him describing her dilemma with New York. Again, the Pope listened intently, and after she finished expressing herself, kneeling before the Pope, looking up at his face, he gently said, **"Not to the East, my daughter, but to the West."** [48]

To be more precise with his statement to her, the Pope went on to say, "The institute is still young and needs financial resources. Go to the United States where you will find them, and with them, proceed to a large field of labor."[49]

This now freed Mother Cabrini's heart to fully commit to New York. This was not the answer she was looking for as she admitted it was troubling to her at first, but she surrendered to the will of God and was obedient to the Pope who was inspired by the Holy Spirit to lead and direct her ministry. She could have easily found excuses due to her compromised health, and fear of water, but she used her weaknesses to reveal and utilize God's strength within her.

Mother Cabrini's journal written at an unknown time:

> In all my trials in life, I should strive to the best of my ability to maintain a strong confidence and trust in the Sacred Heart of Jesus. The person with true faith will never be overcome. Loss of trust in God dishonors him, since it implies he has failed us, which is impossible. It is always we who fail Him by placing obstacles to the work of grace. From now on, I will counteract mistrust with humble confidence in Him. **The more I acknowledge my weakness, the greater will be His power to help me.**[50]

First Voyage to New York

On March 20, 1889, Mother Cabrini and her seven sisters departed from Milan, France on the French Bourgogne steamer which on this particular voyage held 1500 emigrants traveling in third class, and according to accounts, resembled a stable.

Mother Cabrini and her sisters were traveling in second class where they could look down below on the ship's lower level and see the third-class emigrants. In her own words:

> From the bridge near where we were accommodated we could look down on the third class passengers. What a misery! The poor emigrants were lying stretched out on the floor, left to

their anguish, with no one there who was able to help. The doctor made his round, but could do little.[51]

From her sisters' account:

> Our Mother [Cabrini] . . . immediately interested herself in the poor emigrants. . . . Every day she visited the poor Italians in third class, whose accommodations resembled a stable. She never went there with empty hands, but always tried to bring something that might be needed."[52]

Mother Cabrini and her sisters arrived at New York harbor on March 31, 1889. From Sister Umilia's thoughts from the journal, Capietti, "Memorie di S. Madre:"

> Finally, after 12 days of sickness and tribulation, we saw the beautiful Statue of Liberty at about 4 o'clock. Oh, how happy Mother Cabrini was. I could read the joy on her face. She called us together to sing the Ave Maria Stella.[53]

New York Harbor 1889 – Courtesy, Library of Congress

Archbishop Corrigan Challenges

Her first major challenge in New York presented itself immediately after she arrived and was told by Archbishop Corrigan of New York, that they had no place for her to live and set up her convent after being assured prior to her departure from Italy that everything was taken care of. The Archbishop told her she would have to come back at a later time when better accommodations could be arranged. What a heartbreaking thing to do to Mother Cabrini and her sisters who just gave up everything they had and travelled thousands of miles on a steamship to get there. What a waste of precious time, sacrifice, and effort to just pick up and return home.

Nevertheless, Mother Cabrini persisted in deep prayer and perseverance respectively challenging the archbishop offering him viable options to make this work. After a great deal of persuasive effort, she was finally able to convince him to immediately begin her ministry despite the challenges, hardships, and unknowns that lay ahead.[54]

Mother Cabrini and her sisters began their ministry in some of the most dangerous, inhospitable locations in New York City to help primarily the Italian immigrants. They were grossly mistreated and needed food, clothing, housing, and education, all of which she provided for them. Her primary focus was evangelizing them back to their Catholic faith. Mother Cabrini was a hands-on type of leader but was willing to delegate her responsibilities and authority to others which greatly contributed to the success of her ministry. She put all her trust in the Sacred Heart of Jesus to provide for all their needs, and provide He did and more.

Because of her small stature and compromised health, many thought they could take advantage of her. They were gravely mistaken because she had the full power of our Lord Jesus and the Holy Spirit working on her behalf enabling her to do business or whatever else was needed with the shrewdest businesspeople, local government officials, or Catholic clergy. She was quickly able to establish hospitals, dispensaries, schools, and orphanages throughout the area with little funds, but somehow, was always able to come up with the financing at the dismay of those who told her it would never happen.

Columbus Hospital, New York

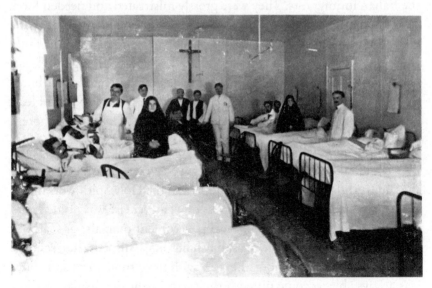

Columbus Hospital – New York with Mother Cabrini and Staff

Mother Cabrini and the Missionary Sisters of the Sacred Heart of Jesus, 1890

Above Pictures Courtesy of The Missionary Sisters of the Sacred Heart
of Jesus and the St. Frances Cabrini Collection, Holy Spirit Library,
Cabrini University, Radnor, PA 19087

Miracle Property Above the Hudson

Mother Cabrini ended up becoming good friends with Archbishop
Corrigan who gained respect for her as she proved herself with the Lord's
help capable of accomplishing difficult tasks by filling the need to help
the Italian immigrants in their time of need. The Archbishop would
often meet with Mother Cabrini and show her the ins and outs of dealing
with life in New York. On one such occasion while outside at Peekskill,
overlooking the Hudson River valley, he pointed out a beautiful piece of
property in the countryside across the river and said, "Now there Mother,
this is where you should establish yourself." Mother Cabrini replied, "May
it please God that Your Excellency prove to be a prophet."[55]

Archbishop Corrigan informed Mother Cabrini that the Jesuits were moving from their Monastery to their Catskill's location on the other side of the Hudson River. He encouraged her to build an orphanage there as it was being offered at an extremely low price and would make a suitable place out in the safety and fresh air of the countryside, away from the problems of New York City life. There was no mention that there was little water on the property thus the cheaper price. Manresa was the name of this lovely property which included two larger houses and a smaller one with farmland and orchards bordered by the Hudson River below.[56] Before all this came about, Mother Cabrini had a dream about such a property which only heightened her resolve to purchase it despite its lack of water. [57]

A few months after she arrived in New York after setting up her ministry now well underway, Mother Cabrini left New York on July 20, 1889, back to Italy.[58] Mother Cabrini and seven sisters returned to New York on April 18, 1890 with this beautiful property along the Hudson still in her heart and mind.[59] Upon her arrival, she wasted little time to go take a closer look at the estate the Jesuits had for sale. These beautiful grounds had the potential to house three hundred orphan girls and removing them out of the slums of New York to this location would be heaven.[60]

She was determined to purchase this property despite the lack of water and placed her trust in Jesus to make up for any deficit. Mother Cabrini ended up purchasing the property and asked our Lady of Graces to intercede on her behalf in finding more water. Her prayers were answered once again as she found a natural spring that provided enough water for all their needs. Prior to this the sisters had to walk down the steep banks to the Hudson River to do laundry and retrieve adequate water supplies for their needs. Her gift to find water in dry areas had only begun. The Jesuits had reservations about selling their property to Mother Cabrini so cheap once they heard abundant water was found.[61]

Main Building, Sacred Heart Academy, Dobbs Ferry, New York

Hudson River Property, Dobbs Ferry

Pictures above courtesy of The Missionary Sisters of the Sacred Heart of Jesus
and the St. Frances Cabrini Collection, Holy Spirit Library, Cabrini University,
Radnor, PA 19087

It was not enough for Mother Cabrini to just take on the challenging task of New York City. She began to spread her ministry to various other areas of the East Coast including Chicago and Philadelphia, and south to New Orleans. She then traveled West, including Denver, Colorado, Los Angeles, California, and Seattle, Washington. Her ministry expanded into Central and South America where she spent countless hours sailing on steamships to distant lands such as Costa Rica, Nicaragua, Panama, Argentina, and various other regions in that area. And this was a person who was once afraid of the water after nearly drowning as a little girl – such a beautiful testimony overcoming her fears, showing that with God all things truly are possible. . . .

Mother Cabrini, 1880 – Courtesy of the Missionary Sisters of the Sacred Heart of Jesus and the St. Frances Cabrini Collection, Holy Spirit Library, Cabrini University, Radnor, PA 19087

Chapter 2

Mother Cabrini's Journey to Colorado

Mother Cabrini Shrine – "The Storm" Continued

While walking down the stairs from the Sacred Heart of Jesus statue, the storm had calmed down significantly. Why did God show us these signs today? What was the purpose? Was He trying to tell us something or was this just another amazing event that had no extra meaning or revelation other than His incredible power and beauty through His creation? Walking down the hundreds of steps gave me time to reflect on what had occurred. I kept thinking this was a sign from God, showing us that turbulent times were ahead.

Little did I know how true this would play out in the following months. In fact, I had no idea what was coming. I often thought of some worldwide event taking place, which most certainly came about with the advent of COVID-19, but I did not consider that my personal life regarding my health would be radically shaken like never before.

I tried not to get caught up in all the gloom and doom but rather, focus on the most important thing – no matter what happens, God is always with us to help us through the storm, just as He was on this day, protecting us, allowing us to enjoy His beautiful creation through nature.

The next day I went back to Mother Cabrini's Shrine as a volunteer to pray and get some more pictures for their social media projects, but this time, the weather was gentler with the perfect clouds for a spectacular golden sunset completely opposite from the day before. We really felt God's healing light.

After taking in the beautiful sunset, we headed down the steps and entered Mother Cabrini's altar to pray. It is so peaceful in there with all the beautiful candles and artwork featuring our Lady, Jesus, angels, and of course Mother Cabrini.

Me praying at Mother Cabrini's Altar

Mother Cabrini's Gift

This wonderful experience at the Mother Cabrini Shrine in Golden, Colorado would not have been possible if not for the strong faith and hard work of Mother Cabrini and her sisters. This beautiful Shrine location provided shelter and well-being for hundreds of orphan children back in the early 1900s up until 1967, and continues to provide a spiritual refuge in the midst of a world gone astray, a holy place, a sacred place, where millions of people from the Front Range of Colorado and around the world can come to seek spiritual renewal, to come closer to the Sacred Heart of Jesus – what a beautiful gift Mother Cabrini has given to all of us!

So how did all of this come about? How did Mother Cabrini from a small town in Italy end up purchasing a beautiful area such as this? It all comes down to her trust, obedience, and faith in our Lord Jesus, showing us that anything is possible if we surrender ourselves to our Lord's holy will.

But for Mother Cabrini, it was just the beginning as she often said the world was too small for her. She travelled to Central and South America in some of the most remote areas of the region. She personally made the voyage to all these places despite her frail health because she understood it was Jesus who commissioned her work and who promised to give her the strength to accomplish it. Mother Cabrini knew full well she wasn't relying on her own strength but rather, through the strength of Jesus, through His most Sacred Heart, where even the impossible became possible. . . .

My focus will be Mother Cabrini's time in Colorado dealing with her orphanages, schools, and retreat centers along with her ministry to the miners in the Colorado Rocky Mountains. I have a special emphasis on her beautiful Shrine located in the foothills of Golden, Colorado which she purchased for the young orphan girls to have a place to go in the summer for retreat, to get away from the city and be out in nature. It was at this Shrine that my family came to know Mother Cabrini and where she has helped us so beautifully in our times of hardship and joy. We have a special place in our hearts for St. Frances Xavier Cabrini and feel honored to be able to share our experiences with all of you.

Mother Cabrini's Denver, Colorado Ministry

After establishing her schools, orphanages, and hospitals in New York and other Eastern US cities, Mother Cabrini had already sent some of her sisters out West. She sent them to establish orphanages, schools, and Catholic evangelization ministries to meet the daily living and spiritual needs of the Italian immigrants who lived throughout these areas with a special emphasis in Colorado, Washington State, and California.

In Denver, Colorado, Father Mariano Lepore, the pastor of the Italian Mt. Carmel Parish in Denver was in need of a school so he invited Mother Cabrini to establish one near his parish. In 1902, the sisters eagerly began their work with 200 children showing up the first day. This was accomplished by the approval of Bishop Nicholas Chrysostom Matz who informed Mother Cabrini that many Catholic Immigrants, ". . . have not received the sacraments for many years. They are exhausted from their labors and live far from a Church, where Holy Mass is rarely celebrated."[62]

https://www.neh.gov/article/mother-cabrini-first-american-saint-catholic-church

Their mission was named Mount Carmel and was established in Mr. Notari's house on Palmer Street. This also served as the sisters' residence and location for the first school of Mount Carmel Parish.[63]

Mt Carmel School, Denver, Colorado

Courtesy of The Missionary Sisters of the Sacred Heart of Jesus and the St. Frances Cabrini Collection, Holy Spirit Library, Cabrini University, Radnor, PA 19087.

Mother Cabrini's personal training of the sisters prepared them for this important endeavor as her disciples going out to proclaim the good news of our Lord Jesus helping those in need.

In great anticipation of her sisters, Mother Cabrini arrived in Denver in 1902. She quickly sized up the situation at hand and quickly went to work emphasizing the main purpose of their mission, "Try to have the interest of Jesus at heart and make an effort to see that Jesus is known and loved. . . ."[64]

Mother Cabrini was also working diligently at this time to establish her mission in Seattle, Washington despite the bouts of ill health she was experiencing at the time. In all her missions, Mother Cabrini's first priority was the spiritual wellbeing of the Italian immigrants. She instructed her sisters to go out and evangelize them, particularly those living in the outlying areas who had abandoned their Catholic faith.

In Denver, Mother Cabrini and her sisters focused on the younger children to receive their first Holy Communion, and those in their twenties, basic religious education.[65]

Mother Cabrini's letter to her students from her travels journal, Denver, Colorado, November 18, 1902.

> . . . On our arrival in this city, the Sisters found a vast field of labour. Though our work extends to every class, without regard to nationality, nevertheless the number of Italians is very great, and this renders our Mission all the more necessary. A School is needed for our children, in order to prevent them from going to the public schools, where they do not receive religious instruction, this being given only in the parochial schools. Apart from the children, the adults think only of gaining their living, and forget all about their souls. There are to be found here young people, up to thirty years of age, who have not made their First Communion yet. There are marriages which have not been blessed by the priest, children not baptized. In the mountains, hundreds of workmen are to be found oppressed by work, living far from the church, where Mass is seldom celebrated, who have not approached the Sacraments for many years; but they are in such good dispositions that they only need encouragement, and if we go to them with Christ's charity, which is all to all, they will, as good sheep, return to God and listen with docility to the voice that calls. . . .
>
> . . . To begin our work, we opened a School at once, to which two hundred children came the very first day. Yesterday we had the pleasure of having it blessed by our worthy Bishop of Denver. He is a man after God's own Heart,

full of charity, zeal and sacrifice, for the good of the sheep entrusted to his care.

. . . It was lovely yesterday morning to see them arrive from all parts, notwithstanding the snow, on which, like a beautiful white mantle, the sun's rays sparkled and covered the earth. They were dressed in white, and they took their places in the centre of the old church, which is now converted into a schoolhouse. The two side aisles were crowded with their parents. . . . [66]

Anti-Catholic Sentiment

During the early 1900s in Denver, there were still stints of the Wild West with violence present making the sisters' work very dangerous and stressful at times.

Just as it occurred on the East Coast, there was a high degree of anti-Catholic sentiment in Denver which opposed the influence of Catholic institutions, especially the schools which contributed to the amazing growth of the Catholic Church in the US. Although the anti-Catholic leaders despised this influence, they could do little to stop it due to the great need for education. The Catholic Church was best equipped to provide this need especially the good works of Mother Cabrini and her sisters.[67]

Despite the hardships, Mother Cabrini and her sisters placed all their trust in the Sacred Heart of Jesus and boldly carried on with their mission. This was true in Denver where the sisters' work became quite dangerous after Mother Cabrini departed for a time.

Not only was there anti-Catholic sentiment to deal with, but there were also factions in the Italian community who disliked certain members of the Catholic Church. On November 18, 1903, Father Lepore, who was the pastor at Mount Carmel Parish, was brutally shot and killed by an Italian radical of the Potenza faction who hated Father. This assassin was also mortally wounded by his own gun during his struggle with Father Lepore. Father forgave him before he died but the assassin hardened his heart even further upon his death.[68]

This of course caused further tension in their community and made the sisters' job extremely difficult during her absence. On February 17, 1904, a mob of Italian immigrants opposing the Potenza faction came out armed with clubs and other weapons in protest, but the sisters, despite the danger, continued with their school classes as the police did their best to keep order outside. The sisters informed Mother Cabrini of their danger and she personally intervened and arrived back in Denver on March 17th which gave them a great sense of relief. Mother Cabrini was able to negotiate a solution to the problem, at least temporarily, and order was restored.[69]

A Bullet on a Train

Mother Cabrini was no stranger to danger. During this time on a train trip out of Denver, on her way to New Orleans after passing Dallas, Texas, a band of rebels started shooting at the train with one of the bullets nearly hitting her. Mother Cabrini wrote in a 1904 letter, "Didn't I write and tell you that I am alive miraculously?" She noted that one bullet "aimed at my head fell to my side, while it should have pierced my cranium." According to the account, Mother Cabrini remained calm while her traveling companion was terrified. After the attack, the train crew couldn't believe Mother Cabrini was not shot. They rushed in to check her condition and surprisingly found her to be unharmed. They asked out loud, "Who was watching over her?" Mother Cabrini told them, "It was the Sacred Heart to whom I had entrusted the journey... they did not understand."[70]

https://cabrinishrinenyc.org/a-bullet-on-a-train/

Queen of Heaven Purchase

As Mother Cabrini left Denver again the sisters began taking care of Italian orphan girls as their numbers were increasing from the dangers of mining and other hazardous activities. When she returned in 1905, Mother Cabrini found the need to expand her ministry to better care for the growing number of orphans. She searched diligently via horseback and buggy all along the Front Range of Denver looking for the perfect site to set up her orphanage. After hours of hard travel, she ended up finding a property at the base of a lake well outside the confines of the City of Denver at the foot of the Rocky Mountains.[71]

When she told Bishop Matz the location she had chosen he thought she was being foolish and said, "No you mustn't go there, Mother. You will be completely isolated. Get nearer the centre." Mother Cabrini shook her head and said, "I have been studying the map Your Excellency. I know the very place for me." Mother Cabrini went on to tell the Bishop, "There I have a large orchard and vegetable gardens. These will help me feed my children. And in the country air they will have a healthy home." The Bishop replied, "But who will look after the orchard and farm? Mother Cabrini immediately replied, "Why our Sisters will look after them. They are nearly all young women from the country and know about such things." With a smile, the Bishop gave his approval. A brief time later the City of Denver had grown into this once outlying area which further justified Mother Cabrini's decision.[72]

Mother Cabrini was inspired by God and His ways are not always our way. This outlying property had an old farmhouse surrounded by many fruit trees which ended up becoming a source of income for Mother Cabrini and her sisters to help support their orphanage. It was named the Villa Regina Coeli, which was soon referred to as the Queen of Heaven Orphanage.[73] The original Queen of Heaven building was rebuilt in 1921 with a much larger structure. The orphanage stayed open until 1967.[74]

https://www.historycolorado.org/media/10733

Some of the Orphans at "Regina Coeli Villa," Denver, Colorado.

Original Queen of Heaven Orphanage Prior to 1921

Courtesy of The Missionary Sisters of the Sacred Heart of Jesus and the St. Frances Cabrini Collection, Holy Spirit Library, Cabrini University, Radnor, PA 19087

Mother Cabrini's sisters were so happy to have this new property to expand their ministry and remarked: "How Good our Mother is, always zealous, lively, happy. Oh, that the good Lord will preserve her for a long time."[75]

Below are Mother Cabrini's own words from her travels journal describing in part the Queen of Heaven orphanage, the surrounding landscapes and mountains of Colorado, and her take on immigration policy in a letter to her sisters as she was leaving from Denver to California:

> . . . How many times have I thought myself almost at the end of my present Mission in the United States, when I have found new work to do, work that I could not have neglected without neglecting the holy interests of the glory of God and the salvation of souls. But now I am in a position to assure you that in a few weeks I shall be with you to rejoice in your virtues, in your progress and in your loving company.
>
> I wrote to you from the summit of the Rocky Mountains, promising to tell you something of my journey to California,

and I do not think you would be disposed to forgive me if I forgot my promise. Hence I steal a little time, at one moment from my Religious and at another from business to converse with you.

I think I wrote to you of my work in Denver for the enlargement of the Orphanage we have in that city for the daughters of our emigrants. It will be enough for you to know that, with the help of the Sacred Heart, always ready to favour us, I have been able to acquire a beautiful property at the foot of the Rocky Mountains, standing upon a pleasant hill which descends with a gentle slope to the banks of the Rocky Mountains Lake. The house, to which a wing is being added, because space is already limited on account of the thirty orphans which are gathered there this first year, is surrounded by trees laden with fruit and enhanced by the proximity of the clear waters of the lake. To the west extends the imposing Rocky Chain with its summits covered with snow; to the east is the beautiful city of Denver. To the south and north are great plains, three-fourths of which include the territory of Colorado.

Meanwhile, seated in a comfortable carriage of the Santa Fe railway, which was taking me to Los Angeles, my glance swept across those immense plains which, around Denver, are dotted with the cottages of our Italian agriculturists, and which, further on, are uninhabited, there being immense tracts still of virgin soil. My thoughts flew to our emigrants, who, in such great numbers, land every year on the Atlantic shores, overcrowding still more the already populous city of the east, where they meet with great difficulties and little gain. In the west there is still room for millions and millions and its most fertile soil would offer occupation more congenial to the Italian emigrants, as well as a field in which to develop their activities and their agrarian knowledge, and to crown their efforts and labours with copious results.

This stream of population must have its course intelligently directed. I know that the Emigration Department is occupying itself with this problem, which is so important for the welfare of our emigrants in the United States. The solution, however, presents great difficulty, not only because of the four thousand miles which separate the Atlantic from the Pacific, but more especially because it is difficult to find good-hearted persons who will occupy themselves with the work and will not speculate in the sacred interests of the poor.[76]

Miracle at Toll Gate Creek

During her fundraising efforts, Mother Cabrini travelled extensively across the Front Range of Colorado looking for donors to help support her growing ministries. She was able to meet many people of various social backgrounds from the super wealthy to the poorest of the poor. Below is one such encounter with a wonderful miracle attached to it.

Mother Cabrini went to many local ranches in her fundraising efforts and ended up at a ranch owned by Irish immigrants who recalled their encounter with her:

> I'd like to share an important story that Betty told me of when Mary (Mamie) was a little girl, and religious sisters/nuns came to their ranch and the neighboring ranches to beg for food and donations for "The Queen of Heaven Orphanage in Denver." Their grandma said, "Mamie, go with the sisters and show them the easiest way to get to the Kennedy's Ranch." As they were traveling in the buggy and were crossing the dry ditch of Toll Gate Creek, Mother Cabrini put her arms around Mamie so she wouldn't bounce out of the buggy. Mamie told Mother Cabrini that they all wished that Toll Gate would become a "live water" (one that is fed by an underground spring), as it only ran good in wet weather. Mother Cabrini said that she would pray for it to become a "live water." Soon after Mother Cabrini's visit, a true miracle happened, as Toll Gate Creek became "live water" and has been ever since. The family was always grateful to Mother Cabrini for this miracle.[77]

https://denvercatholic.org/letter-the-ol-gully-ranch-homestead-mother-cabrini-and-the-miracle-at-toll-gate-creek/

Another Shooting

In 1908, approximately 5 years after the killing of Father Lepore, another priest, Father Leo Heinrich, a non-Italian Franciscan, was shot and killed by an anticlerical Italian. This killing caused more division than the first shooting which affected the sisters' ability to raise funds for their orphanage that primarily cared for Italian children.[78]

Not only did they suffer with this discriminatory burden but later, Denver had an outbreak of scarlet fever and the orphanage for a time was quarantined due to diphtheria. Regardless of the good hygiene conditions kept by the sisters, they still had outbreaks of various other diseases such as pneumonia, typhoid, and meningitis. Despite these hardships, Mother Cabrini and her sisters overcame these difficult obstacles relying on the Sacred Heart of Jesus to carry them through.[79]

Mother Cabrini's work in Denver was focused mainly on the Italian immigrant but she also helped other Catholics and people of different faiths including the non-religious from different nationalities.

Here is a story that really shows the intuition given to her by the Holy Spirit. During this time, a man named Mr. Young approached Mother Cabrini with his daughter Leslie. He wondered if the sisters would accept his daughter and offered to pay them if necessary. The man explained to Mother Cabrini that he was twice married where his daughter Leslie did not have a good relationship with his new wife. Mother Cabrini, in her wisdom, agreed to accept his daughter.

However, it was soon discovered that she had a very difficult disposition and the sisters wanted to send her back home. Mother Cabrini wanted nothing to do with it and said, "Keep her. You will see; she will not only become a Catholic herself, but her father will convert as well. And I will tell you something else. One of these days Leslie is going to become a missionary sister." Mother Cabrini's words all proved to be true.[80]

Chapter 3

Mother Cabrini's Ministry to the Italian Miners

Taking care of the orphanage was not their only responsibility, as they also ran a school and spent a lot of time and effort ministering Catholic teaching, especially to the Italian miners, who worked long hours deep underground in dangerous conditions.

Deep in The Mine

Mother Cabrini and her sisters did not wait for the miners to come out of the ground and come to them; instead, they traveled directly to these mines scattered throughout the Colorado Rocky Mountains. They would go down mine shafts in caged hoists, hundreds of feet deep below the earth, in exceedingly difficult conditions, to meet the miners where they were working, ministering to them, bringing them food, and teaching them the catechism of their Catholic faith. Yes, the sisters risked their lives to show them God's love and the miners really respected the sisters for their efforts making their ministry very effective.[81]

The sisters witnessed firsthand the extreme conditions deep underground and the toll it could take on some of the miners. Mother Cabrini learned here the need for hospitals for the body and ministry for the soul as there were very few priests around the mining camps which further distanced the immigrants from practicing their Catholic faith where many stopped completely. The real gold for Mother Cabrini and her sisters was the salvation of souls and they would travel anywhere to achieve this.

Pietro Di Donato, author of *Immigrant Saint,* so beautifully details Mother Cabrini and her sisters' ministry work to the miners deep underground:

> Men, fathers of families, stripped to the waist, sweated and begrimed, muscles of powerful arms and shoulders straining with pick and shovel against gold-flecked ore, hear the music of a woman's voice. They turn and to their amazement see before them in the shadowy tunnel a fragile, smiling nun. She holds aloft her silvery crucifix.

> "My good brothers, we come down into the bowels of the earth to you in the name of your Creator, He Who pines for your filial love."

> Nuns braved the treacherous depths to come to the men, addressing them in the sweet mother tongue and bringing them the faith of their dear Jesus, the Jesus of their childhood, the very Jesus of their ancestors and progenitors, the saddened Jesus whom, in America, they had forgotten.

> The hearts of these men expanded so that at first they could not speak. They removed their caps, humbly kissed the crucifix in Francesca's hands, knelt, and signed the cross.[82]

Mother Cabrini's letter to her students referring to their work with the miners from her travels journal, Denver, Colorado, November 18, 1902:

> . . . They are fortunate in those villages where the priest goes once a month to celebrate Holy Mass. In the meanwhile there is a spiritual famine, and you may imagine how great is the need of spiritual help. Our Sisters have begun their rounds. They have descended nine hundred feet into the mines, being lowered in a cage hardly large enough to contain them into a shaft about only one square metre wide and cut obliquely in the rock. The compressed air

introduced into the mines makes respiration possible. They have also walked at times several kilometres through narrow tunnels at the same depth, speaking a word of comfort to these poor creatures and reminding them of the eternal truths. It is not difficult to touch on the subject of hell as they walk through these dark tunnels where breathing is difficult, where the only available light is that of a few tallow candles, a pale idea, it is true, but still very expressive of the eternal darkness.

The Sisters, who are performing this Mission for the good of others, find it also advantageous to themselves, for they realise what the world does for temporal gain, and the thought of this fills them with greater zeal to work for the glory of the Sacred Heart and the diffusion of our Holy Religion. To work for the extension of the Kingdom of God on this earth, there is no necessity to go in search of veins of gold, for the smallest act sanctified by a pure intention, and in our case by Holy Obedience and performed according to the spirit of our Institute, is the purest gold, and deposited where thieves cannot steal. Oh, how fortunate are the souls who are called by God to religion! Let us love our vocation with our whole heart. . . . [83]

Mother Cabrini's Mount of the Holy Cross Claim

Mount of the Holy Cross – Thomas Moran (artist) American, born in England, 1837 - 1926. Courtesy National Gallery of Art, Washington[84]

It is true that some miners lost their lives in these harsh conditions increasing the number of orphans in the Denver area. It is also true that Mother Cabrini and her sisters did not like seeing people's lives being exploited but they were not against arduous work if it was done ethically. In fact, Mother Cabrini owned several mining claims in Colorado and New Mexico and was eager herself to make money from these claims to help support her ministry.

A wealthy widow named Julia Edith Dunn who lived in Holy Cross City, Colorado which is in the Colorado Rockies on the slopes of Mount of the Holy Cross, ended up donating half of her property to Mother Cabrini who eagerly accepted it. She at once began the process of staking her claim on Mount Holy Cross to help raise funds.[85]

Below are excerpts translated from Italian from two letters Mother Cabrini wrote in 1904 to the superior of the house of Rome, Mother Gesuina Diotti. In another letter written shortly afterwards, Mother Cabrini mentioned Mrs. Dunn as donor:

> ... Now gold has been discovered there and before opening the mine she was inspired to give half the property to the institute. ...
>
> Mother Filomena will have to learn from that woman the manner in which to procure the mines for us. It seems it would be good to have various claims near the one given us and with time we will work them. First you have to dig a hole in the ground, then ask the government for a claim. I believe it costs $10. Then after a year you can work again a little and then request a license and become proprietor of at least 500 ft. x 1500 ft.
>
> Now, however, look for the money to build, because who knows how long it will be before the mine yields anything."[86]

Mrs. Julia Edith Dunn

Mrs. Julia Edith Dunn living in the rugged mountains of Holy Cross City, Eagle County, Colorado was a remarkable woman in her own right and shared in Mother Cabrini's entrepreneurial spirit and faith in

God. The following article from the Herald Democrat does an excellent job describing this:

> Perhaps the most unusual miner to work the Holy Cross District was Mrs. Julia Edith Dunn, the daughter of an old and distinguished family from the East. Well educated and reared in luxury, Dunn excelled in music and painting. Newspaper reports suggest that a combination of health issues and a failed marriage prompted her to head west with her children. Deeply religious, she chose Holy Cross City as her destination. There she found a cabin and made enough money teaching music and painting lessons to file several mining claims. She hired a couple of miners and worked alongside them to develop the claims.
>
> Two of the claims yielded gold and silver. When Dunn overheard her hired hands plotting to steal the nuggets, she procured a pistol, guarded the ore throughout the night, and sent the men packing to Red Cliff. Dunn sold her claims for a tidy profit, then invested that money in lodes closer to Red Cliff and Leadville. One of her mines was predicted to yield a minimum profit of $500,000. In a camp dominated by rough men, she was notable.
>
> "Any mining man in the west might well be proud of what this woman has accomplished and considering the almost insurmountable difficulties she has had to overcome, the years of toil and struggle in the mountains, her achievements deserve to rank among the greatest in the state."[87]
>
> Herald Democrat, Jan. 1, 1904

https://eaglecountyhistoricalsociety.com/holy-cross-city/

Mother Ignatius Dossena, entrusted to the task of developing this mining property under Mother Cabrini's instructions, had done very little after five years' time had elapsed. When Mother Cabrini was in Colorado in September 1909, she traveled up to the Mount Holy Cross property to pray and rest. Frustrated from the lack of progress, she was determined to get the mining operation in motion. Mother Cabrini wrote, "I would hope to get enough from the mine so that I would not have to send sisters around collecting."[88]

Below, translated from Italian, is a letter from Mother Cabrini to Sr. Ignatius Dossena, July 20, 1909, Mount of the Holy Cross Mining Claims:

> . . . When you have opened a bit of the tunnel and have seen that the business is going well, then you will decide on the license to ensure everything. The names to be given: Providence, Hope, Stella Maris. Send the Money Order for the payment of the three claims. As for taking the lady's share, I will wait to decide when you give me some good news about the place, because with such an exorbitant price, you could have half the mountain. If the news you give me is favorable, I will send a telegram if necessary.

> . . . It will be good to work on those three claims immediately in order to patent them. The name is Elvira De Giovanni. I leave tomorrow morning for Chicago where I will stay two days, then I will go to New York immediately to send the money. So besides being useful, the place is also splendid, so it will truly be a vacation. I would love to see it; the floor of leaves must be splendid and strengthen the lungs. I hope you will bring me at least a pine cushion, as I have asked you.

> . . . I leave you in the Most Holy Heart of Jesus, and in spirit, I am always with you. Guard yourselves and defend yourselves from the ferocious beasts that ruin the soul, and then be assured that no beast will come to harm you. May Jesus bless and console you. Jesus will always come, and He will always accompany you; work hard, for hard work will be your health. With affection in the Most Sacred Heart, M. Francesca Saverio Cabrini.[89]

My Great Grandpa and Family Mining History

Mother Cabrini was an entrepreneur at heart, and loved the freedom and spirit that America offered, taking full advantage of it to help fund her expensive ministries throughout the US and around the world.

Mother Cabrini's help and interest in the Colorado mining era is yet another common bond my family shares with her along with our faith as Catholic Christians. My great grandfather, Billy Boyle, was heavily into gold mining, supervising some of the same gold and silver mines that Mother Cabrini and her sisters took great care and effort ministering to the miners during the early 1900s.

We do not have any records of Great Grandpa ever meeting Mother Cabrini, but he and the sisters certainly crossed paths during their journeys, most likely near Leadville, Colorado where Great Grandpa was the mine foreman for a period back in the late 1800s and early 1900s.

Great Grandpa was also the foreman at several other prominent gold and silver mines such as the Sunnyside Mine in Silverton, Colorado. He prospected on his own as well. According to Grandpa (my mom's dad), Great Grandpa Billy was tough as nails. He was short in stature, like Mother Cabrini, but made up for it with grit. He never looked for trouble, but when it came his way, look out! He was likened to a wolverine when defending himself, friends, co-workers, or his family. Men much taller than him would cower when he became angry. Grandpa said his dad was honest, well respected, and an extremely hard worker. He had a special talent for finding gold and had several major finds attributed to his skills.

Great Grandpa's largest discovery when prospecting for himself occurred at the Neglected Mine located in the mountains of Southwest Colorado near Durango. He discovered an extremely rich vein of gold there and recruited four partners to help finance the large operation. He had finally found his "mother lode." Feeling optimistic about his financial future, he decided to get married late in life. Everything seemed to be going well. He and his partners had a large crew of men working for them and the rich vein discovered turned out to be a very profitable grade of telluride ore which contained a high content of gold with some silver mixed in.

Word of their success quickly spread around the area and according to Grandpa, shortly afterward a company offered them $1 million for the rights to their mine. Great Grandpa was ready to jump on the offer but the other partners couldn't let go of the rich gold, so by unanimous vote the offer was rejected. He did everything he could to talk them into it but to no avail. His experience had taught him that mining was unpredictable and could change as fast as the weather.

After Great Grandpa had been away for a time to manage another mine in Leadville, Colorado, one of his partners high-graded a fair amount of the rich gold, disappeared, never to be seen again. It was rumored that he fled to England and entertained royalty with his newfound fortune and later went broke with nothing to show for it. Shortly afterwards, their mine abruptly ran out of gold which marked the end of the road for them at this particular claim.

I'm sure that Great Grandpa and the other partners looked back many times in their lives, wishing they had taken the generous offer when they had the chance. Just like with many of us today, we find ourselves in the same situation, looking back wishing we had made a different decision. Regardless, the mine became famous in the Southwest and is still recognized today.

My great grandpa, Billy Boyle (second on the right) on his way up to his mine.

Great Grandpa's Neglected Mine with crew that became famous
in the Southwest Mountains of Colorado, early 1900s.

Grandpa Boyle

My grandpa, Warren Francis Boyle, continued his father's tradition and
later purchased several mining claims of his own. The acquisition of one
of his claims was a dream come true. Great Grandpa told him a story
where he came across some drunken miners who were going around
town bragging about a rich vein they had recently discovered. Being a
self-taught expert, Great Grandpa asked if he could examine a sample
of their gold. He claimed it was one of the richer samples he'd seen.

Years later, Grandpa's father told him if he ever had a chance to purchase the claim where the rich gold came from, to jump on it. Great Grandpa believed there was still more gold to be found and Grandpa believed in him with all his heart. When it finally came up for sale years later, he jumped on it.

Thanks to Grandpa, our family still owns this beautiful mining claim located high in the Rocky Mountains. It is nestled in a post- glacial bowl, surrounded on three sides by towering peaks well above timberline. Today, we use it more as a camping and hiking destination to enjoy the beautiful scenery than we do as a goldmine.

Grandpa coming out of his mine.

Grandpa's mining claim property

Warren Francis Boyle

Chapter 4

Mother Cabrini Shrine Property Purchase – Golden, Colorado

After Mother Cabrini and her sisters had successfully established her Queen of Heaven orphanage through many hours of intense work and prayer, she once again went searching long and hard for a location out of the city to where she could take her sisters and the orphan girls to a place of spiritual retreat and beauty, allowing them to get away from all the stress and problems of city life.

Through her experiences, Mother Cabrini had learned the importance of getting out into nature where you could better experience God's beautiful creation, a place of healing and restoration of mind, body, and soul.

In 1909, a year after all the trouble they encountered, she finally came upon a property located in the foothills of the Rocky Mountains, up Mount Vernon Canyon which is just outside of Golden, Colorado.[90]

She purchased this most beautiful and convenient property which was not too far from their Queen of Heaven orphanage, yet far enough to be able to experience the incredible views of the Rocky Mountains to the west and the plains and city below to the east – a perfect place of prayer, reflection, and retreat.

Initially, three sisters established a farm there with dairy cows, grazing cattle, and other poultry and livestock. They would bring up around 20 orphan girls at a time in the more temperate months to experience this beautiful place of retreat where they enjoyed recreational activities in the fresh mountain air and learned how to farm and do other chores.[91]

Tommy Francis, present and longtime head of maintenance and caregiver of Mother Cabrini Shrine in Golden, Colorado, informed me that initially the sisters only took residence there during the spring, summer, and early fall months due to the lack of access and adequate supplies during the harsh winter's from being snowed in. Regardless, Tommy explained that a full-time caretaker would remain on the property year-round.[92]

This property came with a few barns and an old house which lacked an adequate water supply. The sisters initially set up their living quarters in the loft of the larger barn. The sisters had to walk down to the bottom of the canyon each day to get their water which was a strenuous hike. But just like with their property in New York overlooking the Hudson River, Mother Cabrini had a gift from God for finding water in difficult places. After the sisters mentioned to Mother Cabrini their difficulty obtaining water, she took to prayer and diligently walked the grounds searching, telling her sisters, "Lift that rock over there and start to dig. You will find water fresh enough to drink and clean enough to wash."[93]

https://mothercabrinishrine.org/the-shrine

And abundant water they found, bubbling up from a natural underground spring, more than enough to supply all their needs. This miraculous spring on top of a hill where water is not usually found continues to supply all the needs of the Mother Cabrini Shrine and all the thousands of pilgrims who drink from it daily. Tommy informed me that they have an upgraded 70,000-gallon cistern today.[94]

Mother Cabrini wrote, "I can envision many small chapels here where many pilgrims will come to pray." This came to pass, fulfilling her vision with several small chapels of prayer and a beautiful Rosary and Holy Spirit walk on the grounds that provide such a beautiful place to pray for thousands of pilgrims each year.[95]

Mother Cabrini Became a United States Citizen

About this time on October 9, 1909, Mother Cabrini became a naturalized citizen of the United States while in Seattle, Washington. Her attorney there had encouraged her to do this and she finally accepted his advice. This became necessary from all her large real estate holdings and other assets but she also loved America and wrote, ". . . the liberty of the United States, which is unique in the world."[96]

"I can say that there is neither hill nor valley that I have not visited, with an ever-growing admiration for the goodness of the Lord so amply demonstrated in this blessed country."[97]

https://www.neh.gov/article/mother-cabrini-first-american-saint-catholic-church

Mother Cabrini Loved the Rocky Mountains of Colorado:

"I am happy to have a mission in the Rocky Mountains where I always desired to go. I like Colorado. May God be praised!" ~Mother Cabrini[98]

https://www.instagram.com/p/Czlk47tpwqe/

Regardless of her newfound citizenship, Mother Cabrini continued to live out her deeply held Italian heritage the rest of her life. After all, Mother Cabrini was never an immigrant. Instead, she came out of obedience to her pope and bishop to evangelize and catechize the Italian immigrants seeking to find a more hopeful and abundant life.

Stone House

In 1912, on her last visit to Colorado, Mother Cabrini spent her time making plans and arranged a builder to construct the "Stone House" which ended up housing her sisters and orphan girls coming from the Queen of Heaven orphanage. Tommy Francis explained that even in their time off for retreat, the sisters were hard at work as the "Stone House" was mostly constructed out of stone. These stones came from hard work and labor by the sisters, and help from the orphan girls, as they unearthed all these rocks on location with shovels, picks, horses, donkeys, and carts to move the rocks into piles where local stonemasons, who were abundant at the time, began to build this stone structure. According to Tommy, it took several years for completion as it was done little by little in this fashion. It was finally completed in 1914 with the help of Thomas Ekrom, a local builder.[99]

Stone House front and back view, Mother Cabrini Shrine

Procession at Stone House – Courtesy of National Endowment for the Humanities

Tommy further explained that while all of this was taking place, all the orphan girls on-site and in Denver at the Queen of Heaven orphanage had to be fed, clothed, and cared for with medical supplies and other essential goods which was very expensive when you consider three meals a day for hundreds of girls, and all the sisters and staff.[100]

So again, raising funds to continue with their ministry was a constant challenge. Mother Cabrini and her sisters knew that God would provide for them but they also knew they had to do their part, and they all worked diligently towards this necessity in their lives. They raised funds in every ethical way possible including begging long and far from home travelling on foot, and horse and buggy to the local farms and ranches. They also received help from the Bishop, local business owners, wealthy individuals, and even the poor.[101]

Heart of Stone

During that time and place at her Mount Vernon Canyon property, Mother Cabrini decided to dedicate the highest hill on her grounds to the Sacred Heart of Jesus. Mother Cabrini, with the help of a few sisters and orphan girls, rode to the base of this hill on a cow path via horse and buggy. From there they walked up the steep hillside to reach the summit.[102]

Keep in mind, Mother Cabrini was in her early 60s with poor health hiking in rugged terrain, in high elevation over 7,000 feet. Her sisters were always amazed at her ability to accomplish so much with her disabilities. I have made this hike on several occasions with the convenience of the concrete steps now in place and I have personally struggled at times to reach the summit and even failed when going through an episode of POTS which effects my heart rate and energy levels. I can attest to the difficulty it can pose, especially when suffering from a health condition like Mother Cabrini had affecting her lungs. I believe she had angels on each side of her carrying her through life. I do not see how it would have been possible if she relied solely on her weakened human strength.

Their journey up the steep hillside was before any steps or trails were made. I'm sure the young orphan girls loved this adventure along with the sisters.

The view Mother Cabrini, her sisters, and the orphan girls
would have seen standing on top of the hill at sunrise.

As they walked up the hillside each resting point would offer an opportunity for them to leave their problems of city life below and replace it with beautiful views to the east featuring the plains of Front Range of Colorado, and to the north and south, picturesque rolling hills, and the rugged Rocky Mountains to the west. From their high vantage point, they must have felt like eagles soaring high above the earth as Mother Cabrini would often reference her love for flight which she equated to her spiritual detachment from the confines of the world. She often quoted:

> . . . Free yourself and put on wings.[103]

> The soul entirely detached from itself and from everything always flies in holy joy.[104]

> Be holy by loosening yourselves from every little misery that is like so much tar that grounds you on the earth, loosen yourself to be able to fly in the pure air where you will find the ineffable goodness of dear sweet Jesus.[105]

> Be doves my daughters, but try to fly as far as the eagle reaches, which does not stop either on the hills and lower mountains, but arrives at the ridges and there in the living stone shelters itself from turbulence and bad weather. Always united to Jesus, oh! how well one is and how well one works without tiring, with all the enthusiasm, just like those who enjoy the true freedom of the children of God to have completely mastered themselves.[106]

God's beautiful creation was being fully experienced and admired by a future saint and those present on their journey. The path they hiked would be travelled and enjoyed by many in the years to come, well after her time on earth.

When they reached the summit their work had just begun. This was a special mission – a dedication to her beloved Sacred Heart of Jesus. She had them gather white rocks to place in the form of a heart. On top of the Sacred Heart, they built a smaller Cross and then with smaller stones, they formed a Crown of Thorns.[107] I could just image the smiles and pure joy on all their faces as they finished their wondrous work. I'm sure Jesus was there admiring it as well, pleased with his beloved children. Not knowing the details, I could imagine them praying and singing songs of praise and worship to Jesus, and then capping it all off with a nice meal.[108]

Heart of Stones made by Mother Cabrini, her sisters, and the orphan girls.

https://mothercabrinishrine.org/the-shrine

Sacred Heart of Jesus Statue

Mother Cabrini's vision for this property to become a place of prayer for many was coming closer but patience would have to be endured before her dream would be fulfilled. Long after her death in 1954, an Italian artist hand carved a twenty-two-foot-tall statue of the Sacred Heart of Jesus. It was erected directly above the Heart of Stones that Mother Cabrini, her sisters, and the orphan girls had lovingly placed at the summit of the hill.[109] From Heaven, I am sure Mother Cabrini was pleased to see her hard work come to fruition.

According to Tommy Francis, pilgrimage to this retreat property began long before the large statue of Jesus was erected. The sisters would invite visitors to come up to their property for prayer and retreat in limited numbers. Below is a picture of a stone monument that Tommy thought dates to the early 1900s when Mother Cabrini was still present at the Shrine. This stone monument was built directly above the Heart of Stones placed by Mother Cabrini, her sisters, and the orphan girls. When the statue of Jesus was built, they had to remove the stone monument to make way for Jesus but they salvaged the white marble slab with the Latin writing and placed it on the base that supported the new Sacred Heart of Jesus statue.[110]

Stone Monument with the Heart of Stones at its base –
The humble beginnings of the Shrine in the early 1900s –
Courtesy of Mother Cabrini Shrine Museum, Golden, Colorado

After Mother Cabrini's canonization on July 7, 1946, demand increased significantly for the Shrine thus the need and desire to build a place to better accommodate and honor Mother Cabrini and the worship of her beloved Sacred Heart of Jesus.[111]

STATUE OF CHRIST, MOTHER CABRINI SHRINE, MT. VERNON CANYON

Statue of the Sacred Heart of Jesus Early Days – Cooper Post Card Co.

Today's view of the statue of The Sacred Heart of Jesus.

373 Steps of Prayer

The need to better access the new Sacred Heart of Jesus statue prompted the addition of 373 concrete steps with construction commencing on September 11, 1954. The steps were completed in just 67 days which is the same number of years Mother Cabrini lived. These steps were built on the same path that Mother Cabrini, her sisters, and the orphan girls used to gain access to the summit. Along these stairs, the 14 Stations of the Cross were added. Each station was made in Italy of beautiful stone mosaics.[112]

https://mothercabrinishrine.org/the-shrine

The stations begin at the base of the stairs and stop approximately halfway up the hill where the Mysteries of the Holy Rosary of our Blessed Mother Mary begins. They are placed along the balance of the stairway to the summit to allow the faithful to further meditate on the Passion and life of our Lord Jesus.[113]

Tommy informed me that the Luminous Mysteries stations were built later after St. John Paul II officially added the Luminous Mysteries of the Rosary. They built the Luminous Mysteries stations down at that Rosary walk by the springhouse. He further enlightened me about the Ten Commandments located along the summit perimeter with the 11th monolith featuring Moses receiving the tablets.[114] This Shrine has it all, such a beautiful place of prayer.

To make this experience more comfortable, in 1955 the Knights of Columbus added terra cotta benches throughout the long stairway providing a place for pilgrims to rest and enjoy the beautiful views along with prayer and meditation.[115]

The 15th Station of the Cross

In an interview with John McEncroe – long time retired maintenance worker at the Mother Cabrini Shrine in Golden, Colorado, he enlightened me on a subject I was not aware of. I had never heard about the 15th Station of the Cross that was encouraged by St. John Paul II during his papacy beginning in 1978. He emphasized the immense importance of our Lord's Resurrection to be added to the Stations. According to John, many Catholic Churches have added the 15th Station and he spearheaded the effort to get this Station added to the stairway at the Shrine. In 2018, John's vision became a reality but not without its challenges. The original 14 Stations were mosaics designed and made in Italy which would be nearly impossible to replicate. Instead, John had a local family, Tom Merelli, his wife Rosie, and their daughter Madison design and build the mosaics featured on the 15th Station of the Resurrected Christ which turned out to be beautiful. Both Tommy and John built the concrete plaque and delivered it to the Merelli family to complete the intricate mosaics.[116]

15th Station of the Resurrected Christ

John and his wife Carol at the 15th Station

John was inspired to build the 15th Station in part by a large boulder he spotted that was split in half vertically and resembled an empty tomb. St. John Paul II based his desire for a 15th Station from the following Holy Scripture: "If Christ has not been raised, your faith is futile and you are still in your sins." (1 Corinthians 15:17)

World Youth Day in Denver

I believe it was prophetic that St. John Paul II later in August 1993 came to Denver, Colorado where World Youth Day was celebrated with nearly a million youth from all over the world. This was also a historic time for the Shrine where they were tested like never before as 100,000 youth flooded their grounds participating in processions and many other events. Tommy Francis told me that it taxed their resources more than any other time in the Shrine's history but said Mother Cabrini found a way for them to get through it, blessing so many spiritually hungry youth with our Lord Jesus. Tommy said one of the highlights was witnessing St. John Paul II's helicopter flying around the statue of the Sacred Heart of Jesus two times as he prayed over all the pilgrims. This meant that the Shrine now had the presence of two great saints forever blessing this holy place of prayer.

Lord willing, I am really looking forward to seeing the 15th Station onsite once I regain my health enough to travel again.

Miraculous Polio Healing

Tommy Francis in another interview provided me with a beautiful story of healing concerning this place of prayer. During the early 1950's a young child stricken with Polio was brought to the Shrine by their parents where their child was bathed in the spring water. Afterwards, the child was cured of Polio after a period of time with credit given to Mother Cabrini's intercession. The Bohannan family was so grateful that they paid for a beautiful statue of Crucified Jesus to be built at the base of the Shrine steps located on the right-hand side when looking upward. This area has a nice table and gathering place for pilgrims to begin and end their hike, to reflect and pray, as well as just have lunch and other activities. The locals at the Shrine have informally named it the "Bohannan Crucifix."[117]

"Bohannan Crucifix"

A beautiful story is written about this healing in the book, *Cabrinian Colorado Missions*, by Mother Ignatius Miceli, M.S.C.

According to Mother Ignatius, the two-year-old child belonging to the Clifford Bohannan family was healed in 1952. Clifford Bohannan was a member of the Shrine Committee.[118]

After being bathed in the cold spring water, their child was not healed instantly but rather, over a period of time. I found this fascinating as my second healing at the Shrine was delayed as well where it took several months before I had significant improvements.[119]

Mother Ignatius mentioned there have been hundreds of people suffering with illnesses who have sworn in notarized documents that they were healed from the spring water along with prayer at the Shrine. Mother Ignatius's response, "We here at the Shrine maintain that it is the faith these people have and their trust in the Sacred Heart, which they have found in prayer, that heals them." She then quotes Mother Cabrini to her sisters which I took to heart, "that with faith and prayer people would attain health of soul and body."[120]

I received this book from a dear Missionary Sister of the Sacred Heart of Jesus after my book was mostly completed, but I believe it was God's will. If I had received this earlier, I would have focused too much on the Shrine origin details found here instead of finding new information to help complement it. Mother Ignatius's book is packed with historical facts concerning the Shrine and has fascinating in-depth stories about the sisters and orphan girls who called this Shrine home along with the founders and benefactors who helped make all this possible.

Chapter 5

Mother Cabrini – Her Final Years

In 1912, after successfully establishing her plans to build the Stone House at Her Mount Vernon property, which provided a secure expansion and future for her sisters and orphans, Mother Cabrini never returned to Colorado.

It was somewhat of a miracle that Mother Cabrini was able to come back to Denver one last time as she was in Rome the prior year in critical health. She even considered retirement knowing her time on earth was drawing near. When she suggested this to her sisters in the past they were shaken and told her that "they would die for her…" Mother Cabrini with her familiar smile and sense of humor replied, "A lot of good that would do me – to have a pack of dead nuns on my hands! Live and work – that's the best thing you can do."[121]

The sisters secretly sent out a reply to all their houses throughout the world telling them of her plans for retirement. They unanimously affirmed that if Mother Cabrini were alive no one could ever replace her. With that in mind, and by a somewhat good-humoredly decree from Cardinal Vives y Tuto who headed the Congregation of Religious, who issued on her birthday, July 15, 1910, "Mother Cabrini, as up to now you have governed your Institute so badly, I have decided to give you another chance, in the hope that you will do better in the future. You are to remain Superior General." Although like a page from Mother

Cabrini's own sense of humor, the Cardinal laughed, and the sisters present applauded and joined in laughter. Outwardly she smiled, but deep inside her heart, was troubled.[122]

Mother Cabrini out of her obedience to the Church and God, willingly submitted to continue her role as the Superior General despite this not being her own aspiration at the time. Instead, she boldly carried on for another seven productive years before God took her home. . . .[123]

Despite her declining health, Mother Cabrini was able to recover once again while in Rome due to her reliance on God's strength. She steamed back first class from Naples on the NorDDeutscher Lloyd-Berlin to New York, on her last trip to America. She needed to personally attend urgent dealings with Columbus Hospital in New York and other affairs. This was the first time she travelled first class. Due to her compromised health, the sisters wanted to make her travels more comfortable.[124]

Titanic Near Miss

Mother Cabrini was originally scheduled to travel out of England to New York on the prestigious new steamship, the Titanic, which ended up sinking on its maiden voyage. Thank God her trip was cancelled due to her urgent matter with Columbus Hospital. Another example of God looking out for her in a big way.[125]

Soon after her arrival in West Park, New York, she became ill again and cried out, "I am dying! I am dying! Come O death come!"[126] But once again, she recovered enough to travel, and her sisters arranged for Mother Cabrini to go to her Holy Cross Mountain property in Colorado where they hoped she could spend some time in the fresh mountain air to recover more fully.[127]

Her Last Time in Colorado

This mountain is fourteen thousand feet at its summit! Mother Cabrini resided in a log cabin at its base. Living in high elevation has its own hardships where the air is thinner making breathing more difficult. Her compromised lung issues from tuberculosis and being premature at birth made me wonder how she was able to endure basic living up there, let alone trying to recover in such a demanding environment. But, the beauty of God's creation and peacefulness up in the mountains are inspiring and His healing power was surely upon her.

During this time, Denver was suffering economic hardships where her sisters did everything they could to provide funds for their growing needs. They had a shop in downtown Denver selling various items which had to be closed after Christmas due to lack of sales.[128]

Regardless, Mother Cabrini didn't let this stop her but rather, she continued to move forward with her plans to build the Stone House at the Mount Vernon property near Golden along with working her gold mining claims at her Holy Cross Mountain property. Not to mention all her other projects going on back East and around the world. Her many responsibilities required supernatural strength and guidance that came from her beloved Sacred Heart of Jesus.

Return to Seattle

After departing Colorado, she travelled back East for a time. In 1913 she again returned to Seattle to find property for an orphanage. Her health was again compromised but she continued to work diligently to find a suitable property. On foot, she personally searched the hills and woods on the outskirts of the city with a few of her sisters but found nothing. She then decided to study a map of the area which she was good at, and then placed her finger on a particular spot and told her sisters to find it. One sister told her she was sure nothing of interest could be found there but Mother Cabrini insisted they go. Upon returning they told her they had found Heaven on Earth! It was a beautiful estate located on Beacon Hill with a large house and land sloping down to edge of Lake Washington with a view of snow-capped peaks in the background.

The sisters asked her how she knew of this place and she softly replied, "You know about my dreams."[129]

The next day Mother Cabrini went with them to have a look. On their way back, they decided to hitchhike a ride instead of the busy trolley. A woman saw them and asked her chauffeur to pull over and give them a ride. Mother Cabrini took the liberty to explain to the woman that she was interested in buying some property she found to start an orphanage. The woman asked her if she was going to buy it? Mother Cabrini replied, "I will if I can afford it."[130] The woman then asked where it was, and Mother Cabrini told her. After hearing this the woman explained that the property belonged to her husband and said she would help make this happen. The woman argued Mother Cabrini's case to her husband and after some resistance, he submitted and sold the property to her nearly giving it away at such a low price. It gets even better as an anonymous supporter provided the one hundred thousand dollars needed to purchase the property.[131] Talk about a God moment! I love these types of stories.

St. Joseph Medal

From Seattle, Mother Cabrini travelled back to New York to start another orphanage. She was having a hard time negotiating the purchase of a particular property so she pulled out her big gun. While leaving the property after a failed offer, she secretly buried a St. Joseph medal in the grounds before leaving. Of course it worked. Later, the gentleman who turned her down called back a few days later and told her to make him an offer which was accepted.[132]

She later returned to Seattle again in 1915 for the purchase of another property which at the time became problematic as Bishop O'Dea had only approved the Perry Hotel purchase to be used as an orphanage but when the property was finally negotiated at a price suitable to Mother Cabrini, she later realized it would not work as planned. She thought it would work better as another Columbus Hospital but the bishop denied her permission on the feast day of the Sacred Heart of Jesus. She now had a property paying a hefty mortgage with no use. Fortunately, the Bishop later recounted in part by allowing it to be used as a place for physiotherapy and electrotherapy, not exactly what she wanted but better than sitting empty. Along with the fact that her homeland Italy had been drawn into World War I, this latest business venture further added stress which exasperated her already fragile health.[133]

Back to California

Mother Cabrini later travelled to California to rest from the intense business in Seattle. The sisters there were shocked to see how far her health had deteriorated. Regardless, Mother Cabrini took the time off to recuperate in the gentle climate gardening and feeding the birds which helped her to recover at least in part once again.[134]

In 1907, Mother Cabrini purchased this beautiful property in Burbank, California and had a preventorium built for children with tuberculosis. Then in 1917, she had a small chapel built on the hill overlooking her property. Every morning while there, Mother Cabrini walked up the hill to the small chapel to pray to her beloved Jesus renewing her strength both physically and spiritually much like she did while in Colorado and her other beautiful locations around the world.

This small chapel was the last structure she had built which served its purpose beautifully long after her death. It was and still is used by many for prayer and for processions once a year on her feast day in honor of her saintly life. The chapel had to be relocated by the Italian Catholic Federation in the early 1980s to St. Frances Xavier Church grounds in Burbank, California where it stands today. This occurred after Woodbury University planned to demolish it after their purchase of the property.[135]

Despite her illness and stressful hardships, Mother Cabrini didn't let this get her depressed although it was difficult to read her continuance to see how she was feeling. The harder things became, the more she relied on God to lift her up. Instead of becoming bitter, her kindness towards others only increased.[136]

Miracle Healing

Sister Euphemia in California was suffering from a severe form of varicose veins where she could barely walk. Mother Cabrini suggested that she wear silk stockings gentler on the skin. Sister Euphemia went a step further and decided to wear Mother Cabrini's cotton stockings instead. She was instantly cured. Mother Cabrini saw her boldly walking the next day and replied, "What has happened to you? You are all right now." After finding out about her stockings being used she laughed and then quickly changed to a serious face and said, "I hope you are not going to be so foolish as to say that my stockings cured you. It was your faith that did it." This miracle was as testimony for Mother Cabrini's beautification hearing.[137]

Final Days in Chicago

April 18, 1917, barely able to walk, Mother Cabrini left California for Chicago by train to attend some pressing business meetings. When she arrived, the sisters sobbed to see her in such a weakened state. When they insisted she go to bed and get some rest Mother Cabrini replied, "No, I have things to attend to. Besides, a little exercise will do me good."[138]

Mother Cabrini did her best to go about her usual work despite her failing health. Mother Antonietta Delta Casa who was the superior at Columbus Hospital and later became the Mother General was especially concerned about Mother Cabrini's health. She pleaded with Mother Cabrini to go to bed and get some needed rest and not overdo it. Mother Cabrini exercised obedience and listened to her advice.[139]

She was examined by the doctors at the hospital who diagnosed her with malaria, something she already suspected. Her earlier travels to Central and South American had come at a price. She was placed under treatment which helped to reduce her fever, but her pulmonary veins were left compromised. Regardless, she regained some of her strength and was back to her normal work.[140]

She was by no means back to normal health, but she never missed her spiritual exercises with her community when they resumed in July at 5:30 in the morning. Mother Cabrini made the best of her compromised condition and would follow her doctors' orders to drive each day out into the country to enjoy God's beautiful creation which helped restore her. She picked wildflowers and ferns for the hospital chapel and always had her eye out for opportunities to help her order. On her daily drive she noticed all the cows and chickens along the way which prompted the idea of buying a farm to help supply the hospitals in her area with fresh milk, chicken, and eggs. In October of that year, she ended up purchasing a farm in the Parkridge area.[141]

By November, her health took a turn for the worse, and on the 21st, after receiving communion at the altar rail, she fainted while walking back to her pew where the sisters carried her to her room. Once again, later that day she regained her strength enough to continue with her regular activities.[142]

Mother Cabrini did not give up easily and continued to fight on regardless of her poor health. Many people had no idea how severe her condition was as she had the ability to put on a happy face despite her internal suffering. Her guardian angel was surely kept busy looking after her especially during this difficult time for her.

As Christmas neared her responsibilities increased. She became extra active helping to take care of all the last-minute gift giving to her hospital staff, sisters, and those they cared for. When she found out five hundred children who attended school on Erie Street would not be given any gifts due to hard economic times, Mother Cabrini at her own expense bought them all candy.[143]

Mother Cabrini's Final Hour

On Friday December 21, 1917, Mother Cabrini started her day early going to Mass and spent one hour in front of the Blessed Sacrament. Afterwards, she spent her time feverishly wrapping up all the candy for the children and other gifts as if she knew her time on earth was short. She had completely exhausted herself in her labors of love and the next morning she did not arise at her usual time. Some sisters went up to her room to check on her where she remained in bed the rest of the morning. She refused any breakfast because she was fasting in hopes of receiving the Holy Eucharist in the chapel. By noon she was still not able to rise. The sisters asked her what she wanted for lunch. Mother Cabrini told them to bring whatever they decided. At that, she locked her door. Mother Antonietta, who was with her earlier, tried to gain access to see how she was doing but could not enter. She figured Mother Cabrini was getting dressed or praying and decided not to disturb her and would return later to check in on her. Shortly afterwards, one of the sisters was waiting for the food cart in the hall near Mother Cabrini's room and heard her unlock the door. She watched Mother Cabrini's hand reach around the door and pull on a cord attached to a bell to alert the sisters.[144]

In author Theodore Maynard's words who had direct access to the Vatican documents relating to her life:

> . . . The waiting Sister went in quickly with the tray still in her hand to see what was wanted and found Francesca fallen back in a wicker chair. Her nightgown was stained with blood, and blood was on the handkerchief she held to her lips.
>
> Very frightened now the young nun ran to the refectory in the basement, white of face and stammering, "Our Mother! Our Mother!" Followed by the other nuns, Mother Antonietta went with her at once to Francesca's room, after sending for the priest and the doctor. Francesca's eyes were open and her lips slightly parted, but she was already unconscious. There was nothing that the doctor could do, nor could the priest do anything except administer Extreme Unction and give her conditional absolution. Leaning her head against the arm of Mother Antonietta, Francesca turned a last look on her daughters and peacefully died.[145]

Mother Cabrini two years before her death

Courtesy of Mother Cabrini Shrine Museum, Golden, Colorado

Reflection

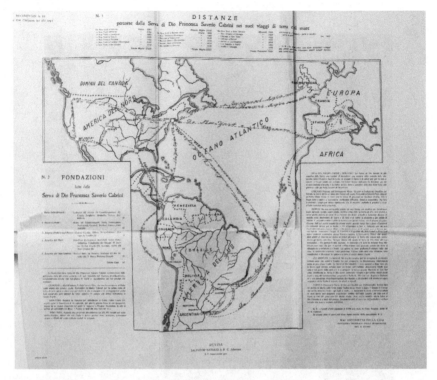

Mother Cabrini's Travel Map – Courtesy of The Missionary Sisters of the Sacred Heart of Jesus and the St. Frances Cabrini Collection, Holy Spirit Library, Cabrini University, Radnor, PA 19087.

Once again, I have to reflect on just how miraculous Mother Cabrini's life really was. She may have died in body at 67 but she accomplished more than most people would do in two lifetimes. She was already compromised in her health but continued to work so hard that her body finally gave out early in life. It's difficult to comprehend the scope of all the work she was doing simultaneously around the world, in Europe, the East Coast of the US, down south in New Orleans, out West in Colorado, California, Washington State, and in Central and South America including other regions of the world. Keep in mind that she was traveling continuously, back-and-forth multiple times to each location throughout her life, via steamship, horse and buggy, railroad, walking, later automobile, or anyway she could keep up with her seemingly impossible schedule and responsibilities.

There is no way Mother Cabrini could have done a fraction of this if it were not for God's supernatural intervention, where He made all things possible for her because she had complete trust in her beloved Jesus. She did all this while suffering with ill health, in constant motion, rarely resting only during intense prayer with her wings outstretched allowing God's grace and Divine love to lift her upwards and forward. This beautiful letter to her sisters really brings this home, "Fly, fly upwards for love, leave the heavy airs of human miseries that oppress your spirit and always live in God."[146]

Mother Cabrini's Canonization

On July 7, 1946, from Pope Pius XII's homily at Mother Cabrini's canonization:

> Although her constitution was very frail, her spirit was endowed with such singular strength that, knowing the will of God in her regard, she permitted nothing to impede her from accomplishing what seemed to be beyond the strength of a woman.[147]

https://www.mothercabrini.org/who-we-are/our-history/

Documented Miracles for Mother Cabrini's Canonization

After her death Mother Cabrini made it to her final destination – Heaven was her prize. The whole purpose of her mission on earth was to do the will of her beloved Lord Jesus, to help herself, and others come closer to Him. I feel confident that she lives present in His glory. Her mission on earth continues to be more powerful than ever. Mother Cabrini joins all the Saints of God who intercede on our behalf in a way not possible while she was on earth. She is now truly flying high above all the problems of the world not burdened by the limits of her frail temporal body but rather, she is completely free to serve and praise her beloved Jesus with no limitations.

While in Heaven, Mother Cabrini did not waste any time as she quickly interceded on behalf of a baby boy named Peter Smith who was born at Columbus Hospital in New York where Mother Cabrini was the foundress. One of the nurses at the hospital accidentally put a 50 percent silver nitrate solution in his eyes, which is basically acid, instead of the prescribed medication. At once his eyes became terribly damaged. I can only imagine how bad the nurse felt after doing such a dreadful thing. Mother Cabrini's sisters spent the night praying and asked Mother Cabrini for her intercession to heal the poor infant Peter Smith who was now blind.

The next morning his eyes were miraculously healed! What a relief that must have been for all involved. There was no other explanation for the healing, making this the first miracle used towards her canonization. Peter Smith was miraculously healed a second time. While an infant he contracted pneumonia that became life threatening. In the same hospital, Mother Cabrini's sisters prayed for him again with the same results.[148]

Peter was later ordained as Catholic Priest on June 2, 1951, which is such a beautiful fruit from his miraculous healings.[149]

The second miracle used for Mother Cabrini's canonization occurred to one of her spiritual daughters named Sister Delfina Grazioli from Seattle, Washington. She was suffering from a life-threatening illness and was given the last rites. Mother Cabrini appeared to her in a vision, and she was miraculously healed. The picture of this nun on her deathbed really tells the story.[150]

Sister Delfina Grazioli on her deathbed
miraculously cured by Mother Cabrini's intercession.

Peter Smith and Sister Delfina Grazioli miraculously
cured through Mother Cabrini's intercession.

https://cdm17305.contentdm.oclc.org/digital/collection/p17305coll9/search
– All Miracles Shown – Cabrini University

Both pictures above related to the miracles are courtesy of The Missionary
Sisters of the Sacred Heart of Jesus and the St. Frances Cabrini Collection,
Holy Spirit Library, Cabrini University, Radnor, PA 19087.

The Years After Mother Cabrini's Death

Mother Cabrini's time on earth ended only after God's will for her was accomplished. Her life's work continued like a well-oiled machine with her ministry still going strong today. More importantly, many souls were saved through it all which was the primary purpose of her work. She was living in the heavenly realm where all things become possible. She gave such a beautiful living example of what can be accomplished if we place all our trust in Jesus. So many times in her life she was misunderstood with her plans because they did not come from worldly origins but rather, she was inspired by God. His ways are not our ways so even her spiritual directors and bishops would sometimes doubt her plans and advised against them, but she would respectfully persist knowing they would work out in the end.

Mother Cabrini's steadfast faith garnered trust in those who initially advised against her plans, but when given some time, they saw that her judgment was prudent. The same was true with the Bishop of Denver who thought Mother Cabrini was foolish to purchase the farmland for her Queen of Heaven orphanage so far away from infrastructure and the people they needed to serve. But Mother Cabrini listened to the Holy Spirit who showed her that this area would soon be swallowed up by the growing city of Denver and that is exactly what happened. Her ability to find viable properties was a valuable gift from God enabling Him to work through her establishing beautiful missions throughout the world.

Granted, none of this came easy for her especially while suffering with poor health but she overcame it through many hours of fervent prayer which strengthened her.

Rejuvenated, Mother Cabrini and her sisters went searching on foot, horse and buggy, railway, and later automobile to help find the perfect property or solution to maintain her hospitals, dispensaries, orphanages, schools, and convents which were expensive to operate making fundraising one of the main jobs required of them.

The World is Too Small...

"The world is too small to limit ourselves to one point; I want to embrace it entirely and to reach all its parts."[151] – Mother Cabrini to Monsignor Scalabrini, 1887

Mother Cabrini's vision to embrace the world became reality and her legacy bequeathed upon her by Christ is still alive and well today.

Note – To view pictures for each chapter online in large format, go to the website listed below and enter the password **2030** after clicking on the Gallery tab found on the header. Please do not share this password online or with anyone else. Thank you and enjoy!

https://stmothercabrini.com

Chapter 6

Queen of Heaven Orphanage and Mother Cabrini Shrine, 1930 Onward

Carl Francis – Head of Maintenance

Again, I had the opportunity to interview Tommy Francis who is the beloved professional caretaker and maintenance professional at the Colorado Mother Cabrini Shrine for over 54 years at the time of this writing. Tommy's dad, Carl Francis, started working at the Queen of Heaven Orphanage in Denver back in 1930 during the Great Depression era. According to Tommy, his dad's initial job was to drive the sisters all around the Denver area to help them fundraise to meet their growing needs. At the time, the sisters were not allowed to drive. According to Tommy, it was not until after Vatican II around 1965 that the sisters loosened their rules, modified their habits, and were able to learn to drive.[152]

Carl Francis, Courtesy of Tommy Francis

Thursday, Friday, and Saturdays were especially devoted to fundraising. The cost to feed and house all the orphan girls and sisters, and to maintain and pay for their property holdings was expensive, as their main source of income came from donations. This was especially true during the early 1940's during World War II when according to Tommy, the orphanage had as many as 250 girls due to the casualties of the war.

Tommy said the sisters would leave early in the morning after their prayers and would not return until well after dark on many occasions out fundraising. It was exhaustive work but necessary to provide for their ongoing ministry. All this took place in challenging economic times especially during the Great Depression when getting donations was difficult.

Fundraising and their daily chores were just one of their many responsibilities. The sisters' highest priority was to properly catechize the orphan girls and the other primarily Italian immigrants back to their Catholic faith. They were missionaries first.

Carl's position with the Queen of Heaven later took on a more expanded role with maintenance projects, picking up food and supplies, along with his initial driving responsibilities. He would also go up to the Mother Cabrini retreat property in Mount Vernon Canyon that was a working ranch in addition to a retreat center for the orphan girls. Carl would deliver weekly provisions of food and other supplies along with bringing up the orphan girls during the summer months. In the springtime he also helped brand cattle and during mid-summer and early fall, he would go up and help cut hay and place it in the barn. Because of the tough economic times, Tommy's dad "had to do a lot from nothing. He would reuse bent nails and salvage anything he could find."[153]

Tommy Francis Working with His Dad

When Tommy was only six years old his dad started taking him along to the orphanage. Tommy, with some laughter in his voice, informed me he was a restless child who would never sit still. Because of this, Tommy's mom asked Carl if he could take him to work which he ended up doing. He put Tommy to work pulling nails to reuse and other chores he could do, and he really enjoyed it.

Mother Ignatius High Country Adventures

I felt inspired to include this short story below about Carl and his family from a book I was recently given, *Cabrinian Colorado Missions*, by Mother Ignatius Miceli, M.S.C. It helps to provide a glimpse of their personalities and life outside the Shrine.

In August of 1955, Carl Francis informed Mother Ignatius that he would be taking them on a mountain picnic the next day. They were supposed to go to Buffalo Bill's up the canyon but Mother Ignatius informed Carl that they were already scheduled to hike there that afternoon, so Carl asked her where she would like to take the orphan girls instead. She replied, "Where the goats go." Later that day, Carl told them to be sure to bring warm jackets and Mother Ignatius replied, "Where are you going to take us?" With a devilish grin he said, "Where the goats go. Just make sure you pack a good lunch. I'll bring a camp stove; I'll make a campfire and warm whatever you bring."[154]

Mother Ignatius and the girls cooked up a feast; roast beef, shucked corn with all the fixings wrapped in foil ready to heat up on the trip. She also added rice and chicken broth along with her famous campfire banana split.

The next day, Carl did not tell Mother Ignatius where he was taking them as they drove up the canyon high up into the Colorado Rockies. This was the first time she had been up to the high country. They arrived at Echo Lake. Carl had them set up camp and they went for a hike. Mother Ignatius's account, "We followed Carl on an Indian trial. His son Tommy, a six year old, hung onto his father's shirt tail. . . ." Carl kept their destination a secret as they hiked. She continues, ". . . When we arrived at our destination, there was a beautiful, wide, blue mountain lake with snowcapped peaks reflecting in it. We had arrived at Chicago Creek. . . ."[155]

This high mountain trip became an annual summer event where Carl would take the orphan girls and sisters up to the beautiful Rocky Mountains where everyone thoroughly enjoyed it. They would start their day early in the morning and come back late in the evening making it a lot easier than camping overnight which required all the extra food and gear. "As we traveled the mountain tops, we would stop near water for our picnics and cook our steaks over a coal fire." Mother Ignatius commented that Carl's wife Elda and their children would always come along on these high mountain adventures where "Elda would prepare our steaks the night before. . . ." [156]

I love this story as it provides such a beautiful snapshot of all their lives including Tommy who just didn't work all the time. He was able to enjoy many outings like this with his father Carl and the rest of his family which helped deepen their relationship.

Carl Francis Camping, Courtesy of Tommy Francis

Later, as Tommy took on more responsibility, he was put in charge of repairing hundreds of bicycles that one of the sisters had obtained from the Denver Police Department. She realized the orphan girls had no bikes, so she went in and convinced them to donate the stolen or lost bicycles that were just sitting in storage. Tommy really took a liking to this work and the gratification he received for providing the orphaned girls with something that brought them so much joy.

After Tommy turned sixteen, in addition to his regular work, and like his father, he started to drive the sisters and orphan girls to their various appointments and other needs. The girls lived in the orphanage up until around the eighth grade before they were placed in a permanent home. Tommy explained that the Catholic Charities Organization set the rules for most of the orphanages in the area including how long the girls would live there. They had all different age groups to take care of.

Sister Rita

Tommy mentioned a fascinating story about Sister Rita who was one of their main fundraisers. When she was still living in New York City around 12-14 years of age, she was walking down the street one day and Mother Cabrini came right up to her and said, "I want you!" Sister Rita quickly replied, "No, no, no. . . ." Mother Cabrini kept telling her, "I want you!" This must have been from the Holy Spirit because on September 8, 1903, Rita took her First Profession and later became a Missionary Sister of the Sacred Heart of Jesus.[157]

Tommy was not sure when she arrived in Denver, possibly travelling with Mother Cabrini at some point. He did know that she was one of the hardest workers he had ever seen. Not only a harder worker but very prayerful. When Tommy drove her around town looking for donations, she was always running her fingers over the Rosary beads praying. While she wasn't fundraising, Sister Rita was busy cooking, cleaning, making jam, or whatever else had to be done. Tommy said, "Her knuckles were gnarled from arthritis . . . but this didn't stop her one bit! She was a very tough woman."[158]

He has a lot of respect for anyone who demands hard work from others but is also willing to work hard themselves, and according to Tommy, Sister Rita was that person. After passionately serving our Lord Jesus, Sister Rita died of a heart attack while mopping the floors on January 16, 1965.

He then brought up another very diligent worker named Sister Rosaria who oversaw all the laundry which was usually scheduled on Mondays. The Queen of Heaven had a large industrial washing machine but no power dryers, so everything had to be hung outside on clotheslines. Then on Tuesdays they had to iron all the clothes where some of the older orphan girls would help them out. You can imagine how much laundry they had dealing with hundreds of orphan girls of all ages.

Tommy said Sister Rosaria never complained and served our Lord Jesus with everything she had. He said this was common with all the sisters who learned by example from Mother Cabrini.

Sister Rita's prayer card – courtesy of Tommy Francis.

The Queen of Heaven Orphanage Closed in 1967

In the mid 1960's due to a lack of orphans, Catholic Charities changed the rules by requiring permanent foster homes for the children at an earlier age, in part making the orphanages unnecessary. Tommy said the sisters had to close the Queen of Heaven Orphanage in 1967. This also occurred to all the other orphanages in the area due to a lack of demand. He went on to say that the sisters tried running a school at the Queen of Heaven for a couple of years but it didn't work out very well, so they decided to sell it. In 1970, after the new convent and chapel was completed at the Mother Cabrini Shrine in Golden, all twenty-three sisters moved up there to begin the new chapter in their ministry.

Tommy said the Queen of Heaven building ended up being demolished in the end. The sisters salvaged a beautiful statue of the Sacred Heart of Jesus from the Queen of Heaven tower and had it transported up to the Golden Shrine. Today it is located outside the entrance of the gift shop as seen below.[159]

Tommy said transporting the Sacred Heart of Jesus statue was quite the undertaking. He had the crane operator from the Queen of Heaven site lower the nearly 1,000-pound statue from around 75 feet up in the tower to the back of his pickup truck, and that was the easy part.

He drove the statue to the Golden Shrine where his dad was awaiting him with a plan. They had an older two-wheel drive tractor with a front bucket along with a road grader. The statue would have to be carefully unloaded into the tractor bucket and tied off and then driven down a steep hill to a concrete pad that was already in place for its new home. Easier said than done. Tommy said, "Of course my dad didn't have a crane ready but instead decided to do it the cheap way. He would always try and save a buck but would usually make it work out regardless."[160] Tommy said he had complete trust in his dad even though the job at hand made him nervous. He was the one who would be driving the tractor downhill, with a precious cargo on board, and of course, he had an audience watching from the near distance.

The pressure was on as Tommy's dad Carl placed a heavy metal chain on the back of the tractor and secured it to the road grader sitting on top of the hill while keeping some tension on it. He then slowly lowered the tractor to help prevent it from sliding down the steep hill potentially crashing into the awaiting concrete pedestal.

Despite all the machine noise, Tommy clearly remembers Mother Consolata, who was the Superior at the Queen of Heaven at the Shrine, yelling at the top of her lungs, "Don't break my statue, don't break my statue!"[161]

Despite all the drama and action, Tommy and his dad were able to successfully position the statue to where they could shuffle it back and forth out of the tractor bucket while upright and place it on the pedestal without incident. Mother Cabrini must have been interceding on their behalf as so many things could have gone wrong with that much weight and equipment on a steep hill. Tommy laughs about it now but at the time, it was a different story. The statue of Jesus ended up being moved again when they recently expanded the main chapel, "but this time with a crane,"[162] Tommy laughed.

Tommy said Mother Consolata was a wonderful hard-working sister who expected a lot out of others but was always willing to do her part and more.

Sacred Heart of Jesus statue moved from
Queen of Heaven building to its present location.

Queen of Heaven rebuilt after 1921 and closed in 1967 –
4825 Federal Boulevard, Denver, Colorado.

Above Photo Courtesy of The Missionary Sisters of the Sacred Heart of Jesus and the St. Frances Cabrini Collection, Holy Spirit Library, Cabrini University, Radnor, PA 19087.

Mystery of the Lost Virgin Mary

During my interview with Tommy, I asked him where they relocated the Virgin Mary statue that was previously located outside the front entrance of the Queen of Heaven building. He couldn't remember what happened to her. Later, after I was given a copy of the book, *Cabrinian Colorado Missions*, by Mother Ignatius Miceli, M.S.C., the mystery of the Missing Virgin Mary was solved. She was relocated behind the main chapel and convent where she stands today in her stone grotto and beautiful bed of flowers, praying for everyone.[163]

The Blessed Virgin Mary statue relocated to the Shrine from the
Queen of Heaven. Photo courtesy of Tommy Francis

I mentioned this to Tommy which triggered his memory. He has so
many things going on at the Shrine that it is easy to forget something.
He then went on to tell me about how the bronze sculpture of Mother
Cabrini and the two orphan girls came about. Mother Ignatius, who
authored the book mentioned above, had this sculpture crated and
sent from Italy to the Shrine. He said it was quite the undertaking. It
weighs a ton which required a crane to lift it and set it in place. Tommy
said it was originally located at the Shrine out in a hayfield away from
everything. It was later relocated to its present location in the Mother
Cabrini Garden which is a beautiful place for prayer and reflection.

Bronze Sculpture of Mother Cabrini and two orphan girls imported from Italy.
Photo courtesy of Tommy Francis

1970 – Sisters and Staff Moved Up to the Shrine

On December 1, 1969, when Tommy was 16 years old he moved up to the Mother Cabrini Shrine by himself 6 months before the rest of his family and stayed at the Stone House. This must have been a time of real independence for him. In the spring of 1970, the rest of Tommy's family moved up to the Shrine after his siblings finished school for the summer break. They all moved to the Shrine where Tommy and his dad Carl resumed their caretaking, maintenance, and other expanded responsibilities which included taking care of the complex water and pump system which was all off grid from city services.

Mother Cabrini Chapel and Convent Early 1970's –
Photo by, Sanborn Souvenir Co.

Mother Cabrini Altar Chapel, Grotto Early 1970's –
Photo by, Cooper Post Card Co.

2024 view of the Mother Cabrini Shrine grounds

By this time, the Shrine staff did not raise cattle any longer, but they did move all the chickens from the Queen of Heaven there along with those already being raised at the Shrine. They had to make their own custom feed which according to Tommy, was time consuming. The Shrine grounds are approximately six hundred acres with multiple buildings, barns, and other outbuildings that kept Tommy and his dad very busy.

Tommy said that he learned a lot about his faith and the trades during his time working with his dad and is very grateful for it.

I asked Tommy if he knew when the first pilgrims started coming to the Shrine. He thought when Mother Cabrini was first beatified in 1938 people started coming in small numbers and after she was canonized in 1946 the numbers started to gradually increase but they were never overwhelmed, which Tommy said was a good thing. He said after the convent and chapel was built in 1970, John Campbell formed a Shrine committee to help organize and plan for the increasing number of pilgrims and to help put their Shrine on the map.

Chapel and Gift Shop Expansion

Tommy said that over the years the number of pilgrims kept increasing gradually which allowed them to keep up with the demand. He was thankful it wasn't like with Fatima or Medjugorje where pilgrims quickly overwhelmed these areas. He attributes this to Mother Cabrini looking after them.

It wasn't until recently that they raised the necessary funds to add on to the main chapel which was starting to get overwhelmed at times. The work began in 2022 and was completed in 2023. They also added on to the gift shop and other areas beginning in the spring of 2020. Tommy said long time Shrine director JoAnn Seaman who is now the Executive Director of the Shrine, was instrumental in raising the over 5 million dollars necessary to complete the work. He also mentioned Fr. John Lager OFM Cap., who is a vital fundraiser and spiritual director for the Shrine. His ongoing spiritual and economic contribution has been a major help and blessing throughout the years. Father and his brothers are part of the Capuchin Franciscan order.

The Church was expanded from around 250 to 450 seats that made an enormous difference. Before the expansion, especially during special occasions, people had to sit out in the lobby to find a seat. I know I had to do this once during a First Communion celebration. Thanks to a lot of hard work and prayers by all the dedicated staff, volunteers, and donors, the Mother Cabrini Shrine is now better prepared for the future allowing even more pilgrims to be blessed by this holy place of prayer.

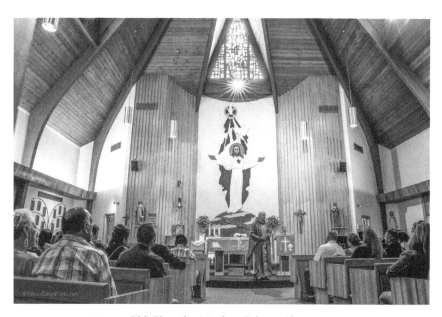

Old Chapel – Mother Cabrini Shrine

Expanded New Chapel – Mother Cabrini Shrine

Mother Cabrini's statue in her new location in the expanded chapel.

Tommy's Thoughts

Tommy takes his job at the Shrine very seriously and has a steadfast devotion to Mother Cabrini and his faith in God. He fully understands whom he is working for:

"Our Job at the Shrine is to bring people to God and God to the people and talking about Mother Cabrini and letting others come and experience this sacred place helps to accomplish this."[164]

Tommy also said, "The amazing thing about Mother Cabrini – she could be worldly without losing her spirituality. She never let the world creep into her spiritual life remaining humble throughout."[165]

In a recent interview posted on the Shrine Facebook account I found Tommy's words to be very inspirational:

Q: "What inspires you the most about Mother Cabrini?"

A: "Mother Cabrini is a hard act to follow. She sets the bar high, and we do our best to keep up. If it were not for her presence on this holy ground, I couldn't do this job. I am inspired because of her humility, her deep faith, and her tireless work ethic despite her frail health."

Q: "What do you want visitors to know about the Shrine?"

A: "What I want visitors to know about this special place is that it is holy ground and deserves reverence. It's a place where a person can find peace in an otherwise unpeaceful world! Many people say they can feel St. Cabrini's presence here. If visitors take their time and go slowly, they will feel that presence, whether it be by inspiration, an idea that seemingly comes out of nowhere, or by an inner comfort that our favorite saint will intercede for them."

Tommy went on to say, "I would like to remain here until 2030 as a tribute to my parents, who sacrificed much in service to Mother Cabrini and her sisters."[166]

https://www.facebook.com/photo?fbid=817842657058253&set= a.229905089185349

Tommy's Family 100-Year Anniversary Hopes

2030 will mark the combined 100-year anniversary of Tommy's dad Carl and his time working for Mother Cabrini and her Missionary Sisters of the Sacred Heart of Jesus.

Tommy's dad Carl Francis, after a lifetime of service to Mother Cabrini's ministry, passed away in 1984 and Tommy picked up the torch and continues with his family legacy of hard work and faith in our Lord.

In an earlier conversation with Tommy, I told him I thought in the future, the Shrine could become a place of refuge for the Front Range of Denver during a crisis where supernatural events would occur comparable with Jesus's feeding of the 5,000. Tommy replied, "There has always been a crisis of some sort going on with today being more of a spiritual one. The Shrine is already providing a place of refuge for prayer, peace, and reflection to help strengthen our faith and devotion to our Lord and this is what Mother Cabrini's Shrine has been doing all along since its inception."[167] Tommy is absolutely right, we don't have to wait, it's already here. . . .

Tommy Francis

In the meantime, Tommy keeps working hard every day to keep the Shrine running smoothly which is a challenging task but one he takes very seriously.

Shutdown

I asked Tommy in a later interview how COVID-19 affected the Shrine. He said they had to shut it down for six weeks out of an overabundance of caution. Of course, this was hard on the Shrine and those who relied on it for their spiritual needs, but Tommy made the best of it. Both he and John had been working on the Holy Spirit Walk project a few years prior and had already made some benches but that was as far as they got. They were too busy to make substantial progress with everything else going on.

During the shutdown, Tommy had more time for this project and he worked on it full-time every day. He then got unexpected help from God, as the county called looking for a place to get rid of fifty dump truck loads of clean fill dirt. This is exactly what he needed to complete the project. He knew Mother Cabrini had a big part in it as this type of thing occurs often. From start to finish, he was able to complete the Holy Spirit Walk in less than a year. Tommy said it would have taken him more than double that time had the shutdown not occurred so not all was lost during that challenging time.[168]

Tommy was in charge of constructing the Holy Spirit Walk, but it was Carol, Tommy's sister and John McEncroe's wife, who was instrumental in the spiritual aspect. While in deep prayer to the Holy Spirit, she was inspired to build the Holy Spirit Walk and was given specific details regarding the design and location.

It sits on the edge of a hill overlooking a beautiful canyon with a stunning view of Jesus in the near distance. Visitors enter the large, intricate metal gate with the Gifts of the Holy Spirit inscribed around its perimeter. For each gift, there is a bench where one can sit, pray, and reflect while enjoying the views. This is a wonderful addition to the Shrine and was made possible by hard work and prayer.

The Holy Spirit Walk was built in times of trouble making this such a beautiful example of Mother Cabrini's life, where even in the most turbulent times for her, God always came through, and even now, her legacy lives on through all those committed to her ministry.

John McEncroe – Long Time Project and Maintenance Worker at the Shrine

Like Tommy, John is a dedicated servant of our Lord who served the Shrine well doing construction and maintenance projects since the mid 1970's. He has since retired.

John and his wife Carol at the new Mother Cabrini Shrine Chapel,
courtesy of John McEncroe

John met Tommy's sister while in college and they were later married at the Shrine in 1976. In 1977 they moved up to the Shrine and lived in a small humble outbuilding near the Stone House until 1983. John had his own construction business so in between jobs he would help

Tommy out with larger construction remodels at the Shrine. In 2015, John became a permanent employee of the Shrine doing mostly maintenance work for Tommy. [169]

John was always very kind and helpful to me while visiting the Shrine and he was instrumental in my volunteer photography work, providing me access to get some incredible pictures that are being used for some of the Shrine's social media projects and fundraisers. There were a few times I was not able to climb the stairs due to my health condition. I developed a good friendship with John and I felt sad when he informed me of his retirement in June of 2023.

Maybe I was just being selfish. After all, John's health was a factor in his decision to retire. On a trip to Israel with his wife in May of 2022, he came down with COVID-19 which exasperated his congenital bicuspid heart valve condition. In August of 2022, John's condition became serious enough that he went in for open-heart surgery to replace his valve and to fix an aneurism. As John put it, he was able to kill two birds with one stone. It was during his operation that he experienced a miracle.

John's Miracle

First some background information is needed to better understand what occurred. Back in 1981, John was asked by Mother Camille Peretti, the Superior at the Shrine at the time, to install frames for some stained-glass windows that were donated from the Villa Cabrini Academy Campus in Burbank, California. This was a private school for girls built in 1944 and run by the Missionary Sisters of the Sacred Heart of Jesus. In 1970, the campus was closed and was later sold in the early 1980s to Woodbury University who removed all the stained glass which was donated to the Mother Cabrini Shrine in Golden, Colorado.[170]

During this time at the Golden, Colorado Mother Cabrini Shrine, there was an open porch to the right side of the chapel where John was instructed to close it in and install the donated stained glass along the length of this new wall.

While John was in surgery fully unconscious from the anesthesia, he saw a vision of deceased Mother Camille. She was standing next to him and he said, "I want you to know that after 41 years they are doing another remodel on the chapel and they are going to finally knock out that wall!"

Mother Camille replied, "We are not going to talk about that now." She then grabbed John's hand and with her other hand, reached up towards Heaven and held Mother Cabrini's hand. He said Heaven was like what others have described, "A gorgeous light with clouds and peace." Then Mother Cabrini said, "John, you are going to be fine." John said the whole vision was spectacular! He came out of surgery just fine and was doing well when I interviewed him just like Mother Cabrini said he would.

John was able to witness other miracles during his time working at the Shrine. He told me about one woman who used to volunteer there who was diagnosed with cancer. She ended up being healed after spending many hours praying there and started working at the Shrine full time. He also mentioned a Native American who he believed was from the Navajo Nation who was also healed from an illness after they prayed at the Shrine. Both Tommy and John said that they heard of other accounts of healings and miracles throughout the years but said that was not the main ministry there. The primary focus is to help bring people closer to God which was Mother Cabrini's ministry.

John's love for nature is one of his common bonds with Mother Cabrini and something I share with him as well. He has sent me pictures of amazing wildlife scenes at the Shrine and does it so easily. It usually takes a lot of effort and time for me to get a good shot with my professional gear while John just points his iPhone and gets a beautiful picture every time. I often joke about this with him.

The Fawn and the Magpie at the Shrine, Courtesy of John McEncroe

John snowplowing waiting for a herd of elk to cross.

Tony Merelli – Longtime Shrine Benefactor

Tommy told me about a longtime friend Tony Merelli whose grandparents used to invite Mother Cabrini and her sisters to stay at their house when she travelled to Denver. Of course, this story was of great interest to me and Tommy went so far as to set up a phone call with Tony which I really appreciated. This was an opportunity to record history, not just matters concerning Mother Cabrini, but for Denver in general.

Tony at the time of my call was 95 years old. He was sharp as a tack and was a joy to talk with. He reminded me of my late grandpa full of energy and zest and was a straight shooter packed with interesting information all with a great sense of humor.

Tony is an engineer by trade and worked for the Denver Water Board working on contracts, water treatment plants, and reservoirs for 40 years before retiring. John told me Tony was instrumental in the original design of Dillon Reservoir located near the town of Dillon, Colorado. Tony and his late wife have four children. He is also a longtime volunteer at the Shrine since the 1940s.

In 1946, Tony designed a functional fountain system at the spring located at the Shrine near where the grotto exists today. At the time it was just spring water flowing from the mountain into a little trough where people would dip in their cups or buckets for drinking water. Tony said Mr. John Campbell did the majority of the work building the fountain he designed with the help of other volunteers. Over the years other improvements were made to the fountain where today it efficiently supplies water for thousands of pilgrims each year and the spring meets the daily requirements of all those living and working onsite as well. Mother Cabrini's miracle spring lives on. . . .[171]

I told Tony my wife is half Italian and her late dad, Ersilio Stoppa, was 100%. He emigrated from Italy to British Columbia, Canada. I went on to tell Tony that her dad had a heavy Italian accent while speaking English and could also speak fluent Italian. Tony said he was upset that his parents would speak Italian among themselves but whenever he came in the room they started to speak English. Years later he asked them why they did that and they said, "We wanted you to be American."[172]

Tony's focus in our conversation was on his grandfather, Michael Notari, who had the Notari House built which was used by Mother Cabrini and her sisters to live there and to start their first school, Mount Carmel Parish in 1902. It was also there that Tony's grandparents came to personally know Mother Cabrini as she would sometimes stay at their house when traveling to Denver. Tony informed me that his grandfather also had Mount Carmel Parish built that he modeled after a similar parish also named Mount Carmel in Potenza, Italy, his birthplace. Both parishes are still standing today with similar architecture.

Tony's grandfather was born in Potenza, Italy on September 10, 1860, and immigrated to the Denver area in the late 1800s. He was married to Rosina Morrato in Colorado on May 21, 1885. They had ten children. Michael Notari's wife passed away in 1909.

According to Tony, his grandfather was nicknamed the "Jobber" by the locals as he had a thriving business helping Italians to immigrate to Denver by charging a fee to arrange for their travels, a job, and a place to live which helped take the risk out of their immigration plans. He was well respected by his community of Italian immigrants and was very generous to Mother Cabrini and her sisters. His grandpa passed away June 18, 1935, and was buried in Fairmount Cemetery in Denver.

Tony continued his grandfather's legacy helping the sisters out wherever he could especially at the Shrine. Tony's brother, Frank Merelli, was instrumental in helping Tommy's dad out with various projects at the Queen of Heaven orphanage. He was also instrumental in helping out with the Golden, Colorado Shrine especially in building the 373 steps leading up to the statue of the Sacred Heart of Jesus along with the new chapel and convent built in the late 1960s and early 70s. Frank and Mr. Campbell who headed up the Shrine committee, helped Tommy Francis and his dad Carl out with many other projects at the Shrine as well.

Towards the end of our conversation, Tony mentioned with laughter in his voice that one of the orphan girls who had grown up later told him that his brother Frank would bring them all ice-cream when they were on retreat at the Shrine in the summer months. When they saw him coming they would sing, "Here comes ice-cream, ice-cream, who screams for ice-cream!"[173]

Tony further explained that Wednesdays are designated for volunteers to help at the Shrine where he consistently helped out on many occasions. At 95 he still goes on Wednesdays to catch up with everyone, not doing as much physical labor now, but more for helping with the morale with his delightful personality and by "saying a few prayers."[174]

Tony Merelli, left, and John McEncroe, Courtesy of Tommy Francis

Both Tommy and Tony have a high regard for each other and have become the best of friends over the years. It has been such an honor for me to talk and get to know them both a little better.

Tony ended our conversation by telling me that Tommy Francis invited him to his retirement party; that won't happen until 2030 if all goes according to plan. I asked Tony if he intended on going and he just laughed and said he would love to. I feel confident that Tony will be there to mark his 100th birthday along with Tommy and his family's 100-year combined anniversary working for Mother Cabrini and her ministry. What a wonderful accomplishment and day that will be although bittersweet to see Tommy retire. God's will be done.

Sister Alice Zanon, MSC

I reserved the best for last referring to Sister Alice Zanon, Missionary Sister of the Sacred Heart of Jesus (MSC) whose role is to minister to the visitors in the grotto, museum, gift shop, and chapel at the Mother Cabrini Shrine in Golden, Colorado.

Sister Alice began her calling with the Missionary Sisters of the Sacred Heart of Jesus in Melbourne, Australia at the age of 23. She was a secretary for an oil company at the time. Sister Alice had a great love for Jesus and wanted to come closer to Him so she decided to go to a Legion of Mary retreat to get some answers concerning her faith. It was there that she met a priest to whom she opened up her heart and personal ambitions of possibly joining the religious life, but she didn't know where to go. After listening to her, the priest suggested that she investigate Cabrini Hospital located in Melbourne where she could use her secretarial skills and spend more time in environment completely open to Jesus. She took his advice and set up a meeting with the Mother Superior the next day to discuss her options. She really liked the environment at the hospital where 22 sisters were based with diverse backgrounds and nationalities giving it "an international flavor."[175] More importantly, it was there she attended another retreat on the Feast Day of St. Michael the Archangel praying all day, contemplating entering the order. On November 13, 1968, she decided to give her life to The Missionary Sisters of the Sacred Heart of Jesus.

A couple of years later she was transferred to Perth, Australia for four years where she attended the Churchlands Teachers College to prepare herself for the classroom. From there Sister Alice went back to Melbourne where she completed a one-year sabbatical to prepare for her final and perpetual vows. She was then transferred to London, England where she received her bachelor's degree in education at the University of London. She was an elementary school teacher in London for 15 years.

From there she was transferred to former Swaziland in the southern part of Africa for three years at Saint Mary's Mission teaching high school. This area offered a school, convent, and a medical clinic similar to the way things were back in Mother Cabrini's time. From there she was transferred to New Orleans in the US where she remained a dedicated theology teacher for Cabrini High School for 22 years. Sister Alice was then asked to retire at the age of 72. She then began searching for a new career path when the Mother Cabrini Shrine in Golden, Colorado offered her a position as their minister to the visitors. She absolutely loved this idea and in July 2017 she moved to Colorado and began her new ministry at the Shrine. At the time of this writing, she still has her ministry there blessing the thousands of pilgrims who come each year. She is fully aware that her life was not left up to random chance but rather, her beloved Jesus was orchestrating everything all along.

Sister Alice mentioned a wonderful story showing how Mother Cabrini was instrumental in her life. After she was established in her ministry teaching, she went back home to Melbourne to visit her family and attended the local parish. When she entered for morning Mass, she introduced herself to the priest and informed him that she was a Missionary Sister of the Sacred Heart of Jesus visiting her family:

> Without saying a word, He took me by the arm, led me up to the altar where he threw back the altar cloth and there, as you probably know that every altar has a relic on it, the relic read in bold letters, Saint Frances Xavier Cabrini! And I got such a shock because all the time I grew up at that parish, as a baby, as a child, teenager, a young woman, she had her eye on me. . . .[176]

Sister Alice was overwhelmed with emotion telling her story of how Mother Cabrini was helping her all along. She also informed me that the priest who helped her at the Legion of Mary retreat just happened to be the parish priest for Cabrini Hospital. At 23 while discerning her vocation, she said she had never heard about Mother Cabrini or her sisters. The Cabrini Hospital was on the other side of town where she grew up miles from her house. This is such a beautiful and powerful testimony.

Today, Sister Alice takes her Ministry at the Colorado Shrine very seriously and thoroughly enjoys doing it. Throughout her life as a Catholic teacher, she has helped bring thousands of children to her beloved Jesus and she continues to minister and council the countless pilgrims today at the Shrine.

Sister Alice Zanon, MSC

Holy Spirit

She is about as close to a Mother Cabrini as one can get on earth. There is no doubt in my mind that Sister Alice is being supernaturally strengthened by our Lord Jesus and through the intercession of Mother Cabrini. She is absolutely in love with our Lord and starts each day out praying to the Holy Spirit asking for guidance on how she can best minister to the visitors. She also spends an hour each day in front of the exposed Blessed Sacrament which she says empowers her. This is in addition to all her other prayers each day with Holy Mass foremost. She told me, "The Lord is beside me, within me, speaking through me, advising me what to say."[177] I thought that was so beautiful and profound. I could feel the Holy Spirit within her flowing onto me over the phone during our interview.

She mentioned that our country is struggling morally and said it was a tragedy. I replied, "That is why God has you here, right now, at this exact moment in history, because he knew from the beginning of time that you would be a bright light in this present time of darkness." Due to her humility, she had a hard time accepting my complement, but it is the absolute truth that doesn't just pertain to Sister Alice, but to each and every one of us. Sister Alice said she doesn't worry because she knows that Jesus is in complete control of all things. I said, "Amen" to that even though I do struggle at times trusting in this truth.

Again, the amount of quality prayer time Sister Alice spends is the key to her spiritual strength and growth; it's just the way it works, and we are always better for it, something that I am trying to learn each day.

I mentioned to Sister that I had planned a trip, Lord willing, to Mother Cabrini Shrine for the first time in over four years in the early part of June 2024 which was coming up soon. I planned to fly because there is no way I could make it over the high mountain passes driving from Durango due to my POTS flare-up and ongoing head pressure issues. But I knew I had to get back to the Shrine to finish my book as I had pictures that needed to be taken and videos for my trailer, and of course, I have been starving for the prayers, peace, and healing that the Shrine offers.

I could only only tolerate a few days due to my health and was not ready to travel but knew I just had to overcome it. Mother Cabrini's steadfast commitment to God's Holy Scripture, (Phil 4:13) during her times of suffering kept going through my mind; "I can do this . . . in Him who strengthens me."

Feast of The Sacred Heart of Jesus

While my wife and I were scheduling the trip to the Shrine online, I tried picking days during the week when it would be less crowded, but the price kept going up almost triple when we didn't include a weekend departure. No matter how many places we tried, the same results. As long as we put the departure for Saturday, the price went down significantly but would mean a longer stay. Regardless, we ended up booking the flight for the Saturday departure. During my interview with Sister Alice a few days later, I mentioned I would try to fly down there in early June, Lord willing, and she quickly asked if I would be coming for the Feast of the Sacred Heart of Jesus Mass at the Shrine on Friday? I mentioned how important it was for me to have my book out in the month of June due to the important Feast of the Sacred Heart, which was everything to Mother Cabrini, but I didn't know the date while planning the trip. And then it hit me like a rock, that was the reason we were having so many problems trying to shorten our visit because if we had, we would've missed the special Mass at the Shrine on Friday by one day. Hit by a rush of emotions, I started sobbing while talking to her, it was embarrassing. I realized at that moment just how much Jesus loves us, and is always looking after us, in every detail, despite all our weaknesses, sinful natures, and hardships we encounter. **WE ARE LOVED!**

It was Sister Alice, through the power of the Holy Spirit working through her, that all this was revealed to me at the perfect time. The power of prayer is unmatched. I know spending time talking and praying with her has helped in part to heal me. It has been such an honor and privilege getting to know her better. After the interview was over and I had time to reflect, I realized that she was the one who interviewed me. She provided counsel and insight without me even knowing it. I had to laugh and rejoice and give praise to Jesus for providing us with such beautiful souls such as Sister Alice in our world. We are truly blessed and have so much to look forward to. . . .

Sister Alice went on to say that the Shrine attendance has nearly doubled since the new movie *Cabrini* came out. She said keeping up with the demand has been challenging but doable thanks to God. According to Sister, as the numbers of pilgrims increased, 70 new volunteers came on board which really helped. I asked her how the priests and other sisters have been keeping up with the demand, and she said a different priest comes each day to say Mass. Father John Lager, OFM Cap., who is part of the Shrine board committee, helps keep things running smoothly.

I was surprised to hear that Sister Alice was the only sister presently at the Shrine full time.

During the interview Sister said, "I am so blessed to be walking in the same footsteps that Mother Cabrini walked at this special Shrine."[178]

Please dear Jesus, continue to provide Sister and all those at the Shrine with Your Divine strength, protection, and guidance through the power of Your Holy Spirit, and Your Precious Body and Blood, Amen.

From Sister Alice Zanon:

> My current ministry is at the Mother Cabrini Shrine. The Shrine is truly a place where people can commune with God, talk to Him about their needs, or just sit quietly with Him. My mission is to be a presence here, welcoming and offering hospitality to the many pilgrims, retreatants and visitors who come here for various reasons.
>
> "Love is not loved" – lamented Cabrini who wrote that the heart that intimately understands the love of the heart of Jesus wants to return that Love.
>
> To be a bearer of the love of Christ in the world today, I need to meet people where they are in their journey with God. I reply to the Holy Spirit to help me sense the needs of other hearts, especially those who are living away from His Love, who are lost and struggling, and need spiritual healing.
>
> What a responsibility, what a privilege, what a joy it has been to just sit down with a brother or sister and listen to their story.
>
> In moments like these, the Spirit invariably inspires me how to respond – perhaps to offer words of encouragement, to share with them what Jesus has done and is doing in my life – to pray for and with that person. I cannot change the past but Jesus and I can work together in the present moment to change the future.

After my interview with Sister Alice, I realized even more that I am not the only one suffering right now. No one is immune – not even a holy Sister of God, especially those involved in the ministry helping to save souls. There is a spiritual battle taking place and we are all right in the middle of it. Prayer is the best defense, especially Holy Mass and the Rosary, and Sister Alice is fully aware of this. During the interview, Sister offered to pray for me and my family which I greatly appreciated, and I offered to do the same for her.

Mother Cabrini to Her Sisters in Times of Trouble

I sent Sister Alice this timeless letter Mother Cabrini wrote to her sisters to help them in their times of trouble. This letter is good advice for everyone, not just her sisters. Sister Alice worked as the English translator for the book, *Free Yourselves and Put on Wings,* which is where this was sourced. She was well aware of this but sometimes we all need a reminder:

> The wind howls; the sky darkens; the treacherous waves rise. The steamer rolls and pitches, upsetting every object, which tumble about like moving bodies. A most terrible storm threatens . . . It does not matter; I have promised fidelity, and I must keep my word. With faith and trust I hope, through God's grace, to go on, always repeating 'Omnia possum in eo qui me confortat.' We are Missionaries, oh daughters, and the Missionaries must never falter because of difficulties and dangers. Rather, confiding in Jesus and leaning on Mary, she does not experience difficulties and passes through danger without noticing it.[179]

A few days later, struggling with my health, I was up praying on the mountain behind our house when a beautiful sunset developed accentuating the spring wildflowers in bloom. The clouds were in motion changing from dark to light in wispy formations due to heavy winds aloft that came down in brisk gusts refreshing my soul. I could really feel the power of the Holy Spirit talking . . . through God's beautiful creation. I felt His presence in a special way, assuring me that all would be well if I continued to focus on His healing light. I felt this was also for Sister Alice whom I was praying for along with other intentions, so I sent it to her.

... I arise today

Through a mighty strength, the invocation of the Trinity,

Through belief in the Threeness,

Through confession of the Oneness

of the Creator of creation.

St. Patrick (ca. 377)[180]

https://www.ewtn.com/catholicism/devotions/lorica-of-saint-patrick-349

Mother Cabrini's Dedicated Workers

To try and sum things up, Tommy Francis, head of maintenance, and all his helpers are the glue that holds together the physical aspects of this Shrine, and it is JoAnn Seaman, executive director, and all her staff who holds together the administrative side, and it is the donors, volunteers, and pilgrims who help make all this possible, but it is Sister Alice and the faithful priests such as Father John Lager and the many others who help keep the spiritual side running smoothly which is the most important element and the reason why Mother Cabrini purchased this property to begin with – to help bring souls to Jesus. They all understand this well with each telling me that it is the Lord Jesus who controls it all, helping them with their hard work, along with the powerful intercession of Mother Cabrini whose presence they feel every day helping them in their enormous but fruitful task of managing the Shrine.

Below are Mother Cabrini's thoughts about those who labored and continue to labor for her ministry. I believe she is well pleased with everyone serving the Shrine:

> I need many subjects but I wish to have only those who are humble, detached from themselves and from their talents, for I am positive that a humble subject can work for fifty or more. Without humility, peace is lacking and grace departs.[181]

Chapter 7

Mom's Mother Cabrini Shrine Miracle

To get a better understanding of my mom's miracle at the Shrine, some background information about my family would be helpful.

Grandpa and Grandma

I was fortunate to have a grandpa on my mom's side of the family who helped show me the emotional and spiritual side of life that my dad wasn't able to give. I was barely old enough to remember when Grandpa had his drinking problem. On one occasion, I vaguely remember lying awake in bed at my grandparents' house around 4 years old when I heard a loud crashing sound of glass breaking outside my open window. Grandpa had come home after being at the bar and decided to throw his empty wine bottle on the brick-paved sidewalk before entering the house. Grandma was waiting up for him and heard the noise. She met him at the door and an argument ensued that caused my little three-year-old stomach to become tied into knots. By the grace of God, Grandpa miraculously recovered from his alcohol problem several years later. It didn't happen exactly the way he intended but, in the end, he was healed.

Desperately praying in an empty church while drunk, he pleaded with God to heal him from his alcohol problem. God didn't deliver him from alcohol that day, but instead he was instantly delivered from his addiction to smoking. From that day forward, Grandpa never had the desire to smoke again. God in His wisdom knew that if he quit smoking, the drinking would follow and that's exactly what happened soon afterwards. With the bondage of smoking and drinking gone, he became the person God had intended all along – a wonderful spiritual leader for our family and a powerful prayer warrior, not only for us, but for others around him. His Irish temper would still get the best of him which gave him the nickname, "The Wild Man," but he had a tender side to him that could melt the hardest of hearts.

Grandpa was born in 1914 at the tail end of the Industrial Revolution. He was one of five children (three brothers and one sister) born in the small mining town of Durango in the rugged mountains of Southwest Colorado. In addition to a few cars, people still used horse and buggy to get around on the muddy pothole and rut-laden dirt streets. Even though mining had long since reached its peak and was winding down, the town was still hardcore which still had the character of the Wild West with all its saloons and other activities typically found in the mining era.

Grandpa told me a story about a hanging that took place near his home. He said it was so gruesome to watch that it almost made him lose his lunch. He claimed that hangings were rare in public at that time and hoped to never witness another one.

I then asked him if he had ever witnessed a gunfight. He was quick to tell me that the movies showing expert dead-on shots from gunslingers were a myth for most people back then. He went on to tell me about the one and only gunfight he had witnessed. According to Grandpa, two men got into a scuffle over an accusation that the other man had stolen his horse. The man accused, challenged the other to a gunfight. Grandpa said that people cleared the street just like in the movies but when the first shots were fired, both men lay on the ground wounded, one hit in the arm and the other in the leg. However, this didn't stop them and they continued shooting at each other with most shots from both sides missing their targets. Before it was all over, each man had emptied their pistols with neither of them fatally shot but they both ended up bleeding to death from their wounds. Grandpa said this was typical in gunfights because most of them were such a bad shot which is contrary to what the movies portray.

Mother Cabrini entered the mining era early enough to witness the Wild West firsthand and was even threatened by gunfire at one point.

Grandpa's youngest brother was confined to a wheelchair most of his life so Grandpa took him under his wing which resulted in a close, symbiotic relationship. His disabled brother was more levelheaded and never developed a drinking problem and was loved by most all who met him. This allowed him to help Grandpa personally with his problems and smooth out their joint business ventures.

They started up one of the first Packard Jeep dealerships in their region. The income from the business helped support not only Grandpa's immediate family and his brother, but also his other siblings. It became a family business partnership which still survives today. Grandpa was always very generous with his time and money and helped family and strangers on a regular basis. He and Grandma had four children (three sons and a daughter).

Like with Mother Cabrini in her pursuit of properties for her growing ministry, Grandpa was searching for a piece of land for their Packard dealership when he noticed a young boy outside without shoes on in the middle of winter. And just like Mother Cabrini, Grandpa was a deal maker so he told Our Lady of Perpetual Help and God that he would buy the boy some shoes if they would help him find a good deal on some real estate. To Grandpa's great joy and surprise, on the same day he bought the boy some shoes, a man offered to sell him a piece of real estate that was divided in two by a railroad track. He thought about it and came up with the idea of obtaining an option to buy with the intent to sell the other half divided by the tracks to another party. The man accepted his offer and within a brief period of time, Grandpa was able to sell the other half of the property for the same price he bought the entire lot for. In other words, he ended up getting the property for his business for free. Grandpa and his brother knew this was from God and they dedicated their shop to the Blessed Mother and our Lord. My grandpa and Mother Cabrini had a lot in common concerning real estate, their love for God's beautiful creation, their interest in mining claims, and foremost, their Catholic faith.

When Grandpa and Grandma first started out with a young family of four kids, they lived in a small home that housed not only their family but also Grandpa's three brothers and aunt. With 10 people living in cramped quarters things got a little hectic, especially for Grandma who just couldn't take it anymore. Grandpa's family members were going through a hard time so he took care of them but he quickly realized he needed a larger home. So he went to the aid of Our Blessed Mother once again and asked for her intercession to help find another home. Shortly afterwards, Grandpa was able to successfully negotiate the purchase of some vacant land that he would later build their larger home up on a hill overlooking the river valley. Of course, this made Grandma incredibly happy as she was the one responsible for taking care of everyone. This helped further Grandpa's devotion to Our Lady who would continue to be with him during important periods of his life. My wife and I ended up purchasing this house on the hill so this blessing has continued through the generations in our family.

Granda's Goldmine

Grandpa's goldmine continues to provide our family with many memorable experiences. He took his mine seriously and made frequent trips that required a lot of hard work in hopes of striking the mother lode. Off and on, he spent the rest of his life, even into his late 80's, searching and dreaming for that promised gold but never found it. Prospecting was just one of many things he enjoyed. His biggest passion was flying his airplane. He often took us on plane rides far and wide. Mother Cabrini also loved to fly but for her it was spiritual.

I once asked Grandpa what he liked the most about living in an age of modern technology. He quickly replied, "the thermostat on the wall." I thought that was pretty funny. It makes sense when you realize that he grew up in a generation where they had to keep a wood or coal stove burning to stay warm, even if it meant waking up in the middle of the night – one thing he would never miss. Instead of finding the mother lode, he blessed us with a wonderful family legacy that will be enjoyed by generations to come. Grandpa passed away at 90 years old and I look forward to being reunited with him in Heaven.

Grandpa, through his special devotion to Mary, and Grandma, who was also a prayer warrior, especially with her Rosary in hand, spent the remainder of their lives attending daily Mass and helping family and strangers both economically and spiritually.

The Novena to the Holy Ghost

Grandpa was extremely dedicated to praying and distributing the Novena to the Holy Ghost to everyone he encountered. He had memorized every word. This is one of the oldest novenas, and to my understanding, the only one officially approved by the Catholic Church. The front cover of the novena beautifully depicts Mary and the Disciples praying in the Upper Room during Pentecost with a heavenly dove and piercing light coming upon them. To this day, Grandpa has many people, including myself, praying this beautiful prayer which can be found at the following website:

https://www.ewtn.com/devotionals/pentecost/seven.htm.

Grandma

My grandma had a lot in common with Mother Cabrini especially coming from a large family farm where many siblings died at an early age. Grandma was also a prayer warrior like Mother Cabrini and they both loved going outdoors and experiencing God's beautiful creation. Grandma was a Registered Nurse by trade and her kindness, compassion, and skillset was appreciated and loved by all she cared for.

Grandma, Mary Blanche Wethington Boyle, was one of sixteen children who grew up on a fruit farm in Farmington, New Mexico. It was sad to learn that seven of her siblings died at or near childbirth. Her parents instilled in them strict biblical principles which laid the foundation that enabled her to survive in tough times. Grandma was very generous with her time and money. She often took me and the family on fun adventures such as raft trips, hiking, jeeping, skiing, and camping where she actively participated as well even into her 80's. Because of her fun-loving nature, everyone she met fell in love with her. Grandma and I were best friends and did so much together. It was she who taught me how to pray the Rosary and was instrumental in my love for God and His creation in nature. She has since passed away but her memory lives on strong in my heart.

Mom and Dad's wedding picture.
My mom's parents and her grandma (left), my dad's parents (right), 1962

Mom and Dad

My parents and grandparents played an instrumental role in my Faith. Like with the rest of us, my dad, Clint Dillon, who has since passed away, had his good and bad qualities. He was polite, never interrupted people while they were talking, rarely cursed, was a genius in mathematics, an extremely industrious worker, and an excellent provider for our family. His weakness was his inability to control his drinking and smoking habits which later cost him his life.

Mom and dad married at a very young age with my mom only 18 and my dad 19. They were both unequally yoked and not yet ready for marriage. Mom was a strong Catholic but religion was the last thing on Dad's mind at the time. Mom was like most teenagers who thought she knew better. She went ahead and got married knowing Dad already had a drinking problem and didn't practice his faith in God. Her decision was ironic as she already knew firsthand the pain of living with an alcoholic because her dad suffered from this disease. When Grandpa was first introduced to my dad, he warned my mom to stay away from him because he had already run into him on several occasions at the local bar. The last thing he wanted for his daughter was another potential alcoholic like himself.

Dad and Mom

Mom didn't listen to her dad's advice and on their wedding day coming out of the church, a few of my dad's friends grabbed him and threw him into the back of their 57 Chevy, took off, and didn't return for several hours. All alone, Mom sat outside on the church steps probably wondering for the first time what she had gotten herself into. Their story was the classic tale of the innocent girl who runs off with a "James Dean" type character and boy did my dad fit Dean's image to a "t." Mom's decision led her and the rest of our family through some good and bad times, and by the grace of God, they stayed married until death took them apart.

Dad was born in 1944 in Mancos, Colorado, a small mountain town that relied heavily on the logging industry. He had two sisters who were over ten years older than him so he basically grew up as an only child. When he was a teenager, his parents decided to move to the Desert Southwest to open up a trading post near Marble Canyon, Arizona. My dad refused to go with them so his older sister and brother-in-law offered to look after him so he could finish his high school years in his hometown of Durango, Colorado. This was a generous offer considering they already had four kids of their own to take care of when money was tight. My dad developed a close relationship with their family and later with my mom, which is why I am here today to tell their story. It is amazing how the decisions we make in life change the course of our own history and future generations.

Though my dad was quite the rebel, he balanced it out with a responsible side. He graduated from college with a math degree and continued on with his education to become a civil engineer. He did all this while holding down a full-time job and two kids already under his belt. My brother was the firstborn, and I came less than a year later. When I was first introduced to my older brother, he smashed a glass ashtray over my head. I guess that was just his way of letting me know who was boss. Later when my sister was born, my parents brought her home with two shiny red fire trucks – no ashtray on the head for her.

After finishing college, Dad landed a job with a large construction company that specialized in road and bridgework. He found himself helping with the structural design of a large cloverleaf overpass in Denver, Colorado, which included estimating the time required, from start to finish, to complete the project. After a successful short career working for someone else, he decided to go off and form his own company. This meant giving up benefits and a steady paycheck but he was an entrepreneur at heart and nothing was going to stop him from achieving his goals. I always respected Dad for his courage to go it alone. He taught my brother and me the valuable lesson of hard work that gave us the confidence to later form our own companies. My dad's hard work ethic and drive was shared in common with Mother Cabrini's. I think I am finding out why I admire and respect her so much. She reminds me so much of those I love and respect in my own family.

Dad claimed to have a belief in God but did not openly practice his faith. The God he believed in was very distant and impersonal, leaving humanity to fend for themselves. This caused strain on their marriage because my mom could never share her faith with him, resulting in a lonely spiritual life. Our family made it a priority to constantly pray for Dad, but to be honest; I had a hard time believing he would ever come to our Lord in an open way. Don't get me wrong, I love my dad and wouldn't have traded him for anyone but our relationship was not complete because God was not included in it. We especially enjoyed hunting and fishing together and this became our common bond.

Dad was emotional inside but rarely outwardly expressed it – we never hugged or exchanged "I love you's." His parents, especially his mom, were stoic in nature and my dad took after them. His dad died when I was young; therefore, I didn't spend enough time with Grandpa in order to develop a relationship. It was not until my mid-twenties that I developed a good relationship with my grandma whom I visited on a regular basis. She was instrumental in setting up our family reunions which kept my dad's side of the family better connected.

Dad's Death

It was late January 1996 when I received a call from my mom. Her voice is usually upbeat, but on this occasion, it was deeply distraught and I knew something was wrong. Without hesitation, she gave me the horrible news that ultimately changed my family's life. My dad was diagnosed with late-term lung cancer but further tests would have to be conducted to confirm the initial results. After hearing this, an intense weakness spread throughout my body and I was overcome with a type of fear that I hope to never experience again.

I informed my wife of the crisis and explained that we would have to leave right away. In a rush, we left late the following evening without checking the weather forecast. About halfway through our trip deep in the rugged Rocky Mountains, we ran into severe winter weather in a wide flat region known for its dangerous driving conditions. Snow blows off miles of flat fields onto and across the road from both directions. A blizzard had come out of the north which quickly became a whiteout. A State Patrol officer set up a temporary roadblock diverting traffic over a steep mountain pass. At least there the snow drifting across the road wouldn't be as bad. Now all we had to worry about was sliding off one of the sharp hairpin turns that worked its way up to the summit of a mountain and then back down again.

Despite the potential dangers ahead, I was determined to reach our destination so we decided to forge ahead. All I could focus on was the crisis that awaited me at the end of our journey.

As we neared Golden, Colorado we drove within a few miles of the Mother Cabrini Shrine but didn't give it any thought. At the time, I knew very little about this Shrine. My mom had invited me to go there on occasion but I always declined thinking it was just a few statues scattered around the mountainside and was out of the way to get there. Thank God we were able to literally plow through the snow without incident and we safely made it to my parents' house.

As we sat parked in their driveway, part of me wanted to turn around and go back and pretend this nightmare wasn't really happening. I knew seeing my dad eye to eye would be extremely difficult considering the fact that our relationship was never expressed on an emotional basis but instead, it was a working relationship.

My brother and I from an early age had worked for my dad in his construction business and our personal conversations were usually limited to what was accomplished at the end of the day's work. If we weren't working together we were usually off hunting or fishing. It was times out in nature that we had our best conversations. Don't get me wrong; as I explained earlier, my dad was an honest, hard-working, intelligent man, but like the rest of us, he wasn't perfect. Though Dad by the grace of God, was able to quit drinking ten years before his diagnosis of lung cancer, he could not stop smoking no matter how hard he tried. Our family knew his habit would eventually make him sick but when it finally occurred, we were still taken by surprise.

I never really understood what kind of relationship Dad had with God. He didn't go to Church with our family and he rarely talked about Jesus with us. We often talked openly about our Lord when Dad was in our presence, but he usually sat there silently, not engaged in our conversations. I often wondered what he was thinking about when we shared our Christian experiences. He was an analytical type of thinker and was a genius in mathematics. As with many other brilliant minds, faith in something you can't prove on paper can be difficult to accept.

After much thought, we got out of the car and my mom immediately greeted us with concerned, tear-filled eyes as we exchanged hugs. We found out that my dad was staying at the hospital overnight as they had conducted another series of tests. I was actually relieved that he wasn't there which gave me more time to mentally prepare myself for the inevitable. It was late so we all went directly to bed. Surprisingly, I quickly fell asleep but awoke in the middle of the night and had forgotten about Dad's condition. After lying there for a moment, my memory came back and the reality of the situation set in hard, which left me tossing and turning the rest of the night.

Early the next morning, exhausted, we headed to the hospital to see my dad. When we arrived, my hands were drenched with sweat and I wondered if I could even go through with it. Never before had I been placed in such an awkward situation. I told my wife and mom that I wanted to meet with him alone and they understood.

While walking down the hallway that led to his room, I saw a man in a green hospital gown sitting in a wheelchair, staring out the window.

I've rarely seen my dad in anything other than his normal clothes and never in a wheelchair, so at first glance I didn't recognize him. It was a shocking sight to see him sitting there looking so helpless. My brother and sister arrived at that moment which made me feel better having someone else with me when facing Dad. As we all walked closer, he broke out of his gaze and saw us coming. I could tell that he was embarrassed to be seen that way. He had hardly been sick a day in his life and had just recently climbed a steep mountain while elk hunting. Yet there he was, humiliated by his condition, but he knew he had no choice but to face his dilemma.

The closer we got to Dad, the faster my heart pounded and I realized it was going to be harder to face him than I had anticipated. I clearly remember my first words, "Hey Dad, is this really happening?" He just slowly shook his head and nodded in acknowledgement. For the first time, we saw tears well up in his eyes which sent a series of painful emotions running through my heart. Dad explained that the test results confirmed that he indeed had late-stage lung cancer and was only given several months to live. It was unfortunate that he had to get this horrible news on his birthday. We all told him not to give up, that we would be praying for him, and would do everything we could to help out. I told Dad that I would stay as long as necessary to help them get through this crisis. This was tough stuff, something unlike I'd ever experienced before and hoped would never happen again.

In the following days, the usual procedures were administered, radiation, chemotherapy, and laser treatments to help reduce the size of the tumor to enable my dad to breathe better. We were all praying for a healing and we shared this with him. The first month would see my dad in and out of the hospital which gave him little time to work so I had to take over all the jobs he presently had going and began soliciting new contracts to help them out financially. My mom, who is a licensed dietician, had to continue working to help pay for the bills that kept pouring in from all the medical costs. On top of it all, my parents were in the last stages of building a new home and had a lot of work left to finish.

Despite our efforts, Mom and Dad were still short on money so we decided to rent out a large shop building located on their property.

We told Dad our plans and he agreed it would be for the best. To our amazement, we were able to rent the building out to a company who operated their business just a few miles down the road. All they needed it for was storage and agreed to let us use one-quarter of it for our own needs. The rent was almost exactly what Mom needed to cover the house payment. Little did we know that Dad had asked God to help us rent it out and God's quick answer to my dad's prayer helped build his newfound faith. These were trying times, but our family pulled together and through Christ's grace, we were able to keep our heads above water and continue forward.

Through the month of February, the cancer in his lungs became more aggressive and grew rapidly. His doctor claimed it was the fastest growing cancer he had ever seen. That wasn't good news and from that point forward, they increased the laser treatment used to help burn away the tumor to free his air passages. The cancer was growing so fast that it was literally plugging up his lungs. After the treatment he would feel better, but within a few days the cancer would grow back and new treatment would be required. As things got worse, we intensified our prayers and openly laid our hands on Dad and asked God to heal him.

March came and his condition had turned for the worse, to the point that the doctor told us that he only had a few days to live. The doctor felt he had no choice but to be more aggressive with the laser treatment and warned us that Dad probably wouldn't make it through the procedure. Regardless, Dad decided to go ahead with it. Just in case, we all came to the hospital to give our last good-byes. I got the strangest feeling thinking it could be the last time on Earth I would see him. Although it was difficult, I told Dad for the first time that I loved him.

I'll never forget the way my brother reacted as the nurse began wheeling Dad off towards surgery. He just waved his hand and said, "Good-bye." Dad responded with a brief hand wave and replied, "I'll be working hard building a house for all of you in Heaven." We never expected a comment like that and wondered if he was trying to tell us that our prayers were not in vain and that God had touched him in a miraculous way? Regardless, it gave us hope that he had come to know our Lord. It turned out that he survived the laser surgery and God had given all of us a second chance. He felt much better but was still too weak to come home. After a few weeks went by he once again took a turn for the worse so we all went to his bedside and gathered for prayer. Something happened that night that only God could be responsible for. As we were about to pray, Dad reached out his hand to take mine. This made me feel extremely uncomfortable. First of all, this was the first time he had offered to openly pray with us and second; we had never held hands before. Uncomfortable or not, I grasped his hand and we all prayed the Our Father. To say the least, it was a very special moment. God's presence was with us that night and Dad received a miraculous healing, physical and spiritual.

Several days later the doctor was amazed at how much better he was feeling and even suggested that we take him home for a few days. We all thought his physical healing would be permanent. I picked Dad up from the hospital late in the afternoon and remembered how anxious he was to finally come home again.

As we were pulling down the long narrow driveway leading to his home, I couldn't help but notice what a beautiful evening was unfolding before us. The sun was just starting to set behind the majestic Rocky Mountains and the sky was lit up with a dazzling fiery red that appeared almost angelic. To me, it was as if God was doing it just for my dad and this special gift didn't go unnoticed. Dad proclaimed, "What a beautiful sunset God has given us! After spending so much time in the hospital I now realize how much I've taken all of this for granted." What he said might not sound profound to someone who didn't know him, but to me, it was as if the gates of Heaven had opened up and portrayed all its glory! Our whole family had prayed for years for Dad to accept Christ and I had my doubts that it would ever happen. But there on that special evening, he was letting me know that he had come to believe in our Lord.

My mind flashed back to the moment nearly five years ago when I travelled to Medjugorje in former Yugoslavia, high atop Cross Mountain, all alone, on that cool May night, when God told me to pray for my dad's conversion. At the time, I had many doubts that he would ever convert, but right before my eyes, ears, and heart on that beautiful sunset evening, my dad's conversion proved that what may seem impossible can become possible. I gave thanks and praise to our Lord for this wonderful miracle that had taken so long to occur.

That evening, our family had a joyful family dinner. Later, after everyone had gone to sleep, I lay awake staring out the window deep into a starlit night. Intently praying, God inspired me with the following words, "I am more concerned with the soul than the body."

A few days later, Dad suddenly became worse again and we had to take him back to the hospital. It seemed like it all happened so fast. They ran some tests and found out the cancer had spread to his liver which all but guaranteed the outcome. He had a severe reaction to the contrast die used to conduct the test and his scarred lung tissue caused from all the laser treatments started to hemorrhage. His lungs soon filled with fluid and my mom stood by his side all night and prayed with him. She encouraged him to say Jesus as he breathed in and out which brought him some needed comfort. Dad slowly passed away in the loving arms of my mom and early the next morning on a cold snowy day, I received word that he had died.

I'll never forget going to his hospital room and seeing Dad in a reclined position with his lifeless, pale body just lying there motionless in his bed. This was my first close-up experience with death and it changed my life forever. The reality of death was now real and I quickly became aware of how fragile life could be. The need to always be ready to meet Jesus took on a whole new meaning – there is nothing more important than spending eternity with Christ. There is no source of human pleasure that can compare with this wonderful gift that awaits all who are written in the book of life.

Mother Cabrini really understood this well, that Heaven is the most important. That is what strengthened her resolve to be fearless and accomplish so much in her earthly life despite her many weaknesses.

We cannot be like my dad who took the chance of missing out on Heaven most of his life. He was very fortunate to have had the necessary time to accept Jesus. Dad faced several near-death experiences that could have jeopardized his relationship with Christ but God in His mercy repeatedly saved him.

Car Accident Miracle

Soon after my dad passed away, I nearly lost both my wife and son to a terrible car accident. The driver responsible for this accident was a young teenage girl who had several friends with her. My wife was stopped at a busy two-lane highway to turn left into my mom's driveway. There were several oncoming cars so she had to wait before turning. As she looked into her review mirror, she could see a car coming off in the distance. As the car got closer, it appeared it wasn't slowing down. She then looked forward to see if any oncoming traffic was coming and just as she began to make her left turn, the car slammed into the back of her car traveling over 50 miles per hour. The impact was tremendous and it sent her car spinning into the oncoming traffic lane. The automobile that hit her was much larger which added to the force of the collision. None of the passengers from the other vehicle were hurt but the driver came out screaming hysterically, apologizing for the accident. She was too busy talking with her friends and failed to notice my wife's car stopped in front of her. It was only at the last second that my wife turned left to try and avoid the collision that helped reduce the impact by channeling more of the energy to the right side of the car which in turn helped to save my son's life. Because of this, there was more damage to the right back side of the car than to the left. My son was in the backseat on the left side. That morning before the accident, my wife changed his car seat from the right to the left side and didn't know why. I don't think this was a coincidence; rather, the mighty power of God was at work.

God had indeed performed a miracle. The impact from the other car had cracked the back of our son's car seat in half. If the impact had penetrated any further, our son would not be alive today. God through his great mercy and love, held the other car back just enough to allow our son to live.

After I met them at the hospital I was beyond joyful and relieved to see them both alive and well. We both praised Jesus for miraculously protecting our family. My son ended up suffering a mild concussion and after a precautionary CT scan, the doctors said they didn't see anything of concern.

Later in his life, he became symptomatic regarding vertigo issues and found out through testing that his inner ear was damaged from the accident which can cause an assortment of issues. A low salt diet really helped. He has lived a fully active life but at times it can become debilitating. My wife suffered some injuries as well but after being rehabilitated, she has been able to lead a normal life. We all realized that it could have been much worse.

Mom's Heavenly Encounter at Mother Cabrini's Shrine

In my mom's words after Dad had passed away while she was going through a painful grieving period:

I Love her! We have the Mother Cabrini Shrine in the hills around Denver! It is a Holy Place. The statue of the Sacred Heart stands at the top of the hill overlooking the city! Many pilgrimage to this place. There is a statue of Mother Cabrini in the church and she has piercing eyes. The grandkids think she follows them around the chapel when we go there! I've experienced a miracle there while attending mass in the lower outer courtyard!

My husband Clint had passed away from lung cancer. I was in tremendous pain. There was a Mass in the outer courtyard of the Mother Cabrini Shrine on a Friday afternoon at 5:30 pm and I wanted to go after work. It was one of those hell days at work and doctors kept consulting me even as late as 4pm with a TPN Consult and consult for diet instruction of a patient. I finally finished at 4:40pm and headed up the highway jammed with cars; I was in rush hour. Mass had already started by the time I got there. I went down into the courtyard, and it was sprinkling with rain. I looked for a place I could sit and saw an older lady who had a trench coat on smiling at me from across the courtyard and motioned me to come so I headed in her direction. Sitting down next to her and trying to calm myself, as I was upset about being late to Mass. In a few minutes when I had regained my composure, she reached over and quietly said to me, "I'm so glad you made it!" I looked at her to see if I knew her and I didn't know her. She just smiled at me and said the same thing again! She had gray hair and appeared to be in her late 70's or early 80's. During mass it started to rain lightly again so she shared her umbrella with me and shared her song book with me! She was so kind and gave me GREAT comfort! After Communion, she touched my arm and said again, "Thank you for coming!" I asked her, "Do I know you; you have been so kind to me?" She just smiled at me and didn't say a word. After Mass was over, we started walking towards the stairs up and out of the lower courtyard! I was behind her and I was going to talk to her some more and find out how she knew me when we got up the stairs and on the road. Again, I was right behind her but when I reached the top of the stairs and on the road, she was gone and I looked for her everywhere! My heart was swelling with appreciation for her incredible kindness as it helped to ease the pain of the loss of my husband. I then walked the Stations of the Cross that are on the grounds of Mother Cabrini's compound. The stations go up to the top of the hill where the huge statue of the Sacred Heart is and overlooks the city of Denver. That day carried me through the next week and sometime after with a certain amount of joy mixed with pain as I realized that God cared and sent someone from Heaven to console me!! Who knows, maybe it was Mother Cabrini as so many miracles have occurred there. That place was my source of comfort for years after Clint died. My family would join me in going there and the grandkids loved it there and were so happy! Thank you, Lord, Jesus for your comfort and kindness!

When Mom was ten years old, she used to sit by a small seasonal waterfall located above her house and write poetry about the Blessed Mother Mary to whom she had a strong devotion. This is the type of thing future saints did, like Mother Cabrini who sailed her little paper boats down the river with imaginary missionaries on board to evangelize China. My mom reminds me a lot of Mother Cabrini with her passion to help bring others to Jesus. Mom also reminds me of St. Bernadette of Lourdes whose life at an early age was similar in several ways. They both had a special devotion to the Virgin Mary, attended Catholic elementary school, and due to their lack of knowledge in certain subjects were often ridiculed by the nuns who taught them. Mom struggled with math, but she was an excellent writer and poet and won a school-wide contest with a poem she wrote about the Virgin Mary.

Years later, Mom's faith was put to the test with the loss of her husband, but she has kept her faith in Jesus, with her devotion to Mother Mary and our Lord strong as ever, helping her through the trials in life.

I have always considered Mom to be a saint. She has stood by me and the rest of our family as our steadfast matriarch through the thick and thin, putting her own interests aside. She does this for everyone. May our Lord Jesus continue to bless, protect, and comfort His beloved daughter all the days of her life.

> My pretty little Rosary
> I say it everyday.
> I ask our Blessed Mother
> In a very special way
> To guide, protect, and pray for us
> Through her Divine Son
> For each day that is given
> And those not yet begun.

Teresa Louise Boyle - Age 10

Chapter 8

My Journey

Thanks to Grandpa, praying the Holy Spirit Novena helped save me from many years of hardship especially while I was in high school. By the grace of God and prayers from family members, I was able to remain drug free, although I did have a short bout with alcohol. I constantly had students at my school asking me why I didn't do drugs and I simply told them I didn't want or need to. Most of them respected my answer but occasionally I would get harassed over it.

While at a party, someone would offer me a beer, but before I could say no, friends around me would tell them I don't drink, almost as if they were my own personal guardians. This went on for a few years but then something happened to change all of that.

I thought I was invincible until I made a bad decision by slowly playing around with alcohol that quickly got out of hand. I had also developed a relationship with a girl that only compounded the situation. Before I knew it, my life was quickly out of control. I knew I had a problem because I couldn't stop drinking with just a couple of beers. Instead, I would keep drinking until I blacked out. This was the most vulnerable period of my life. My friends claimed that I ran across a busy six-lane highway with cars forced to slam on their brakes to avoid hitting me. How I wasn't killed was a miracle. The next day I couldn't remember anything about the night before. I was told that I once went up to a big football player's girlfriend and started hugging her right in front of him. Lucky for me, he just laughed at my miserable condition and didn't pound me into the ground.

I remember my homecoming dance where I became so intoxicated that I fell all over the place while trying to dance with my girlfriend. One of my teachers noticed my behavior and booted me out the door into the cool fall night. My girlfriend escorted me to my truck where she left me alone in my misery. Lying on the floorboard on the verge of passing out, I briefly remember throwing my guts out, feeling like I was going to die. I pleaded with God to save me and told Him if He would stop the pain, I wouldn't drink again. I don't even remember how I got home that night. I was such a hypocrite because I used to make fun of some of my friends when they made a fool out of themselves while drinking.

During that time I also made the mistake of letting my relationship with the girl get too serious which caused me to abandon my friends and even quit the track and field team. When my coach found out, he was furious. He called me into his office and tried to knock some sense into my head but I didn't listen. I can still hear his words when he told me that I would look back one day and regret what I had done. When he saw that I wasn't responding, he grabbed my shirt collar and pushed me up against a wall and threatened to punch my lights out. He claimed the only thing holding him back was the threat of being fired. Looking back, I wish he would have knocked some sense into me – it would have saved a lot of heartache.

Premarital sex can be as addictive as drugs or alcohol and can be just as dangerous to our health and soul. I know firsthand that it is difficult to date someone for a long period of time and remain celibate. Not only can it result in pregnancy or a sexually transmitted disease, but it will also leave you feeling guilty, empty, insecure, and ultimately, it can destroy your relationship with the other person and with Christ. God created sex to be fulfilling between a husband and wife. Anything outside of marriage will only lead to despair. Leaving yourself pure for your future spouse is the ultimate gift to them and more importantly, it is pleasing to God.

Later in my life my wife and I became certified marriage preparation ministers at our local Catholic parish so don't lose hope if you are suffering the same fate as everything is possible for God.

Unfortunately, I wasn't thinking about that at the time. Then one day it came to a head when I got into an argument with my girlfriend while driving drunk. I stopped on top of an overpass in the middle of the road, got out of my car, and started walking away. At this point I knew things had gotten out of control so I knew something had to change. By God's grace, I stumbled on one of the Holy Spirit Novena booklets my Grandpa had given to me and decided to give it a try. The novena takes nine days to finish and each day I gained a little more strength. Directly after finishing the ninth day, something happened that changed my life forever.

My Vision

I find it very difficult to share the following but think it is important enough to risk potential ridicule or disbelief from others. I had just finished the ninth and final day of the Holy Spirit Novena in 1981 around 10:00 p.m. while sitting up in bed with the light on. I was getting up to brush my teeth in the bathroom located down the hall. After a few steps towards the door, I was suddenly shocked and alarmed to see a beautiful woman dressed in a robe with a head covering standing at my door opening. She had a warm loving smile on her face. Startled and embarrassed, I immediately jumped back into bed. From there, I had another brief look at the woman. She looked to be in her late 20s or early 30s but her face was very kind and mature with a motherly appearance about her. Her beauty radiated from her heavenly presence. No words were spoken, just her smile and warm eyes that pierced into my soul. Then she disappeared. It all happened so quickly.

Still a little shaken up, I peeked around the corner down the hallway to see if she was still there. All I could see was the cloth depiction of the Sacred Heart of Jesus we had hanging on the wall. I continued down the stairs to where my parents were up watching TV and ran in to tell them what had just occurred. I couldn't believe I did that in front of my dad who would surely think I was crazy with such a story. To my surprise, he didn't say a word but just listened as I briefed my mom. She immediately commented that maybe it was the Blessed Mother? I didn't know what to think at the time.

Artist rendition of my vision – *Our Lady of Open Doors*.

After a restless sleep, I awoke the next morning still in disbelief to what had occurred the night before. I wondered who this woman was and why she came to me. The thought of the Blessed Mother Mary sent chills throughout my body. While I was contemplating all of this, an inner voice deep in my soul told me to stop having premarital sex. So that evening, I met my girlfriend and told her what had happened. I could tell she thought I was a little crazy and she burst out crying when I told her we had to stop having sexual relations. She told me I didn't love her anymore and took it personally. It was definitely a difficult moment but I knew I had to do it. I wasn't perfect afterwards by any means, but I did have the strength to finally stop which would not have occurred without divine help. I ended up breaking up with her and stopped drinking as well.

Something really did happen that night that helped me have the strength to overcome my weaknesses. Going forward, I continued to take baby steps. I definitely wasn't without my struggles but I had finally been freed from the bondage that would have destroyed my life and others around me if left to continue. If it really was Our Lady who came to my aid, it wasn't because I am special or a good person but rather, just the opposite – I was really messed up and needed divine help to overcome it.

Sacred Heart of Jesus Revelation

While writing this book, I was hit with a revelation. We had the Sacred Heart of Jesus picture on our wall outside my room. This is more profound than I had realized as there is great power in displaying this sacred image in our homes. Back in 1673 in France, Sister Margaret Mary Alacoque began to receive visions of Jesus with specific focus on His Sacred Heart. In her vision, Jesus told Sister in part, ". . . I promise you that my heart shall expand itself to shed in abundance the influence of its divine love upon those who shall thus honor it and cause it to be honored."[182]

Jesus made twelve promises to Sister Margaret for those who honor His Sacred Heart and cause it to be honored. Promise number nine stood out for me as it pertained to my story. "I will bless those places wherein the image of my Sacred Heart shall be exposed and venerated."[183]

https://ewtn.co.uk/article-why-is-june-the-month-of-the-sacred-heart-of-jesus/

I am so thankful to my Mom for having the wisdom and love to hang this beautiful and powerful image of our Lord's most Sacred Heart in our hallway. And now looking back, and through all my experiences at the Shrine, I can now see that Mother Cabrini, whose whole ministry was based on the Sacred Heart of Jesus, was helping us back then, and was preparing us for the present times through her powerful intercession to the most Sacred Heart of Jesus.

Discovering Medjugorje

A couple of years into college, I got to the point where I didn't need a girlfriend but rather, I just wanted to have friends. My life had become so much better without a serious romantic relationship. In fact, I went nearly five years without dating a girl and it was one of the best times of my life. Most importantly, this was when I became "born again" and truly dedicated my life to Christ. I was staying with my grandparents off and on during that time and was thirsty for God. My grandpa and grandma became my mentors, with Grandma teaching me how to pray the Rosary which really helped me overcome weaknesses and strengthen my relationship with Jesus.

Via a random letter sent from the Marian Movement of Priests, I first discovered the phenomenon of Medjugorje that had been occurring since June of 1981. The newsletter fascinated me as I learned about the visionaries who were about my age claiming to have daily visions of the Blessed Virgin Mary in the remote communist village of Medjugorje, (former) Yugoslavia. The more I read about it the more I wanted to know. At first, I didn't get the connection that Mary started appearing there in 1981. When I finally did, it really got my attention as that was the same time I had my encounter with the woman dressed in the robe after finishing the novena. I hadn't thought about it very much since but then after a few years had passed, it resurfaced in a big way. Maybe it really was Our Lady, I thought, or maybe it was a saint, an angel, or other heavenly body? I did know that I had experienced many fruits since that day occurred.

Later, I found a newspaper written by Wayne Weible who did an excellent job detailing all the events occurring there at the time. I called their organization to ask for a few extra copies and they sent me a box containing hundreds of these papers, so I started handing them out to people. Mary was asking us to fast on bread and water on Wednesdays and Fridays, monthly confession, and three hours a day of prayer which included the Rosary, daily Mass, and Holy Scripture readings. I took all of this seriously and started to faithfully live out Mary's messages. I even went to confession for the first time since my Confirmation. I was really on fire for God and had also developed a beautiful devotion to Mary which really made me want to go and see Medjugorje firsthand. Unfortunately, I had very little money as I was helping my grandparents rebuild some of their commercial buildings that needed repair in exchange for room and board. About that time, my sister informed me about the reduced airfare tickets. Then Father Svet told me that a person would know when it's time to go to Medjugorje because they would be called in their heart. I felt like I was being called but had no idea how I was going to get there. Then a way opened rather quickly just as Fr. Svet had said it would.

Medjugorje's Impact on My Life

The beautiful story of Medjugorje is extremely complex with many roads that lead us to Jesus through Mary. Medjugorje has not just been about changing world events but rather, how this special place of prayer has impacted the individual. I can speak for myself that my life has changed for the better since learning about this place.

God was always there caring for me even when I didn't deserve it. During that period of my life, I was in worse shape than I even realized and is why I feel God sent the Blessed Virgin Mary and His Holy Spirit to my rescue. I am very humbled that our Lord saved me from my self-inflicted misery.

Through God's mercy, I grew in faith and strength. I found myself praying more, especially the Holy Spirit Novena. I used the rosary beads to keep track of the seven Glory Be's required in the novena. I loved using the Rosary in this way but didn't know how to pray it.

I finally asked my grandma to teach me how to pray the Rosary as she was the expert. She provided me with some literature that provided a step-by-step guide. This beautiful prayer highlighting the life of Jesus, Joseph, and Mary brought my relationship with God to a new level.

Regardless, I still had many struggles, and they continue today, but now I can overcome my adversities, not through my own strength, but through our Lord's.

I also thank my mom and grandma for all their prayers and my grandpa for showing me how to pray the Holy Spirit Novena that helped open my stubborn heart long enough to allow the Holy Spirit to gently guide me in the right direction. Things would have been completely different for me if I had not received all this help when I needed it the most.

I really enjoyed college because I was in a better state of mind due to my newfound prayer life. I had completely stopped drinking alcohol, wasn't dating anyone, and was extremely busy trying to balance my studies with work. Regardless, I was happier than ever.

It took me six years to graduate from college because I had to work full time to pay my way through it but it went by like a breeze. I graduated with a degree in Environmental Real Estate and Finance. It combined business with the environmental sciences such as biology and ecology. I was fascinated by the natural world and loved business as well so I incorporated both majors into one degree.

In my early years of college, my brother and I bought our first duplex and we quickly learned that real estate investing wasn't easy. We had to completely renovate it and after many long hours we finally rented it out which allowed us to break even on our mortgage payment. Whenever we had a vacancy, it was very difficult to make the payment. Grandpa was a real estate broker so my interest in real estate probably came from him.

Although I was doing much better in my prayer life, I still had a long way to go. My love for money reached a peak after graduating from college. I was on fire to make millions in real estate and quickly registered to take my broker's exam and felt very fortunate to pass it on my first attempt. The word spread quickly as Grandpa called me soon afterwards to congratulate me on passing the test. He also had a hidden agenda as he now saw an opportunity for Grandma and himself to winter in California to avoid the deep snow and cold weather of Southwest Colorado where they called home.

Grandpa came right out and asked me if I would consider running his real estate company while they were gone for six months. I immediately got a sick feeling in my stomach as I knew his small town of Durango, Colorado had limited opportunities. I appreciated his offer but that was the last thing I wanted to do, as the Denver real estate market was very affordable at the time due to a market crash that was on the verge of recovering. I wanted to start buying houses in large numbers and I saw managing his small one-man real estate office as a dead end.

I told Grandpa that I would consider it and get back to him. He was determined and kept calling me and even asked my mom to talk me into it. "This will be a good opportunity and valuable experience for you," he claimed. Grandpa's persistence paid off. I ended up moving there and found the market to be very depressed. I told Grandpa that I would only stay until he returned. There were rusty real estate signs everywhere as properties would take forever to sell. Prices were cheap but I failed to see the investment opportunities that would later turn out to be quite substantial. Back in the 1980s you could buy an average sized home in town for $30,000.00. Today, the same home would cost around $750,000.00. This area was invaded when the big cities around the country started to fall apart, especially after the California riots and earthquake occurred back in the early 1990s and recently after COVID-19 in 2020. Since then, this area has become extremely expensive with mostly lower paying jobs and so the local saying goes, "If you want to make one million here, you better bring two." Small towns all over the Western US suddenly had swarms of people searching out a "Mayberry" type existence that was safe from crime, disease, and all the problems associated with larger cities, not to mention the beautiful scenery around here.

When I first arrived, it was very difficult to sell anything as the market was still a few years away from exploding. Grandpa, through a family partnership that he set up, had two commercial buildings that he leased out. One of the buildings had become vacant. This is the property where he claimed the Blessed Mother helped him acquire it after he bought a poor young boy some shoes after he saw him walking down the street barefoot in the middle of winter. The property needed some serious work as the former tenant ran an auto repair shop. They had completely trashed both the inside and out with grease and old car parts scattered throughout. Because of the poor real estate market, I decided to focus my work on cleaning up the building and getting it leased out again. I had plans to convert it into retail space as the building had high ceilings even though it would require an enormous amount of work. Regardless, Grandpa agreed with my plan and he borrowed the necessary funds to start the remodel.

Hungry Homeless Man

Later that week after beginning the remodel, I was sitting in my truck going over some paperwork when I suddenly had a strange feeling that someone was watching me. I looked out my open window and was startled to see a man nicely dressed in western wear standing only a few feet away, staring at me. When he saw me inch, he apologized for startling me and asked if I had any money he could borrow. I never expected that to come out of his mouth considering how well kept he looked. He didn't look like someone who needed money. He went on to tell me that he had recently lost his job in another state and was just passing through but had run out of money several days before. He claimed he hadn't eaten a meal since.

As with most people, I never give money to anyone on the street because you never know whom you are dealing with and what they will use it for. The last thing a potential alcoholic or drug addict needs is money. I thought about it for a moment and told him I would be happy to buy him a meal at the fast-food place across the street. I asked if he wouldn't mind walking over to the drive-up window where I would order and pay for his meal. He agreed so I drove over and placed the order. I doubled everything including dessert.

When he saw that the order was ready, he eagerly came over to my truck and I handed it to him. With a quick thank you, he hurried over to a grassy area along the curb and started to devour his meal. He literally looked as if he was starving to death the way he was gobbling his food down. I stayed at the edge of the main road and watched him as long as I could before another car came up behind me which forced me to leave. At first it was almost funny watching him, but then my smile turned into tears. How could someone in our country become that desperate in such a short period of time? His clean appearance probably caused others to not take him seriously. I had to wonder how many people rejected his plea for help before I met up with him. Before I left, I told him where he could find a shelter and I could only hope that he listened to my advice.

I know if that were me, I would have had a hard time swallowing my pride. I learned firsthand that it doesn't take very long for someone to become homeless. It could happen to almost anyone if they do not have family or friends to help them. To be left on your own, hungry and scared without a home must be the worst feeling in the world. At the time, I wondered if the man was really an angel sent by our Lord to test me because he just didn't fit the bill of a homeless person. Today however, I have seen this so many times that I realize this problem is real, especially in our present times.

Mother Cabrini's life was full of these kinds of encounters where she met struggling people daily in far worse conditions providing them with a helping hand in their time of need. It would just take me several decades before I found out about her beautiful contribution to our struggling world.

Although I was extremely busy, I found time to pray and started going to daily Mass early in the morning for the first time. Receiving daily Eucharist was a real turning point in my faith. It allowed me to experience Christ in a more intimate way. I became closer to Jesus than I ever thought possible. Prayer was no longer a burden but rather, something to look forward to. I found myself wanting to do acts of charity so I volunteered whenever I could.

As I mentioned before, this is the period when I was born again in the Spirit and when I first met my wife. I can't imagine what my life would have been like if I hadn't made the decision to move. It would be a lot different. That is why it is so important to be right with God. When we are in prayer, God's calling for us becomes clearer. Being open to the

Holy Spirit makes all the difference when trying to discern direction in our lives. Having a close relationship with Mary as our intercessor to Jesus has been instrumental in my life. Mary has taught me invaluable lessons and wisdom in which to live out my faith.

Canadian Angel

During that time, my life felt complete with no need to start a serious relationship with a woman. However, little did I know that God was busy making plans for me. While volunteering at a soup kitchen run by the Missionaries of Charity (late St. Mother Teresa's order), I met a young Canadian woman who had come down from British Columbia, Canada, to volunteer her time. It had almost been five years with little interest in meeting another woman but when I first saw her, it was as if my spirit leapt for joy.

Later that evening while lying in an unfamiliar bed, I prayed extremely hard that God would allow me to become better acquainted with her. The next day, the sisters had planned a birthday party for my uncle who dedicated his life helping out the Missionaries of Charity in their work with the poorest of the poor. His birthday was to take place at a small lake surrounded by tall Ponderosa Pine trees located a few miles out of town. This was also my last chance to get to know the Canadian girl because it was her last day before returning home.

I had recently been to this lake while taking a group of Navajo Indians up into the hills to track wild turkeys and deer. It was an opportunity for all of us to get out of the city and back into the wilderness where we could experience their native hunting grounds. As soon as we arrived, they jumped out of the truck and were on game trails within minutes. It was refreshing to see how excited they were while out in nature away from all the problems that tore them down. Even more amazing was their ability to take a raw piece of wood and shape it into the form of an animal using only a pocketknife. Their skilled hands and their ability to perceive every detail in their surrounding environment was unmatched. To keep it authentic, I brought some hard-earned elk steaks that I had taken earlier that fall. After the afternoon hike, we fried up some elk steak over a natural fire that turned out to be delicious cooked that way. We first gave thanks to Diyin (God in Navajo) and then we all ripped into the wild meat. For a moment it felt like we were living back several hundred years ago in a time when that type of life was the norm. On that day, I formed a bond with my new friends that would not be broken.

Because of my positive experience at the lake, I felt optimistic that good things would also happen at my uncle's party. I prayed to have a chance to talk with the Canadian girl and my prayer was answered. Though my conversation with her was brief, I thoroughly enjoyed being in her presence. To my disappointment, the party quickly came to an end and I couldn't get up enough courage to ask for her phone number.

Little did I know that my grandpa, who had come with me to attend his son's birthday party, was watching my every move. He came up and quietly asked me if I had gotten her phone number. When I told him no, he couldn't believe it! In a loud voice he said, "Are you going to just sit there and let her get away? If I were your age, I would've already had her number and gone on our first date!"

Grandpa couldn't take it anymore and decided to take matters into his own hands. I remember feeling mortified when he waved her over to where we were standing and abruptly asked for her father's number in case he needed information about British Columbia's real estate prices. Like me, Grandpa was a real estate broker so this old business line worked like a charm and he felt proud to have helped me out. I had never seen him do anything like that before and wondered why he felt so compelled?

Several weeks later, I gathered enough courage to call which completely caught her by surprise. During our conversation, I found out that she never gave me a second thought after meeting me. Embarrassed, I explained to her how my grandpa had used the real estate thing as an excuse to get her number. To my relief, she thought the whole thing was funny and told me how blessed I was to have such a great grandpa.

Looking back over the years, I can clearly see how God has directed my path. When God is in control, things work out for the best. I also thank God for Grandpa who took time out of his life to look after my better interest – if it were not for his persistence, I would have missed out on this wonderful blessing of my new family. Though Grandpa has passed away, I look forward to being reunited with him in Heaven.

Letters

Feeling refreshed, and full of hope for the future, I started writing long letters to my "Canadian Angel" as I commonly called her:

May 31, 1990

Dear Canadian Angel,

I want to start by saying that I love you in a very special way. I'm still not exactly sure what type of love this is. This has to be a Godly love because this love brings me closer to Him. It feels so comfortable, so natural, so easy to express. I thank God for this! I guess I should think of it as a sisterly love but it just feels different from the love I have for my sister. I guess I shouldn't think about it so much and just let things be.

I do know one thing for sure; you are a very special friend to me. I will take time out for you before anyone else. Believe me, I have been so busy after returning from Medjugorje that I haven't had time to unpack yet.

To tell you about my trip to Medjugorje would take a thousand pages. I'll tell you one thing, it has changed my life forever! My faith has become so much more important to me. My experience has in a way, almost ruined me in this world – all I want to do is pray and worship God! I have lost my ambition to make lots of money as this desire has been replaced with heavenly things.

When I came back from Medjugorje, it was like seeing for the first time. We do so many things that are totally worthless – we are so busy in our lives but if we are not doing it for God, what good is it? We need to focus on the eternal! This trip did exactly what I had prayed for. It brought me to a new understanding of God.

He became so real, I see Him differently now, and it is like having a new pair of spiritual eyes! My life has more meaning and purpose. This trip was far greater than I could have imagined! There is no material thing in this world that I would trade for this experience as my sister and I were so fortunate to visit the edge of Heaven!

So many graces were given to us. If only we could live and follow them, as I know this is the truth. Many miracles took place. We felt the breath of God touch us as we all prayed together for the whole world atop Apparition Hill. I know this is the way God intended our lives to be. It is unfortunate that we have strayed so far from God's will. "Please God, help us to see your light, your truth!"

I felt the presence of the Holy Spirit descend upon us in a physical manner like when someone touches you! It was so intense, so powerful; that this special presence instantly cured a bad cold I was suffering from. This all took place during a talk with Father Jozo who I believe is a living Saint. Both my sister and I experienced miracles so touching that at times it became hard to believe they were actually occurring in such frequency. I had never cried so many tears of joy – it was overwhelming!

I also want to thank you for your last letter. You really opened up for the first time by expressing your feelings. This is what I have been praying for, to become closer to you – to get to know you better, and to be able to talk to you about anything.

There are times when I wonder if I have wasted part of my life focusing too much on God. I wonder what my life would have been like if I had pursued my earlier dreams of becoming rich in real estate. Would I have been happy or completely messed up by removing myself from the only source of true happiness? I see some of my friends who are already successful as far as the world goes. Believe me, I know I shouldn't think this way but I am challenged with these types of thoughts. Living a worldly life is very tempting. To help counter this temptation, I look back in my life when God wasn't so important to me and I quickly realize that focusing on Him is the right decision.

Living for God in today's generation is totally against the grain of society. Living for something we cannot see is not very cool in our world. We would rather live for the tangibles, things we can get our hands on, show off, and even make them part of our identity. We go to great extremes to acquire them. Yes, I get caught up in all of this so please pray for me.

It relaxes me to write to you; in fact, I love to write to you. I especially like to read your letters. The fact that you have begun to open up to me makes me feel so good! It helps me to gain confidence in our friendship. I want very much to know you better but I understand this cannot be rushed as this takes time. Trust must first be established through experience and I hope you can eventually learn to trust me with anything.

I was so excited to see your letter upon my return from Medjugorje. Before reading your letter I was worried that something was wrong and that you were drifting away from me. Your letter helped to clear this up for me.

Like Father Svets said in Medjugorje, let God lead you and ask for His will for you – He always has the best answer. We must strive for holiness to receive God's will for our lives.

You have many graces awaiting you. . . . I'm serious; I can see God working in your life.

Addressing your comment about suffering, I would not ask for it even though we can offer it up. Instead, we need to pray constantly, always asking God for His will, and then if suffering comes our way, we can offer it up for the conversion of sinners as our Blessed Mother has asked us to do.

I hope you don't think I am lecturing you? I have been praying very hard prior to writing you. I asked the Holy Spirit to help give me the right words to say to you. The Blessed Mother Mary really cares for you. Ask her to intercede on your behalf to her Son. Seek refuge in the Immaculate Hearts of Mary and Jesus. There you will find peace.

As evident in my letter, I was deeply in love with God and was starting to fall in love with my future wife as well. The greatest fruits from my experience in Medjugorje have been my closer relationship with God and of course, my wonderful wife and son! I was overflowing with love during that time and God knew that I was finally ready to express this newfound love in a holy way. This really taught me that it is always more important to get your life right with God first before getting involved in a relationship. With our Lord on board our chances for a successful relationship and eventual marriage are greatly increased.

To make a long story short, after many hours of phone calls, long letters, and eventually meeting in person again on several occasions, we developed a serious relationship and eventually got married. I thank God daily for bringing us together which has resulted in many years of happiness and our beautiful son Noah. However, we have not been immune to the daily struggles of marriage and raising a family. We have had to draw on Christ's strength to make it work out for the best.

Patrick and Melisa Dillon's wedding picture.

Patrick, Melisa, and Noah Dillon

Our Greatest Gift – Our Son Noah

Our greatest gift on earth is our son Noah. He has always been our pride and joy and the greatest blessing in our lives and continues to bless us in so many ways. He was born two weeks prematurely as my wife had a difficult time carrying him with constant bouts of pre-term labor during her pregnancy. She was prescribed bed rest and had to be careful with physical activity beginning in her sixth month of pregnancy. Through the grace of God, he was born healthy and full of zest, ready to explore life.

As a child, Noah grew up loving our Lord in a special way. He loved to pray and read books about Jesus and the saints. He also loved the outdoors and was always outside playing, fishing, and exploring. He is a natural at sports and played mainly soccer and baseball. Baseball was his first love and he was really good at it playing first base, catcher, and pitcher. It was on the mound while pitching that he learned self-discipline and the ability to handle pressure. People would often comment how composed he was even when the bases were loaded and the game was on the line. This would later prove to be valuable experience for him in dealing with his career as a professional photographer, artist, and musician.

He graduated from college with a degree in Exercise Physiology, but he had other career ambitions.

He had a strong desire to be a creative artist in Hollywood, California, which is next to impossible to be successful. Many people including us, his parents, told him it was a very difficult path, but Noah refused to listen and kept on pursuing his dreams just like Mother Cabrini did when those around her said it was impossible. Both of their dreams are completely different yet similar, as Hollywood today can be just as brutal and challenging as it was in the inner city of New York at the time Mother Cabrini first arrived there to help the suffering Italian immigrants.

Noah has always had a strong drive to succeed in everything he took on. His dream to become a world-class photographer/artist and musician was no exception. Yes, it was brutal at times trying to break into this industry and yes, he has caused us great anxiety on many occasions, but Noah, through his hard work and determination, is now living out his dream.

He has photographed some of the biggest legends in the industry and has recently obtained a music contract with Atlantic Records. Who would have thought that someone from the small town of Durango, Colorado could go so far without any contacts, in such a demanding, brutal, and competitive environment as Hollywood?

The keys to his success are similar to Mother Cabrini's. He never lost his Catholic faith albeit he has struggled at times to maintain it in such a secular environment. This is true for our youth in general where the culture is all about "me." And like Mother Cabrini, Noah has struggled to overcome a physical disability that he suffered from the car accident making things more difficult for him.

Noah has never been the kind of person to be star-struck, which puts the celebrities he works with at ease. They often say there is something special about him, and yes this is true, but I know that the presence of God in him is what these people are feeling.

He is not out for the money but rather he has a strong drive to make good art and is willing to sacrifice long hours to accomplish this. Some may look at certain projects he has published and wonder if he is even a Christian, but being one of them, Noah understands how the youth think today and how to reach them. He does this in subtle ways that are highly effective and has reached lost souls though his non-traditional ministry efforts. Believe me, there are times when I get frustrated with him over his work but just have to wait and be patient, and for the most part, I usually see how he was right. Sometimes he is more blatant in his message. On one occasion back in 2021, he carried a handmade 10-foot tall 2x4 cross painted white on his shoulder for over 10 miles from Hollywood all the way to the Santa Monica Pier. Noah completed his journey at the edge of the Pacific Ocean. It was very moving. A person filmed him unknowingly along the way. The reaction he received was mixed, from people honking in approval, to strange looks from passersby. I asked him why he did it and he said, "Why not."

It would probably be easier if he were an Exercise Physiologist and maybe someday he will pursue this field, but for now he is travelling around the world doing his work and we are proud of him for working so hard pursuing his dreams. He has taught me to go beyond my comfort zone and fear to pursue things important to me even if it seems impossible at times. We are proud of Noah regardless of what he was doing. Our hope is that he keeps his faith which is not easy, especially in the industry he is in. Our part is to support him however we can and of course pray for him, a lot. . . .

Recently, while writing this book heavily engaged in one of Mother Cabrini's journals, Noah called me stressed out at the Las Vegas Airport while standing in line trying to get through security. His flight was leaving in 15 minutes and there were over 100 people in front of him in the TSA line. If he missed his flight, he would have to pay nearly a thousand dollars extra for his camera gear rental as it was due in Los Angeles later that day, not to mention the disruption it would cause to his busy schedule.

I was just reading prior to his call, about how Mother Cabrini in these situations would completely place her trust in Jesus knowing full well who was in control. If her steamship were not on schedule due to weather, she would praise our Lord for the turbulent high seas and threatening skies turning a stressful moment into a delight for her. Mother Cabrini knew there was a reason for everything, including a delay.

I explained all of this to Noah who by this time said making the flight would be nearly impossible. But I knew he called me at the right time, and this would become a valuable spiritual lesson for both of us. I felt Mother Cabrini's presence and knew deep down that Noah would make his flight against all odds.

I then said, let's pray, "Dear Mother Cabrini, please intercede to Jesus on behalf of Noah to help him make his flight. Your will be done Lord." It was as simple as that. But in my mind I thought, "If he doesn't make his flight, it could damage his faith." There I was succumbing to doubt myself. Right after we prayed, we talked about faith for a several minutes and then he had to get off suddenly to check in. I kept thinking to myself, "Jesus, we place all our trust in You."

I didn't hear from him after 15 minutes or so and then his text came roaring in . . . "Made it." I was overcome with God's joy and thanked our Lord and Mother Cabrini for their help. This was a real faith builder for my son and I. Praise be to you Lord Jesus!

Throughout my life I have let fear, insecurity, and other means limit myself too much at times underestimating what I could have accomplished with God in control. This doesn't mean I have to be famous like my son, or a great saint like Mother Cabrini; rather, it just means I must do the will of God with all the talents and gifts He has bestowed upon me – with all my heart and soul. If I do that, it is good enough.

Chapter 9

Shrine Encounters Interwoven in My Life

Going back to August of 2019 from the beginning of Chapter 1, where we were praying the Rosary at the Shrine caught in the thunderstorm.

After our wonderful visit to see family and visit the Shrine, we made the long journey home to Durango. The first few months were fairly calm. Summer faded into fall and on February 03, 2019, my wife and I were fortunate enough to make another trip up to Denver to visit family again. Of course, we also planned to make another trip up to Mother Cabrini's Shrine where everything looked different in the wintertime, providing a fresh new perspective.

While at the Shrine on a cold winter afternoon, all the clouds had disappeared leaving little hope for a nice sunset as we cautiously made our way up the 373 steps that lead up to the statue of the Sacred Heart of Jesus.

This time hiking up to Jesus would be more difficult as a winter storm had recently hit the area leaving some of the steps covered in thick ice making it somewhat treacherous. Thank goodness for a secure handrail otherwise it would've been impossible to navigate. The maintenance crew had done a wonderful job clearing the snow but there's only so much they could do.

On the way up I had a lot of time to reflect, and kept telling myself to not get discouraged because of the lack of clouds for a sunset but rather, God would have something better awaiting us, something that I couldn't imagine, and this gave me hope as we carefully forged our way up the mountain passing by the beautiful artwork featuring all the Stations of the Cross and Mysteries of the Rosary.

Reaching the top, we were greeted by Jesus along with our Blessed Mother, and St. Mother Cabrini nestled underneath her beloved Jesus, and of course the beautiful 360-degree views in all directions.

There's a special feeling of holiness and hope on top of that beautiful mountain unique to this area alone, where our Lord feels so close with everything seemingly more possible.

Despite the lack of clouds, the horizon was filled with vibrant colors and the distant city lights began to sparkle with the stars starting to appear from the heavens as nightfall was quickly approaching.

Everyone else I was with had already headed back down so it was just me up there alone when a beautiful subtle light began to gently glow on the west side of Jesus, with the Virgin Mary statue standing below. A beautiful heavenly scene began to commence. Mary was looking up at her Son where I could feel the love between them radiating in my heart all the way down to the millions of people of Denver below. It was a beautiful spiritual moment participating in this heavenly gathering. I offered up thanksgiving and prayer to our Lord Jesus Who is always watching over us, Who deeply cares for us, along with His Blessed Mother Mary.

It was truly a night to remember, to know that we are not alone, because God is always with us, every step of the way, as this is His great promise to us all.

This time at the Shrine there was no ominous sky, just God's beautiful love and creation in motion. The prayer time after coming back down was always the highlight. We all met up at Mother Cabrini's altar, lit a few candles, and prayed for family conversion, those who were sick, and those who were struggling in any way.

Problems Begin

Unfortunately, when we returned home late in the evening at my mom's house, our beloved dog Abbey, who was nearly 16 years old in seemingly perfect health, was lying on the floor in pain and hardly able to get up.

Earlier that day she had eaten a lot of coyote and rabbit poop. I thought it made her sick like it had in the past so we thought it would wear off again. But this time it seemed different, she was sicker the next day and didn't recover after our long trip back home to Durango.

Abbey became worse before going to bed. Early the next morning I heard her collapse on the floor after getting up from her bed and knew something was terribly wrong, hoping it was just a bacterial infection. Upon arriving at the vet, the doctor examined her stomach and instantly felt something wrong. He got the ultrasound machine out and said, "Look here, she has a large tumor in her abdomen." I replied, "It has to be some kind of mistake, she had been eating a lot of poop which could have caused an infection." The veterinarian said it's possible but he wanted to do an X-ray. After getting the results rather quickly it told the story – a large tumor the size of a grapefruit was growing out the end of her spleen, and he said it's almost always cancer.

She had been doing so well before with no signs of a large tumor. This all came on so suddenly that we hardly had time to comprehend the seriousness it entailed.

The doctor woke me up out of my denial and said he needed to operate as soon as possible because the tumor was rupturing as the vascular structure of the cancerous tumor had started to burst and she was literally dying from lack of blood. He asked me what I wanted to do. We could euthanize her, take her home and try to make her as comfortable as possible, or we could choose surgery and remove the spleen and tumor. Without thinking it over I decided on surgery because there was still a 25% chance the tumor was benign. A biopsy confirmed Canine Splenic Hemangiosarcoma. It is a very fast-growing cancer that grows its own blood vessels that will eventually rupture, which happened to our Abbey.

She was part of our family, as most of you understand this close bond we have with our animals. Our Abbey was no exception and we loved her dearly. In fact, she was a special dog given to us by God. Abbey was also our certified emotional support animal where my son and I took her with us on many flights to help calm both our conditions. She was such a good traveler, so calm and loved by all. Her perpetual puppy like appearance even into old age was an instant draw to others who would come running up and say, "Can I pet your puppy?"

Answered Prayers

This was no ordinary dog and our family considers ourselves very fortunate to have owned her. She was a beagle lab mix and was found by the Humane Society roaming in a parking lot at a busy shopping center. My wife and son, who had been checking often, went to the pound to see if any new dogs had been brought in. Sure enough, there she was trapped behind bars eager to greet them with a wet kiss. My son instantly fell in love with her so they called me at work to come and see her. It was love at first sight for me as well so I gave my son the go ahead to claim her. She was on a seven-day hold before anyone could take her home and the time spent waiting for that day was torture for my son.

The day finally arrived, and he woke up early to get there as soon as possible. They planned on arriving before it opened because they knew how popular she was and expected a lot of people to come for her. When they arrived, no one else was there to my son's great relief. He quickly jumped out of the car and placed himself in front of the locked door ensuring that he would be first in line when they were due to open in an hour.

Awhile later, an employee walked out and asked him if he was waiting for a dog and he nodded yes. He then asked if it was the beagle. My son smiled so big that he could hardly respond with another yes. The man told him there was a long list of applicants for this dog but it's usually first come first serve as long as he was qualified. This gave my son hope. He had prayed a long time for a good dog and it appeared his prayers would soon be answered. Just before the pound opened, an older couple showed up who also wanted the beagle. About that time the doors were unlocked and a worker came out saying there were five applications for her. He then informed the older couple that he would interview my son first since he was there before them. Shortly afterward, he reviewed the older couple's application and within minutes, the worker awarded the beagle to my son. After hearing this, the older woman started crying. My son felt sorry for her but the excitement of his new dog quickly overshadowed any bad feelings. We all became very attached to Abbey as she became a very special part of our family.

Abbey ended up living for a month after her surgery to remove the tumor and for a short time, became much better. But then the cancer spread to her heart which proved to be fatal. She didn't suffer very much through it all as she was actively running around and begging for snacks several hours before her heart ruptured. Soon afterwards, she passed away in my arms. . . .

What a blessing Abbey turned out to be, not just for us, but to all those she came in contact with. This whole experience really taught our son the power of prayer. For me it is a reminder that we can never take advantage of our time on earth as we never know what lies around the corner. To always be ready, not in fear of what's to come but rather, in courage and faith in God our Father who will make all things new no matter what we face. The following Holy Scripture is helpful in times of suffering.

"I consider that the sufferings of this present time are as nothing compared with the glory to be revealed for us." (Romans 8:18)

Abbey and our Son

Health Issues

Prior to Abbey's passing, back in early 2008 during the "Great Recession," problems started coming in from all directions. The worst was the loss of my health. Without warning, I awoke in the middle of the night and felt my heart beating extra hard. I remember feeling very weak and could hardly get out of bed to go to the bathroom. After finally standing up, tachycardia set in while walking over to the bathroom. This was a scary feeling that made me wonder if I was having a heart attack. I went back to bed and after several hours of worrying, I finally fell asleep. This continued into the next day and my wife had enough and demanded I go to the hospital to get checked out. I knew she wouldn't take no for an answer so I agreed to go. Why is it so hard for men to get help?

On our way there, I started feeling better because my adrenalin kicked in. I told my wife all the things she would have to take care of if something happened to me. I couldn't believe I was talking that way – it seemed like a bad dream. When we arrived, I was anxious to go into the clinic for fear of what the doctor might tell me. After the usual waiting time I was finally attended to. I explained my symptoms and the nurse immediately hooked me up to an EKG machine which checked the electrical balance of my heart. To my relief, the test came out negative and everything looked normal with the exception of my heart rate which was near 100 beats per minute. The nurse then checked my blood pressure and found it to be slightly on the high side at 135/84. My usual rate is 110/70.

The doctor was then called in where he completed a quick exam and asked me to explain my symptoms. He then had the nurse test my pulse and blood pressure lying down, sitting up, and finally standing up. The results confirmed that while standing up my pulse was much higher than sitting or lying down. He concluded that I was severely dehydrated. He explained that when a person is dehydrated, the blood thickens because of the reduced water content making it much harder for the heart to pump. He also said the blood volume is reduced which also makes it extremely hard for the heart to pump efficiently. Simply put, my heart was struggling to pump the thick, molasses-like blood running throughout my body. He ordered two liters of IV solution to help re-hydrate my body and I felt like a new person after the treatment. I couldn't believe that something so simple would work so fast.

Later that evening, I was still a little nervous to lie down because the heart palpitations from the two previous nights were still fresh in my mind. As I laid on my back my heart started to palpitate so I jumped up out of bed and it stopped. This was disheartening because I thought my problems were over. Anxiety started settling in and my body went into high alert the rest of the night. This vicious cycle went on, over and over and left me with little or no sleep.

In the morning, I called the hospital and explained my situation. The doctor told me to try sleeping on my right side because that position would have the least amount of pressure applied to the heart. He told me that my heart might still be irritated from the effects of dehydration.

Several weeks had passed and the heart palpitations increased. At first they only came on while lying down but later they started occurring during the day while sitting and standing up. On one occasion, it got so bad that I went to the doctor's office while having them and they caught it on the EKG. To my surprise, the doctor told me not to worry about it and said he sees this on a regular basis. I asked him what I could do about it and he told me there was nothing that would help. He tried to comfort me by telling me that it wasn't life threatening and I would just have to get used to it.

This was not what I wanted to hear. I left the office frustrated and even more determined to find some answers. I had the EKG records forwarded to a local cardiologist who examined them and later informed me that he didn't see anything that looked potentially harmful and told me to come in if the symptoms persisted.

I was determined to get my body back into good health and was willing to do anything to accomplish this. My mom is a registered dietician so I also sought her help on a regular basis. I found magnesium worked best for my condition. I also dramatically changed my diet, eliminated high fat content, and processed foods. Through trial and error I discovered that by eliminating processed sugars and wheat, the indigestion that always accompanied my heart palpitations was eliminated. Because of this, I switched over to a gluten free diet.

After a week went by, to my great relief the heart palpitations stopped! I still had a slight pressure feeling in my chest and upper abdomen, especially after eating a meal. My mom explained that it could be due to my radical change of diet because my body was still trying to adjust to the new food intake. I can almost certainly attribute the magnesium for helping stop the heart palpitations. Having made progress was a good feeling and I thanked Jesus for helping me. The heart palpitations only reoccurred a few more times and only when I was under a lot of stress.

Through it all, I kept asking God, "Why all the testing?" Was God preparing me for something in the future or was it just bad luck that would soon fade away as time moved forward? I got so caught up with all the problems that I temporarily abandoned writing a book I was working on at the time called *Steadfast Christian*. I wondered if my recent illness wasn't an attack from the evil one to try and stop me from finishing it.

Despite all the trouble, God kept blessing my business with abundant work, almost double the average for a given year which helped pay for all the medical bills with money left over to put into savings. If work had been slow on top of all the other problems, we would have been in real trouble. God promised that He would not allow us to go through more than we can handle, and once again, He was true to His Word. (Isaiah 41:10)

"Fear not, for I am with you; be not dismayed, for I am your God; I will strengthen you, I will help you, I will uphold you with my righteous right hand."

Several years later, I continued to have episodes of tachycardia despite all the changes to my diet. I finally found out why my heart had become so sensitive. After many hours of research, I could not find an answer nor could any of my doctors who kept telling me it wasn't dangerous and just deal with it the best I could. It was actually my wife who finally diagnosed me properly. I had a form of Postural Orthostatic Tachycardia Syndrome (POTS) which is rare, especially for men.

With the advent of Long COVID, or "long-haulers," which is a form of POTS, it became a household name and put POTS on the map. Because of this, more funding has become available to help find a cure which is a good thing.

My Cardiologist put me through several exams, such as an Echo Cardio Stress Test which all came out completely normal ruling out heart disease or structural defects of the heart. I also did a tilt table test which tested negative for syncope which was a good thing as some people with POTS can pass out from low blood pressure. My blood pressure was normal. My Cardiologist ended up loosely diagnosing me with orthostatic intolerance which is a form of POTS. This can be caused from genetics or a bad virus affecting the vagus nerve, or even from a lack of exercise called deconditioning. It is rare and effects women more than men. The medical field knows very little about POTS and there is no known cure even though some people grow out of it after they have reached their mid-twenties. Treatment includes Beta Blockers and other pharmaceuticals, extra salt intake, and hydration to help keep the blood volume higher which can help alleviate some of the symptoms such as an elevated heart rate, palpitations, and overall weakness.[184]

Through research, I also found limiting tyramine containing foods helps to reduce heart palpations and tachycardia considerably in my case. Tyramine is a byproduct primarily from aged foods such as cheddar cheese or any food or drink that is aged during processing. This also includes different kinds of meats or other foods that have been aged, along with leftovers that have sat in the fridge overnight.

Tyramine helps to release adrenalin and other stimulators that increase the heart rate. Too much tyramine can also cause headaches which is where most of the research is directed.[185]

I used to eat cheddar cheese as a snack throughout the day and wondered why I was getting so many heart palpitations. When I stopped, the heart palpitations greatly reduced. I also found that using ice packs on my body helps when in tachycardia, along with cool water splashed on my face. This helps constrict the blood vessels increasing blood volume, making it easier for the heart to pump blood.

St. Theresa of Avila suffered from passing out a lot from an unknown heart condition that left her bedridden on many occasions throughout her life. I wonder if she had a form of POTS as her journals reveal similar symptoms.

Jesus Claimed Mother Cabrini's Heart

Mother Cabrini suffered from heart palpitations as well with one such bout that lasted over a year, but this was not from POTS but rather, a mystical experience. While deep in prayer pouring out her heart to Jesus,

He came to her and said, "My beloved, your heart is mine. I want it for myself forever, so I take it from your breast because for now on, you will work with my heart." Mother Cabrini felt her heart being torn from her breast and for over a year, she had unusual heart palpitations that her doctors couldn't explain. This experience brought her much closer to Jesus's Sacred Heart.[186]

I guess I could consider Mother Cabrini the patron saint of heart palpitations.

From 2008 onward I was able to get my POTS under control and live a more normal life working, and going up into the high elevation of the Rocky Mountain Alpine to do my landscape photography which is a very challenging environment for any condition.

My POTS would flare up for a period of time and then go into remission, but it would usually take months of slow transition for the remission to occur. Unfortunately, it only took one trigger to put me in full POTS again so I had to learn what these were and avoid them whenever possible. Pushing it too hard especially at high elevation above 10,000 feet was one of the main triggers. Regardless, this is where I spent many hours photographing the high alpine three days a week during summer months. I had to be careful hiking too far and intense, or else I could get a flair up that could last up to six months or longer. POTS is a difficult syndrome to deal with in many aspects. For one, people don't take you seriously, especially the doctors because most of the time, even when you are feeling terrible, your outward appearance looks fine. This includes family members who think it's all in your head. Regardless, I can vouch that POTS can be horrific at times.

I included my past health issues because they have a direct relationship with my experiences at Mother Cabrini's Shrine. Also, having this condition makes me appreciate all the hard work and travels Mother Cabrini accomplished despite her compromised health.

First Healing at the Shrine

My mom had been asking me to go to the Mother Cabrini Shrine for many years and I kept coming up with excuses not to go. Finally on

October 15, 2017, I finally made my first pilgrimage there and could not believe I had neglected to go all these years. My experience there exceeded all expectations. I felt like I had gone back to Medjugorje. Opportunities to pray and hike were everywhere. Maybe this was God's best timing for me as Mother Cabrini always said that our Lord is in complete control of our lives where everything happens for a reason.

While there, I received a healing. I was struggling with POTS before going and really struggled during the long drive over the high mountain passes from Durango to Denver. Arriving at the Shrine with my wife and sister, due to heavy weakness and an elevated heart rate, I was having a hard time getting out of the car and walking over to the springhouse area. My sister told me to drink some of the spring water but I was a little cautious, thinking it could be contaminated by all the hundreds of people drinking from it. I overcame my worries, said a prayer, and guzzled down a large, white paper cup full. At first I didn't feel anything, but a few minutes later, I noticed I wasn't as weak and my heart settled down. I walked up the stairs with little effort to the Bohannan Crucifix which is located at the base of the main steps leading up to Jesus. There, we talked to some ladies my sister knew from Church who had read my book about Medjugorje and they were excited to talk about it.

I remember feeling stronger with my heart calm for the first time in several months. I knew something had happened deep within my body. The others started walking up the 373 steps towards Jesus and asked me if I was able to go? Cautiously, I told them I was feeling better and decided to give it a try. To my great astonishment, the walk turned out to be no problem at all. My wife was pleasantly surprised, knowing how bad I was previously. I kept waiting for my symptoms to reappear, but they didn't. Instead, I forgot about my condition and started living my life to the fullest, thoroughly enjoying the Stations of the Cross and the Mysteries of the Rosary on the way up.

Looking out at the incredible views I was in awe of all the beauty. Upon reaching the Sacred Heart of Jesus for the first time, I was overcome by tears of joy. . . . I praised Jesus for healing me and I thanked the Virgin Mary and Mother Cabrini for interceding on my behalf in such a special way.

This is how I first met Mother Cabrini and her Shrine. It was the beginning of a special spiritual relationship with her that only became closer, every time I went to the Shrine. I was feeling so much better the whole time I was up in Denver, and this continued even up in the high altitude when travelling back home to Durango. This was the real deal, I couldn't have been more thankful.

Second Pilgrimage to the Shrine

A little over a month later on November 22, 2017, we travelled a second time to Mother Cabrini's Shrine. My wife and I went there on a retreat to stay overnight which was a wonderful experience. We crossed the beautiful Rocky Mountains and high plains to get there from Durango and I tolerated it well once again. As we arrived at the base of the Front Range at sunset, only a few miles as the crow flies from Mother Cabrini's Shrine, the sky blew up into vivid colors with the most unusual sunset. I pulled our car over in order to capture what was unfolding above. It was as if Mother Cabrini was welcoming us back with a beautiful image of the Sacred Heart of Jesus.

We were not going to the Shrine that evening but instead to my mom's for an early Thanksgiving dinner with all the family. After a wonderful feast and time catching up with everyone, the next day we left for the Shrine excited to begin our retreat.

It was there that I met John and Tommy for the first time. My encounter with John was friendly as he was very helpful in letting me take pictures of the statue of the Sacred Heart of Jesus in the evening. I planned on donating the best pictures to the Shrine. It was so wonderful to be up there all alone with my wife in perfect peace and beauty as a nice sunset was lingering well into darkness. I gave it my best effort to capture it the best I could. I used my commercial flash to light up Jesus which enabled me to maintain the lighter exposure of the sunset in the background. I must have taken 100 shots with my flash going off repeatedly for half an hour.

Well, this got the attention of Tommy Francis, the main caretaker. We could see a pickup truck quickly coming up the private access road that leads to the top where we were. A man jumped out of his truck and walked sternly towards us, and in a loud voice, "What are you doing up here . . . you are not supposed to be here after hours!" He put the fear of God in us as he came closer. I yelled out, "John your worker told us we could come up here and take some pictures since we were staying overnight at the retreat center." Tommy kept coming towards us in the dim light without responding to my appeal. When he was within a few feet he stopped and said, "John never mentioned you coming up here. I am sorry for hollering at you both." In a big sigh of relief, we both apologized to Tommy for making such a commotion on top of this holy hill. In the end, we were all laughing together. I didn't blame Tommy for getting upset with all the flashing lights going off where he might have thought the hill was on fire or who knows what?

This is Tommy's Shrine to take care of and he was just doing his job. I would have done the same. Since our initial meeting on the hill, I have had the chance to talk with him on several occasions. He is a wonderful man and devout Catholic who takes his job very seriously where nothing gets past his watchful eyes. Today, they have added security cameras to make his job a bit easier dealing with thousands of pilgrims each week.

After getting some wonderful pictures, we headed down the steps to our awaiting room for the night.

My wife and I at the Shrine that night.

Unfortunately, I had become so excited once arriving that I climbed the 373 steps leading up to Jesus way too fast. I literally ran up there. We were both really tired from our busy day but went into the main chapel to pray for an hour or so before retiring to our room for a good night's rest.

About an hour after going to sleep, I awoke feeling terrible. My POTS had come back full-strength causing chest pressure and tachycardia to the point I couldn't get back to sleep. This was disheartening because I had been doing so well since getting healed the last time we were there. After praying, I was finally able to drift off to sleep for a few hours but I planned on waking up early morning to get some pictures of the sunrise, preferably at the statue of Jesus. However, that was now out of the question.

About an hour before the sun came up when it was still dark outside. I felt pretty awful but slowly gathered up my gear and went by the chapel to ask Jesus if he could please let me have enough energy to take some pictures. Surprisingly, I felt somewhat better with my heart calming down a bit so I headed outside towards the bottom the stairs leading up to Jesus. I still wasn't feeling well enough to make it all the way to the top so I prayed I could at least make it far enough in order to get a better vantage point for the sunrise that was still below the horizon but was just starting to give out its light. I kept reminding myself that my condition was not dangerous, so I slowly walked up the stairs to about the halfway point where I set up my gear in preparation for what was to come.

The clouds were perfect for a nice sunrise as there was a nice gap on the horizon that would allow the rising sun to break through the thick cover above. Then the holy moment occurred. . . .

The Holy Moment

Suddenly, out of the predawn, the most beautiful bells and chimes started ringing a wonderful tune coming from the direction of the main chapel. At that moment, the clouds started taking on a beautiful reddish glow. I thought I had died and gone to Heaven it was so beautiful! As a professional landscape photographer, I have experienced many incredible sunrises, in some of the most beautiful places on earth, but never have I experienced a moment quite like this. It was a spiritual moment where God was blessing me with His wonderful gift of creation mixed in with heavenly sounds of bells and perfect stillness that penetrated my inner soul. It was healing to be present in such beauty. . . .

I tried hard to pull myself together to capture the glorious sunrise unfolding before me. The beautiful red crosses that are along the stairway were the perfect backdrops along with the city lights of Denver below with the sky on fire with variations of red and golden tones. It was just Jesus and me, all alone, to witness this incredible moment. I was able to get some shots that at least captured the scene, but as always, you have to be there in person to truly capture the moment. The sunrise kept going and going giving me plenty of time which I really appreciated, because I was able to sit back and take it all in which is rare in this type of work where split seconds can make the difference in getting the shot.

When it was all over, I felt rejuvenated in mind, body, and soul. I even had enough energy to walk up the rest of the steps to see Jesus who was lit up by a golden glow. Maybe I just needed a reminder of my POTS so I would really understand who was making me feel better?

I sat up there with the beautiful sunrise all but gone but the peace and quiet all alone with our Lord was even better as I had time to pray and reflect.

As I was sitting there praying, one of the first families of the day had made it to the top where I introduced myself and we had a nice chat. In my Facebook prayer group we were giving special attention to a young girl who was diagnosed with brain cancer. I often carried her picture around with me and asked the family if they would be willing to join me in prayer for her healing and they were very generous and happy to.

After a heartfelt prayer, we said our goodbyes and I hurried back down in order to attend Mass where I was sure my wife would be awaiting me, wondering if I would make it on time.

I kept feeling better the rest of the day on our retreat even after we took a long hike around the grounds. I received a renewed healing at sunrise. I was fine travelling back home over the high mountain passes and continued to do well into the next year. The following May of 2018, we travelled to Malibu, California to see my son and photograph the spring wildflowers, along with driving through Zion National Park and other locations on the way back home. We also went to Chimayo, New Mexico on pilgrimage so we really packed it in since I was feeling so well. Then to top it off, in late May, I went on a high alpine hike crossing through

2 feet of snow at times to reach a 13,000-foot summit in the San Juan Mountains. The year prior I was able to drive up to the high alpine but not hike very far in this harsh but beautiful environment until now. It was such a triumphant moment for me to hike back up there with my trusted dog Abbey even thought it was very cold on top of the world as I praised and worshiped our wonderful creator God.

A month after I climbed this peak, we had a dreadful wildfire that closed down all the mountains around us and the air quality from all the smoke kept us indoors more than we were used to. As soon as the fire was brought under control in late June, and the Forest Service roads were reopened, I headed up to the high alpine to catch the wildflowers now in season. I tried exploring a new four-by-four road that was very steep, narrow, and rocky. About two miles up the road I had to stop as the rocks became too large for our truck to continue. It was too narrow to turn around, so I had to back out the whole way which placed extreme strain on my neck from intensely looking backward as I was trying to keep from sliding off the step mountain. By the time I made it back down to the main road it was getting close to sunset. This was the main reason why I came to begin with so I hurried up the road to set up at a familiar spot to try and capture some columbine wildflowers with the saturated golden light right before sunset. I barely made it as the sun was setting so I jumped out of my truck and quickly walked up a steep hillside to a nice clump of wildflowers, bent down, and captured a beautiful scene from God.

While bending down, I started to get chest pain and my heart began to palpitate which turned into heavy tachycardia. I thought for sure I was dying from a heart attack. I loaded up my gear and my faithful wife who was with me drove us back home which was an hour and a half drive. On the way down I started to feel a bit better but once home, I had a rough night's sleep.

I went in and had my heart checked the next day as I was still feeling pretty rough. They did the regular EKG including a blood test to see if I had a heart attack and once again everything checked out normal. Later, I had another Echo Stress Cardiogram that checked out completely normal. One thing is for sure, that episode up in the high alpine definitely put my POTS on fire for the next 4 months or so. I even resorted for the first time to take a low dose Beta Blocker only as needed when a tachycardia event flared up. The wildfire effects and deconditioning from lack of exercise and/or the strain placed on my neck backing down the steep 4x4 road must have been the trigger for my POTS flare up. I learned that a vagus nerve injury caused from my neck being twisted too hard can affect my heart rate and other bodily functions.[187]

https://www.webmd.com/brain/vagus-nerve-what-to-know

Continued Healings at the Shrine

The first healing I received at the Shrine back in October of 2017 lasted about 9 months. Then I went downhill again after the high-altitude incident in July of 2018 just mentioned above. It wasn't until I went back to Mother Cabrini's Shrine on November 23, 2018, that I found relief again. On this Thanksgiving pilgrimage I was still pretty bad with POTS and couldn't make it up the steps to see Jesus. Most of my family had come with us and they all walked up the steps to see Jesus. It was a cold day but beautiful as usual. Later, we all met back at the Mother Cabrini altar by the grotto where my family prayed over me which was a very humbling and joyful experience. They also walked down the stairs to get me a cup of spring water from the fountain because I was not able to. I felt a bit better afterwards but not as good as the first time. We came home after a day of needed prayer and I slept really well after getting to bed early that night.

The next morning, I awoke early to catch a sunrise at my mom's house who has wonderful views of the Front Range Mountains. I felt good enough to go out and walk a half mile and captured some nice shots, praise be to God. At 10 a.m. in the morning, I had a meeting with my mom's parish priest. He is a wonderful man of God who spent over an hour saying different healing and deliverance prayers over me. I also had confession. I came back to my mom's house feeling rejuvenated and started jogging around her property to give our dog Abbey some exercise tolerating it well while doing it but felt pretty rough afterwards, obviously over doing it. That night I struggled a bit with tachycardia but felt better the next morning on our way back to Durango.

Sunrise, Front Range Mountains from Mom's House.

Christ the King Statue

About an hour and a half into our journey, we stopped at an overlook off Highway 285 to view the large 55-foot-tall Christ the King statue located above Camp Santa Maria retreat center near Grant, Colorado. This statue when built in 1933 was said to be the second tallest statue of Jesus in the world. Our family has always made it a tradition to stop here and say a prayer to Jesus.

Christ the King

As we pulled over we were met by a vanload of Catholic sisters who got out to admire their beloved Jesus. I got out as well and greeted them. As usual they were all very joyful and friendly although I did not know what order they belonged to, nor did I ask. I told them about the Mother Cabrini Shrine in Golden and they said they would love to go there on retreat sometime. I pulled out several Mother Cabrini relic cards that the Shrine provides and gave it to them as a gift and they loved it very much. We all went on our way full of our Lord's love, joy, and peace.

Baby Jesus

The rest of our high elevation trip home was a bit rough on my condition, but we made it in good time. Upon our return, I still struggled with POTS the rest of the week but was still doing a lot better than before our trip. On the following Sunday we went to Mass and it was there that Jesus let me know that everything was going to be ok. We were sitting towards the back on the left side of the Church where there is stained glass featuring the Presentation of our Lord with Baby Jesus in Simeon's arms standing with St. Joseph and Mary. Right before Holy Communion, I felt someone staring at me and I look up and saw Baby Jesus locked in on me with the most intense love. It was so overwhelming that I started weeping uncontrollably. My wife looked over and asked what was wrong and I just pointed up to Jesus and she just smiled.

When it was time to walk down the aisle to receive the Holy Eucharist, tears were still streaming down my cheeks. I tried to get my emotions under control the best I could feeling embarrassed that others would notice. I wiped my eyes dry just before receiving Jesus and hurried back to our seat. As soon as I sat down, I looked at Baby Jesus again and the emotions flared up again causing me to cry like a baby which is something that is exceedingly rare for me. I just could not hold back the intense love I was experiencing. After Father said the ending prayer I quickly rushed out of Church leaving my wife behind. I had to get out of there before people saw me in my vulnerable condition. When my wife came to our car she told me that Father noticed that I bolted out of Mass in a hurry and asked if everything was ok?

Presentation of our Lord Jesus seen at Mass

The following month I still struggled at times with my health but was much better than before. This second healing took more time to develop than the first. God was trying to help me get to the source of my problem and He showed me through a heavy metal blood test that my arsenic levels were elevated from eating too much brown rice and almond butter. When I stopped eating those two items known to contain arsenic, my healing really took off. The next several months were so much better, praise be to our Lord Jesus.

This was the second time I received a healing that originated from the Shrine. For whatever reason I don't get a complete, long-term healing there but rather, it seems Mother Cabrini wants me to keep coming back for maintenance. I have to laugh about this but it's true. Regardless, I really appreciate her intercession for me and the relief it provides.

So not only has the Mother Cabrini Shrine become my place of spiritual renewal but also a place of healing for me with both needing periodic rejuvenation. I guess that just makes sense and I am thankful for such a beautiful place for a healing remedy.

Then COVID-19 Hit

After a rough second half of 2018, I stabilized in 2019, and was able to easily climb the stairs on several pilgrimages to Shrine including the one in August when we got into the thunderstorm as detailed earlier in chapter one. I still believe the scenes from Heaven we witnessed that day were prophetic in nature, as a warning of what was to come. Early the next year in 2020 COVID-19 was detected around the world and in the United States. Things quickly escalated when the first deaths were reported and especially when scenes from Italy and other countries showed hospitals being overrun with COVID infected patients with many dying.

A considerable portion of the world literally shut down for a period, warranted or not. My son living in Los Angeles, California, sent us videos of the usually busy freeways nearly deserted, in the middle of the day, like a scene from a science fiction thriller. Newsreels from Italy showed the usual murky waters around Venice clearing up as dolphins and other sea life suddenly appeared as boat traffic had drastically reduced. Even in our little town of Durango, Main Street was empty with people hibernating in their homes.

For me it was an opportunity to go out into the mountains and have it all to ourselves. I could park my car on the highway and take landscape pictures around the Purgatory Ski area with no worries of any cars coming. It was completely deserted.

Mother Cabrini just missed the Spanish Flu pandemic of 1918 and was sheltered from World War I while living in the US; but it grieved her knowing that her homeland of Italy was at war. Her sisters went through it all . . . the Spanish Flu and COVID- 19.

My health was pretty good at the time which I was so thankful for making it easier to wear masks in public places. That would have been really difficult with full blown POTS affecting me.

We continued our lives as normally as possible and practiced good sanitary measures and wore our N95 masks as needed at work, Church, and shopping. I needed to take extra precautions due to having POTS as the COVID virus could raise havoc on my vagus nerve exasperating my already compromised condition.

Things were going well considering the pandemic was upon us until my wife's dad passed away from a condition unrelated to COVID. Tragically, she could not go to her dad's funeral because Canada had closed its borders. She had to attend via Zoom, which was better than nothing, but it was hard on her and the rest of the family.

Like everyone else, we did our best to get through it all. Feeling better for the most part with my health really helped. I was sad that we couldn't go visit the Shrine during this time as I felt it was too risky for my condition.

Mercury and Arsenic Poisoning

Then suddenly, about a year later my health took a turn for the worse in October of 2021. My POTS was under control for the most part although there were some rough times after the 2020 elections with all the politics swirling around where I became too emotionally involved which can be a trigger. But this time it wasn't from POTS or COVID. It was something I would never have expected. It came in like a thief in the night.

My symptoms started with heavy stiffness and irritation on the back of my neck which gradually spread up the sides of my face to my forehead. Fatigue and weakness then set in throughout my body followed by minor ataxia affecting my motor skill functions, especially in my hands and legs along with some speech difficulty. Then a very irritating form of head pressure and "buzzy" feeling set in which I later referred to as **"mercury head."** It was scary stuff.

I finally had enough and went in for a complete blood workup. The culprit was heavy metal exposure in the form of mercury and arsenic as well as being deficient in copper. My doctors didn't seem too concerned about the double-digit mercury and arsenic levels in my blood but I certainly was. They said there was not a lot they could do about it as the levels were not high enough in their opinion to cause concern. They told me to find and stop the source of contamination and let my body do the rest. I had been eating a lot of wild caught cod from Alaska to help supplement my chicken. I have to be careful eating too much red meat and other foods high in iron as my blood iron levels were usually too high pointing towards Hemochromatosis. This is a condition that causes too much iron buildup in the tissues and organs.

In 2022, I tested positive for heterozygous (gene from only one parent) Hemochromatosis which is usually benign for most cases with less than 2% becoming symptomatic, so I guess I am one of the unfortunate lucky ones . . . but at least I know now. Homozygous is where a person acquires this gene from both parents which pretty much guarantees you will become symptomatic at some point in your life. I tested for Hemochromatosis nearly a decade ago and was negative so it can be beneficial to retest as lab errors can result and today the technology is more sensitive.[188]

I stopped eating red meat which helped lower the iron levels but I got tired of eating mainly chicken so I decided to get more variety by eating cod.

I quickly went to work doing more research on heavy metal exposure. The Internet is flooded with information regarding how to treat mercury toxicity with many chelation protocols that could potentially cause more harm than good. The last thing I wanted was to redistribute the mercury to other parts of my body, especially my brain. I knew about the high content of mercury found in tuna and other larger predatory fish but I didn't realize that cod could also be a problem.

I ended up testing the cod I was eating at a local lab and the parts per million of mercury was on par with tuna fish and the amount of arsenic was off the charts. This was shocking news for me. I had been poisoned by arsenic before as written earlier by eating too much brown rice and almond butter but I had no idea it could be this high in fish.

I tested other food and drink I was consuming on a regular basis and was further shocked to find out that pretty much everything was contaminated with lead and arsenic in trace amounts. My diet was fairly limited from eating gluten free and low iron, so I was eating a lot of the same things. As my mom the dietician keeps reminding me, eating a well-diversified diet is so important which can be challenging for some like me with limited options. My story is a good example of why blood testing for heavy metals is so important especially if you are eating a limited diet. The blood test may determine if a person is presently being contaminated by heavy metals as they will accumulate in the blood. The hair test is better for long term exposure even after the source has been eliminated. I chose to do both.

I immediately stopped the mercury and arsenic sources such as the cod, and over a period of 4 months, my mercury and arsenic levels dropped from double digits down below 3 ug/l which was expected as mercury has a half-life of around 90 days. I made improvements concerning the ataxia and speech issues as the months progressed, but my head pressure, body fatigue, and weakness became worse at times. I found out that mercury leaves the blood quickly where it is mostly stored in fatty tissues with most excreted out the digestive system, but fish contains methyl mercury which easily crosses the blood brain barrier allowing it to absorb deeply into the brain where it is really difficult to remove. Traditional chelators such as DMSA do not cross the blood brain barrier, so it is of little help.[189]

I found out that mercury, which is a known neurotoxin, does many other harmful effects to your body. It depletes essential minerals along with the reduction of white blood cells which made it even more important that I take extra precautions to help prevent COVID or other illnesses since I had become immunocompromised.

The worse symptoms for me are the head pressure, body fatigue, and weakness. It can become worse especially when I go to higher elevation above 8,000 feet where my head pressure increases. This is unfortunate because this is where I love to spend time photographing God's beautiful creation. It also prevents me from traveling to Denver over the high passes to visit family and Mother Cabrini's Shrine which has been an exceedingly difficult cross to bear. I never had head pressure or any other head issues before I got mercury poisoned.

Studies have shown that mercury can remain in the brain for over 20 years which is discouraging, but through research, I found a natural chelation protocol that can cross the blood brain barrier, but unfortunately, it has put me into tachycardia on a number of occasions. Our bodies like to pull the mercury out of the blood and hide it in areas like fatty tissue which includes our brain. Once a chelator grabs hold of the mercury, it pulls it out into our blood stream where it passes through the heart and other organs, and if the chelation bond is weak, it can let go and drop the mercury in these sensitive organs causing adverse symptoms. That is why it is important to use a chelator that has a stronger bond to mercury and won't let go potentially dumping it in a worse location, such as the heart or brain. This is called redistribution. Heavy metal chelation should always done under your medical provider's guidance – this is something you do not want to do alone. That does not mean you shouldn't seek out additional information to help complement your care.

It is sad and unfortunate that mercury and other heavy metal contaminants have adversely affected our oceans and waterways throughout the world, even reaching the most remote and pristine areas of our planet.

The food chain starting with small plankton is very efficient at cycling these heavy metals where it eventually becomes exponentially compounded as it moves up to the top of the food chain, i.e., shark, swordfish, tuna, other large predatory fish, and land animals.[190]

I have found firsthand we have to be careful what we eat, especially the quantity, because it is usually little by little that wins the race, whether the outcome is good or bad for our health. I have also found that staying active even when feeling bad is super important. Our bodies just work better when we move. Walking has been the best exercise for me several times a day along with getting up from the computer or other seated activities every 20 minutes to do some stretching exercises.

I won't go into further detail about all of this but will say that this has been an eye opener for me and has changed my life. I majored in the environmental sciences back in college and decided to go back and refresh my skills learned and recently became board certified through the American Association of Natural Wellness Practitioners (AANWP).

I want to help as many people as I can to not go through this terrible condition and have set up my own company, Team 3 Health, LLC to do just that. My website below has lots of information concerning this topic that you or a loved one may find helpful.[191] https://team3health.com/

Dealing with POTS has been a walk in the park compared to being poisoned by mercury and arsenic. The intense head pressure at times along with weakness and other issues have really been a challenge.

That said, I feel fortunate and thankful to God to still be able to function in daily living. Through testing, my doctor said my reflexes are not compromised and I have the full use of all my bodily functions. I know several people I work with who are bedridden from mercury poisoning.

Longing for Mother Cabrini's Shrine

At the time of this writing, it has now been over 4 years since I have travelled up to Denver or anywhere for that matter. As COVID has waned down with the rest of the world back to a more normal life, I have not been so fortunate. My problems have come from another source.

Heavy metal poisoning has also worsened my POTS which has made things even more difficult. It has now been over two years since becoming poisoned and things are still rough at times. I have had MRIs and other scans from the top of my head down to my waist with nothing of major concern showing up. There have been incidental findings of bulging and degenerative discs in my lower back and a reversal of lordosis in my cervical spine which means that my neck is curving in the wrong direction. This can be caused by poor posture, a previous injury, or a number of other things. Who knows, I could have had it from birth or even the mercury neurological effects on my cervical muscles and tendons causing spasms which can be another trigger for this condition. I have had bad posture most of my life looking down at my phone and computer which can cause what is commonly referred to as "tech neck." My wife has often told me to stand and sit up straight, but I never listened to her. I wish I had now. The reverse spinal curve in my neck could be the reason for my POTS all along as it puts stress on the vagus nerve that controls many bodily functions such as regulating the heartbeat. This has been a real learning experience for sure.

Four plus years and counting I have not been able to go to Mother Cabrini's Shrine which has been a real cross for me as this place of prayer has been my healing remedy prior to this. It has been so frustrating to be trapped in my town and not being able to travel. But out of all the negative, my condition has forced me to stop being a control freak by trying to rely on my own self-merits. Instead, I have been crushed to the point that I have finally realized that God is my only way out of this or anything else. In fact, He has been the solution all along but my stubbornness and pride have prevented me from realizing this.

Consecration and Confraternity to Jesus Through Mary by Saint Louis-Marie De Montfort

The past few years as my physical condition has worsened, my soul has become stronger. My confessions, according to my priest have been deeper and more meaningful. My prayer life has increased significantly and my quiet time with our Lord more profound. My desire to be with our Lord is stronger than at any other time in my life except back when I had my "born again" experience in my youth.

Back in 2017, I completed the *Consecration to Jesus Through Mary* authored by Saint Louis-Marie De Montfort. This was a true blessing and a life-changing experience. See below link for instructions on how to complete the consecration.[192]

https://www.ecatholic2000.com/montfort/secret/secret.shtml

Then in 2020, I took a step further and joined the *Confraternity of the Most Holy Rosary* instructed by St. Louis De Monfort. By joining this confraternity, I promised to pray at least one mystery of the Rosary every day for the rest of my life. This was one of the best spiritual things I have done, and I thank God for preparing me and my family spiritually. See below link for instructions on how to properly join and pray the Rosary.[193]

https://www.youtube.com/watch?v=9JJFxDohpsU&ab_channel= insight856

Stronger Spiritually and the Illumination of Conscience

I am going through an illumination of conscience like no other time in my life.

I am being convicted by things that happened early in life all the way up to the present – things I never really gave much thought to, or had completely forgotten about, or just didn't want to face – but now it seems I can't run anymore or pretend it never happened, because now these things have become so much clearer, more important, and necessary to exam. These things are coming at me from all directions, a bit overwhelming at times, and are convicting me exactly the way they should, and God is using this to help bring me closer to Himself and Heaven.

My time in confession has increased, becoming so much more important and necessary, so much deeper with more conviction, sincerity, and honesty. I can't think of anytime in my life that this has been more intense, the need to examine my conscience, a time where I feel God has put me into the fire to help purify my sinful soul, out of His great love for me – all for my own good.

By no means do I think this is the final illumination of conscience or the "Warning" prophesied by St. Faustina of the Divine Mercy revelations but rather, I do believe this is helping me to prepare for this great day where God will give each of us the chance to return to Him, out of His great love and mercy for us. And I do believe with all my heart this great day is near![194]

https://v-catholic.com/marian-messages/st-faustina-our-ladys-prophecy-and-the-great-sign-of-mercy/

God's Gift to Us, Our Suffering

Although very difficult and even painful at times causing much suffering and hardship, I thank our Lord Jesus for this special gift of love and mercy that is helping to bring me closer to Him. I want to share His mercy and love with others. I have seen this same act of mercy happening to others in my life and it may be occurring to many of you as well.

I have learned the hard way that maybe God has allowed this suffering for a reason. Just maybe it is necessary for me to go through this to better love and serve our Lord. God has used and continues to use my suffering to help lost souls.

That said, I do not like to suffer. I will do almost anything to get better. But I have learned through my own experiences and through some good advice from others, especially through my spiritual advisor, that wasting my suffering is not the way to go. So yes, it is ok to dislike suffering, but while it is occurring, why not offer it up and let it do some good.

That is one of the beautiful things about the Catholic Church – we can offer up our suffering for reparation of the conversion of sinners and for our own sins. Suffering can be used as grindstone to make us stronger in our faith. We can share in our Lord's sufferings on His Cross which is a powerful force. Suffering can actually be a gift if put to good use instead of wasting it on self-pity and despair. A work in progress for me – easier said than done but necessary.

Below is a letter I wrote to my fellow prayer warriors back in June of 2022 sharing thoughts on my own sufferings and a prayer given to me by my spiritual advisor. I have learned that many people are suffering right now in various ways:

> Speaking for myself and for many of you, there is no other way to sugarcoat what has been going on. It has been brutal. . . .

> Never before have I/we been challenged to the very core of our existence and faith like now. It is overwhelming to say the least. I am not talking about the crazy evil events taking place around the world and in our own communities which is horrific enough. Rather, I am talking about a personal affliction of suffering that seems to have a grip on me (and many of you) that I cannot shake no matter how hard I try, no matter how hard I pray to God to release me from this grief. It is overwhelming. . . . I have felt rejected and abandoned by God, "Why would He allow me to suffer like this if He loves me?"

> But even in this seemingly terrible dark place of suffering, I still have inner peace and hope that God is using my suffering for the conversion of souls and to transform me where a better day will come, because "this too shall pass," and His eternal glory awaits all those who Love Him.

> I have been so fortunate to have a wonderful spiritual advisor who has been there by my side guiding me through this heavy trial and I want to share with all of you, the prayer he taught me that has sustained me and even let me thrive in this difficult situation.

> I encourage you all to say this prayer below daily and reflect on it often which helps turn our suffering into a gift rather than a curse, and allows us to not waste our suffering but rather allows God to use it for His glory:

> "I am God's beloved son! I am God's beloved son! I am God's beloved son! Or, I am God's beloved daughter! I am God's beloved daughter! I am God's beloved daughter!

I savor my suffering as a gift from God, and to you Mary Mother of God, I give you my most precious gift, my suffering to do with it as you will to honor your Son Jesus! All in honor of the Blessed Trinity. . . .

I do this because,

When LOVE (God) gives, LOVE returns. . . .

So I give you God my gift of suffering, just as Your Son Jesus on His Cross gave back His gift of suffering to You and all of us. Amen."

In addition to the above prayer from my spiritual advisor, I hold on dearly to this Holy Scripture: (2 Corinthians 4:7-18)

The Paradox of the Ministry

But we hold this treasure in earthen vessels, that the surpassing power may be of God and not from us.

We are afflicted in every way, but not constrained; perplexed, but not driven to despair;

persecuted, but not abandoned; struck down, but not destroyed;

always carrying about in the body the dying of Jesus, so that the life of Jesus may also be manifested in our body.

For we who live are constantly being given up to death for the sake of Jesus, so that the life of Jesus may be manifested in our mortal flesh.

So death is at work in us, but life in you.

Since, then, we have the same spirit of faith, according to what is written, "I believed, therefore I spoke," we too believe and therefore speak,

knowing that the one who raised the Lord Jesus will raise us also with Jesus and place us with you in his presence.

Everything indeed is for you, so that the grace bestowed in abundance on more and more people may cause the thanksgiving to overflow for the glory of God.

Therefore, we are not discouraged; rather, although our outer self is wasting away, our inner self is being renewed day by day.

For this momentary light affliction is producing for us an eternal weight of glory beyond all comparison,

as we look not to what is seen but to what is unseen; for what is seen is transitory, but what is unseen is eternal."

Amen. . . .

Update – Return to Burbank, CA, Mother Cabrini Shrine

After five long years, by the grace of God and intercession from St. Mother Cabrini, my wife and I were finally able to return and go on pilgrimage to the Mother Cabrini Shrine in Burbank, California while visiting our son Noah. (This took place after the first publication of the book.) We were given a private tour of this beautiful Shrine by Carmelo Sabatella, President of the Italian Catholic Federation (ICF), Mother Cabrini Chapel Committee. He revealed the Shrine's fascinating history with its beautiful artifacts and relics from the days Mother Cabrini and her sisters lived and prayed there. Mother Cabrini had originally purchased this property in 1907. In 1917, she had this small chapel built on the hill overlooking her property.

In 1944, the Missionary Sisters of the Sacred Heart of Jesus built and ran the Villa Cabrini Academy Campus on this property which was a private school for girls. This beautiful educational campus for girls was expanded into 22 buildings on 30 acres. In 1970 due to staffing shortages and other related problems, the campus was closed. The following year, the Great San Fernando Earthquake destroyed half the buildings. Then in the early 1980s, the property was sold to Woodbury University. More detailed information was provided in Chapter 5, Back to California, and Chapter 6, John's Miracle.[195]

Mother Cabrini Shrine Mural, Burbank, CA, and the Dillon Family

Chapter 10
Mother Cabrini Shrine Facebook Journals

In this chapter I have included some of my Facebook posts relating to the Mother Cabrini Shrine in chronological order. They are mostly unedited except removing a name mentioned or other detail when necessary.

I hope these experiences at the Shrine, and the impact it made on my life can bring you some hope and joy as much as it has for me and my family.

Back at the time I was involved in an international prayer group where we put together a prayer list that was carried around the world to Fatima, Lourdes, Medjugorje, Bosnia-Herzegovina, Knock, Ireland, etc. I would take this prayer list with me everywhere I went such as Chimayo, New Mexico, The Missionaries of Charity at Gallup, New Mexico, Mother Cabrini Shrine, Golden, Colorado, British Columbia, Canada, Malibu, California, the high alpine of the Rocky Mountains while doing my photography, on my daily prayer hikes, and many other places all to offer up prayers of healing for the hundreds of people around the world who requested to be on this list for themselves or for a loved one in need.

After meeting with my spiritual advisor, he advised me to take a long break from our prayer list as it was starting to become overwhelming and cautioned that something of this nature needs heavy spiritual guidance and protection. This may have been in part what was causing myself and others involved to lose their health. I was obedient to him and stopped working on the prayer list in late 2019.

It was during this time that I posted journals about my experiences at Mother Cabrini's shrine and other places of pilgrimage. Mother Cabrini was woven in tightly to my experiences where I feel she was with me in my travels. After getting to know her in 2017, I feel we have become close spiritual friends and I pray with her often. Other than the Blessed Mother Mary and Saint Joseph, Mother Cabrini has been my closest mentor and favorite Saint.

Below I posted in chronological order my posts on Facebook describing my experiences at the Shrine and places of pilgrimage in-between. It was here during these experiences, that I became better able to relate to Mother Cabrini and her travels as our common bond was serving our Lord:

August 4, 2017, Preparing for Pilgrimage to Shrine

I was overwhelmed today with so many hurting people asking for prayers around the world. Some who lost a loved one, another who worried about their unborn baby who may not live through birth, and another who is suffering from an illness and yet others who asked for undisclosed prayer requests.

The more I pray about it, the more compassion and love floods my heart for them. I've personally experienced gut-wrenching trials and I know how painful it can be.

Being a professional landscape photographer, I decided to do something special and go up in the high country of the Rocky Mountains, free from distractions and where God's creation is most powerful to me. I spend a lot of time there for that reason alone. I printed out a copy of all the people who liked my post and those who messaged me asking for prayer. The list was long. I decided to attach my favorite picture of Mary to the prayer requests and place this in my shot.

While driving up it was overcast with little hope for a decent sunset. Up I went to almost twelve thousand feet (12K) just above the timberline. I arrived late in the evening and noticed the sun was starting to break free. What happened next was amazing. I get to see plenty of beautiful sunsets, but this one was special. I ran up to a patch of wildflowers and was suddenly overwhelmed with the most intense brilliant reddish-golden light. It radiated everything around me. It was a warm light that penetrated my soul. I placed the picture of Mary and all the prayer requests in the patch of wildflowers and resumed the Rosary I had been praying on the way up there for everyone.

All the while, I was shooting off pictures of this amazing site. I could feel God's warm loving light wrapping around me. I was praying for everyone, but one person stood out in my mind. His name is John and he had just passed away. I could envision John walking toward Jesus's brilliant light as He walked into our Lord's loving arms for all of eternity!

San Juan Mountains with Mary and prayer list at sunset.

Oct 15, 2017 – First Time at Mother Cabrini's Shrine, Golden, CO

St. Mother Cabrini, British Columbia, our Prayer List, and Pilgrimage

Visiting Beautiful British Columbia is hard to match with the beautiful prayer hikes I was so fortunate to take . . . but the surprise of my trip happened in Colorado on the way home at St. Mother Cabrini's Shrine located just West of Denver. I have driven past this Shrine many times and never paid a visit . . . I'm not sure why but I never did . . . Until now!

What a gift this place of prayer is . . . It is like a mini Medjugorje with the Church, the mountain hike with the Stations of the Cross, and a large statue of the Sacred Heart of Jesus on top to greet you . . . Mother Cabrini was a marvelous woman who followed God by taking care of orphans in the Denver area. . . .

She purchased this beautiful property high above Denver for a place for the orphans to go away on retreat. Just like with Lourdes, she and her sisters dug for a water well and they miraculously hit a spring that has provided water for this shrine ever since.

Without planning anything, I ended up meeting several people that have been to Medjugorje and one woman that had predicted an earthquake that occurred only 2 hours after talking with her on the phone . . . I brought this up in an earlier post.

We all got together at the base of the hill and prayed for Lelia's complete healing and for everyone else on our prayer list. We also prayed for all those affected by the fires, hurricanes, earthquakes, and other natural and man-made disasters going on in our world today.

It was truly quality prayer time! We then proceeded up the mountain to do the Stations of the Cross where I offered up a prayer for Lelia and all on our prayer list at each station. I felt like I was back in Medjugorje!

On top, at the large statue of the Sacred Heart of Jesus, I was overwhelmed with the smell of flowers. I thought it was just me but then my wife said she also smelled the flowers before I said anything to her. . . . All the flowers on top were dead from the cold fall temperatures. I have only had this experience a few times before, once in a Church while praying the Rosary. I feel confident that Mary was there with us in our presence . . . The power of the Holy Spirit was also really present. . . .

This was a short but wonderful pilgrimage that I will most certainly do again, soon! God Bless everyone!

Oct 20, 2017, Mother Cabrini's Worn-out Shoes

Two pictures, one video, all beautiful, all created by God for a specific purpose, but one really stands out for me. . . .

On my recent trip to British Columbia, Canada, and the Pacific Northwest of the US, I was blessed to witness many marvelous sites. God's beautiful creation was all around me which provided a perfect environment for prayer for all of you!

I was overcome by His beauty with each day a unique perspective of His wonders!

But as mentioned before, my last-minute decision to visit Mother Cabrini's Shrine in the mountains of Denver, CO was the highlight of my trip. And the shoes worn by Mother Cabrini posted here have made a huge impression on me. I can't get this out of my heart, mind, and soul. . . .

These shoes of hers tells the story of an exceptional woman of God who put the needs of others first in her life, especially those in most need at the time – the orphans who were abandoned by society – the outcasts left to fend for themselves.

She offered up her body as a living sacrifice so others might have some joy in this sometimes-cruel world.

Her battered shoes tell her story better than any words can. . . .

This is what it means to be a saint! Her life sounds remarkably like the life of St. Teresa of Calcutta! These two wonderful women have provided all of us the example of what it means to become a saint through their example – something for all of us to emulate in our walk in faith. . . .

Just as they found the strength in God to achieve marvelous works of charity, we can all do the same. . . Sainthood is not limited to only a select few but rather, we are all called to become saints. This is our calling as Christians! We may not be officially recognized by the Vatican or the world, but God knows our hearts which is most important!

I have had the wonderful opportunity to witness many of you here who are already saints going about your business loving, caring for, and helping those in most need.

It has been an honor and privilege to have fellowship with all of you . . . I thank God every day for your presence in my life!

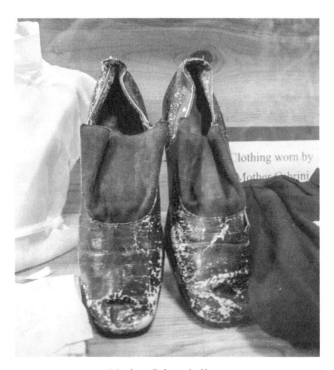

Mother Cabrini's Shoes

Nov 22, 2017, Mother Cabrini Shrine Retreat Announcement

**Happy Blessed Thanksgiving to all of you, no matter what country you are from!

Is there a more beautiful sight than college students on fire for God, taking time of their busy schedules to pray for precious Lelia and for all of you and your needs . . . I think not!

A group of students recently came with me on my prayer hike to pray for all of you. . . . This is proof that God is alive and well in our youth . . . the future of our Church. . . .

In fact, God's love and Divine Mercy is on fire right now, and all we have to do to tap into this great fire of love is to TRUST IN JESUS, as Fr. Gaitley reminds us in his wonderful book, *33 days to Merciful Love.* . . .

God's Mercy is overflowing right now as never before, and trust in Jesus is the conduit to this wonderful grace. . . .

As we are quickly approaching Thanksgiving with family, friends, and even strangers, those who are left out, we can fully appreciate all the wonderful gifts that God has given us and will continue to give to all of us!

***SPECIAL REQUEST!!! I will be making a private retreat at Mother Cabrini's Shrine in Denver, CO this weekend. . . . This retreat is specifically set up for prayer time for Lelia and for everyone else on our prayer list that all of our heartfelt prayers can be answered for them for a complete healing and any other need. . . . God wants all of us to be whole and this is what my/our steadfast prayer will be for all of you this weekend on this special prayer hike and retreat. . . .

As always, we are not alone in our prayers but rather, we rely on the prayers of all of us coming together in communal prayer for each other. . . . This is the most powerful form of prayer so I humbly ask that all of you prayer warriors please join me in my praying this weekend for all those in need. . . .

And expect great things from our Lord Jesus!! He is with us, He loves us more than we could ever know, He wants to heal us, to protect us, to give us abundant Joy!!!

We can rejoice in this, and lift up or hands and hearts in praise, thanksgiving, and worship, to our most High God Who cares for us!!!

God bless everyone and have a blessed Thanksgiving!

Through the powerful intercession of all the saints, in particular for this occasion, St. Faustina, St. Therese, St. Margaret, St. Teresa of Calcutta, St. Mother Cabrini, St. John Paul II, St. Padre Pio, and our most precious Virgin Mary, Pray for us for a special healing for all those in need on our prayer list and all those who need help right now . . . Amen!

Nov 25, 2017, Second day at Mother Cabrini Shrine, Thanksgiving. . . .

At sunrise this morning, it was just me, Jesus, and Mary atop the hill watching God's beautiful creation unfold. . . .

I feel like I'm back in Medjugorje with everything here at the Mother Cabrini Shrine revolving around prayer, Mass, confession, hikes to the beautiful statue of Jesus, Mary and St. Mother Cabrini and other holy things. . . .

Praying in the empty chapel in complete stillness has been one of the most rewarding things!

I also had another Priest prayer over our prayer list and over Lelia's picture for her after Mass! There is a group of missionaries from all over the world present and I'm going to have them pray for everyone as well. . . . This weekend is all about prayer for me and for many of you!

I'll be adding a few more images to this post as they are taken. . . .

God bless you all!

Blessed Mother Mary sunrise at the Shrine.

Mother Cabrini Shrine, Dec 02, 2017

The following day after returning home from Mother Cabrini's Shrine, which was last Monday evening, we were blessed by the most beautiful sunset. It developed on our prayer hike so I ran towards the top to catch the view. It felt as if I was being helped in some way as I didn't tire or lose my breath. I have tried to do the same thing before which nearly killed me. . . .

The sunset was on fire by the time I reached the top radiating it's beautiful reddish golden light across the land and sky. One of our Facebook friends lives in the same area and they too were able to witness this amazing display of God's creation from their home. We don't often get sunsets like these, so it was a real treat. It was so bright that I almost needed sunglasses to view it.

Maybe it was St. Mother Cabrini giving us a goodbye present. . . . So much wonderful prayer took place at our retreat at Mother Cabrini's Shrine with major prayers already answered. It was such a blessing to be in a constant state of prayer the entire time. It was also heavenly to hear the bells and chimes going off every hour outside while praying on the hill and elsewhere.

The Holy Spirit was truly present as I was overwhelmed by His great Love for us as I prayed with all my heart for a healing for Lelia and all on our prayer list . . . .

Please continue to pray extra hard right now as people on our prayer list are in serious need.

We ask you dear St. Mother Cabrini and St. Francis to intercede on behalf of Lelia and all those on our prayer list that Jesus can provide them with relief from their suffering and make them all whole again, whether it is related to health, financial, spiritual, mental, or anything else that causes us to suffer. We ask this through the precious name of Jesus our Lord!

God bless everyone!

April 29, 2018, Praying in the Moonlight with Jesus

Late last night late in the evening I was up praying for everyone atop a mountain on a beautiful moonlit evening . . . .

When I approached the massive statue of our Lord Jesus, I was greeted by the most warm and loving scene. Jesus was glowing in the beautiful moonlight as if raising His prayers up to Father God in Heaven. He was praying for all of us, fully aware of all our needs. . . .

I knelt and joined Him in prayer on this special moment and pleaded with Our Lord to hear our cries and His presence became overwhelming as a sat there in awe, all alone with Jesus in this beautiful comforting light.

Jesus is with all of us no matter how bad or good our situation in life. Holdfast to our Lord and He will give us the necessary strength and courage to go forth in great hope and expectation.

As Christians we have a lot to look forward to as we know that our trials are only temporary. That better day is already upon us as we sit present in the loving arms of our Lord!

We have prayer warriors praying now all over the world with our prayer list in Medjugorje soon and today in England on the Rosary on the Coast. If you haven't already, please join us in prayer this week in a special way as we lift up our petitions and our praise to Jesus, through the powerful intercession of Our Lady joined with St. Mother Cabrini – a powerful team. . . .

God bless everyone!

Jesus and the Moon – Mother Cabrini Shrine

May 19, 2018 – Mother Cabrini Chapel, Burbank, CA

Pilgrimage to Our Lady of Malibu and Mother Cabrini Shrine in California

It was so nice to take a road trip around the beautiful Southwest part of the US with its deep canyons and light painted desert landscapes. We also had a pleasant stay in Southern California along the gorgeous Pacific Ocean visiting our son.

As beautiful as it all may be, the highlight of the pilgrimage has been the wonderful people God has brought in our paths such as Alexis Walkenstein who we had the great privilege meeting at this same Church last fall. Her book *Ex Libris – Fulton J. Sheen* is out now and I'm just starting to read it and loving it. . . . It was Alexis who told us about the Mother Cabrini Chapel in Burbank, California where we had a chance to visit on our last day. Unfortunately, it was closed when we went but it was still an enjoyable experience seeing this humble little Church that helped so many young children throughout the years. The chapel was relocated from its original location up on a hill according to the literature found at this site.

Mother Cabrini Shrine Burbank, California

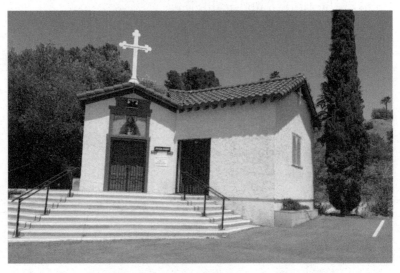

Mother Cabrini Shrine Burbank, California

November 25, 2018, at the Mother Cabrini Shrine

Another wonderful pilgrimage at the Mother Cabrini Shrine in Golden, Colorado immersed in prayer for everyone – hiking and the beauty of God's creation – everything that I love. . . .

The steadfast Italian Saint Mother Cabrini who left her mark throughout the US and abroad continues to bless us with the fruits of her labors.

Here at this particular Shrine, I can't think of a more beautiful location to be inspired by God's beautiful creation with the majestic Rocky Mountains looking west and the Great Plains and city lights below, not to mention the incredible sunsets and sunrises often seen here. . . .

Saint Mother Cabrini accomplished so much because she placed her trust in Jesus for everything and her great works are a testament to her steadfast faith and perseverance in accomplishing God's will for her.

Nothing is impossible for God and her life is the perfect example of this.

More than anything else, trusting God is the answer to solve any problem or to bring joy into our lives. Taking the good advice from a local Priest here, our goal is to always strive to accomplish God's will in our lives even when is hurts. . . . Trust, love, patience, perseverance, and lots and lots of prayer to our Heavenly Father is the key to discovering what God's will is for us and having the wisdom, strength, and courage to live it out even when the road ahead is unclear.

At the Shrine we lit a candle for a special intention for all those in need of healing. God bless everyone and may the joy, peace, and love of Christ Jesus be with you always. . . .

Lit Candle for healing at the Shrine

August 9, 2019 – Handing out Mother Cabrini Relic Cards to the Homeless

I was out this morning trying to minister to the homeless and they ended up ministering to me as usual. They are usually very open talking about God, more so than mainstream society from my experience.

I did this with all of you in mind but especial those here who do not have the physical strength to go out and do this for themselves, so I ask you to be in prayer with me during our Rosary for these poor souls who feel rejected, lonely, abandoned by society . . . And yes some are there by choice, but they are still hurting and in need of prayer just like all of us are. . . .

In our town there's been a large increase, and some are committing crimes but most are just trying to survive, so we are challenged to show love, but at the same time, we have a responsibility to protect our communities and maintain law and order which is no easy task. I've had to call the authorities to remove them off our hill because they start fires when everything is really dry which is obviously a bad situation.

After giving out Mother Cabrini relic cards to some of them and explaining who she was, they are now in Mother Cabrini's hands . . . The blessing will come roaring in for them. . . .

I definitely do not recommend that any of you try this on your own, as it can be quite dangerous . . . This morning an intoxicated man started to harass me and while talking loudly unintentionally spit on my face . . . so I kept my distance.

God bless everyone today and beyond as we trust and pray, glorifying our Risen Lord. . . .

From February 2020 onward I have not been able to travel to the Shrine due to COVID restrictions and especially after being poisoned by heavy metals in October of 2021. But God always provides no matter our circumstances. I have felt Mother Cabrini's intercession for me on several occasions where she has worked through my sister to comfort me during my hardship. I really appreciate my sister praying for me when she travels to the Shrine. Her efforts have been fruitful and healing for us both.

Below are more of my Facebook posts while I was not present at the Shrine but was there in spirit. . . .

November 16, 2022 – My Sister's Prayers at the Shrine

Answered Prayer –

I was praying asking the Sacred Heart of Jesus and the Immaculate Heart of Mary for some help on Sunday, the Feast Day of St. Mother Cabrini, asking our Lord if I could get a little relief while having a pretty rough day . . . This was about 3 p.m. Then around 4 p.m., I suddenly began feeling remarkably better. I thought to myself that someone else must have also been praying for me . . . .

I felt better throughout the rest of the evening and into the next morning when I noticed a text from my sister I had missed that she was praying for me at Mother Cabrini's Shrine. I texted back and asked if she was there right now and she replied back, "No yesterday on her feast day. . . ." I asked her what time it was when she was praying and she said around 3:45 p.m. . . .

Oh my!!! The same time I started feeling so much better. I had no idea she was there praying for me and had written her intention for me to get well in the prayer request book where many pilgrims pray daily for others and their own. . . .

No doubt Mother Cabrini on her feast day was giving us a special blessing . . . She has already done this over the years and now she has interceded for me when I really needed it . . . I got the relief I needed and prayed for . . . Prayers are truly answered. . . .

Praise you Jesus, Thank you Mary, Thank you St. Mother Cabrini. . . .

Thank you, dear sister. . . .

Sister Praying at the Shrine

July 7, 2023 – Sister Praying with Candle Lit

Pray for us dear St. Mother Cabrini. . . .

Someone very special just sent me these pictures after lighting a candle for me and family . . . May the Sacred Heart of Jesus bless her abundantly. . . .

And may God bless and protect all of you through the Precious Body and Blood of His Son Jesus . . . especially your children and loved ones who are struggling with the evil spirit of unbelief. . . . May Mary the Queen of Heaven intercede on your behalf crushing the head of the evil one. . . .

Lit Candle for healing at the Shrine

July 13, 2023 – Mother Cabrini and I Praying at the Shrine

Picture posted was from the past where I was hanging out and praying with one of my favorite saints – Mother Cabrini, before the world and my life dramatically changed back in 2020 . . . I knew rough seas were ahead but had no idea how drastic it would be and how personally challenging it would become.

Spiritual growth has been the main fruit of these difficult spiritual exercises that so many of us are going through now. . . .

Through it all it has been comforting to know we have such wonderful intercessors advocating for us to overcome these tough times.

Thank you Blessed Mother Mary and all Saints of God for your steadfast prayers and love helping to us draw closer to Jesus.

God bless and special prayers for all of you. . . .

Me and Mother Cabrini praying at the Shrine.

March 8, 2023 – New Mother Cabrini Movie

When watching the new St. Mother Cabrini movie . . . Remember who she really was and is . . . A humble, kindhearted, obedient, faithful, beloved Catholic Missionary Sister and servant of the Sacred Heart of Jesus.

She completely relied on Jesus for everything in her life.

EVERYTHING. . . .

St. Mother Cabrini was a missionary first with the conversion of souls and bringing people back to the holy Catholic Church foremost with a special emphasis on the Italian Immigrants.

Mother Cabrini's words:

"In whatever difficulty I may encounter, I want to trust in the goodness of the Sacred Heart of Jesus who will never abandon me. Jesus, please continue to do everything for me, even though I am so unworthy! I will turn to Mary, Mother of Grace, so that she may render me less unworthy of your heavenly assistance."

Amen . . .

Source unknown.

See my Facebook account at Patrick Dillon where we can pray and share in God's blessings.[196]

https://www.facebook.com/profile.php?id=100017309984734

Chapter 11

Mother Cabrini the Mystic

Mother Cabrini was certainly a remarkable sister of Christ with all her many attributes, talents, and gifts, but I had no idea that she was also a mystic. In my research I found very little information relating to this until I read *Journals of a Trusting Heart,* by Sr. Patricia Spillane, MSC. It was there that her life as a mystic was so beautifully revealed.

Mother Cabrini had mystical revelations from the Sacred Heart of Jesus and the Virgin Mary. In one such encounter while praying in front of the Blessed Sacrament exposed on the altar, she was struggling with a decision to accept a mission that could possibly place her sisters in danger and was begging our Lord to help her decide. She then saw the Host on top of the revolving world emitting a brilliant light where Jesus showed her the places, in writing, where she must travel to glorify His holy Name. She could not read most of it because it was in a foreign language. Regardless, this gave Mother Cabrini great comfort and confidence to accept this great mission given to her from God.[197]

Mother Cabrini was blessed to see her beloved Sacred Heart of Jesus in shining white robes where He positioned His hand over His Heart pointing to His name inscribed in blood and said, "Go! With this name in which you have so much faith, your voyage and work will be blessed."

This gave her the confidence and strength to overcome her fears and doubts of traveling overseas.[198]

Life of Prayer

This vision from Jesus would have been extremely helpful for her to make wise decisions without hesitation. But for most, becoming a mystic doesn't happen overnight; rather, it takes many years of dedicated devotion and prayer, and Mother Cabrini was no exception. She spent many hours in retreat in deep heartfelt prayer to her beloved Jesus. She began her steadfast prayer life as a little girl in her native homeland of Italy. From there, Mother Cabrini nurtured a relationship with Jesus that continued to grow and blossom as she went through various hardships and triumphs throughout her life.

In her early years, she admits that she did not yet understand the power of offering up her crosses to Jesus, but as she matured in her faith, this became one of her greatest gifts which enabled her to go beyond her own weaknesses and hardships to accomplish things seemingly impossible. She did it all through the strength and power of our Lord Jesus as she was well aware.

This allowed her to replace fear with faith, eliminating all the obstacles that opposed God's will for her. Studying Mother Cabrini's life has been such an inspiration to me and a great joy! I have learned so much from this blessed saint and I'm thankful to God for her beautiful life on earth.

Mother Cabrini was able to accomplish so much because she placed herself and all her works to the Sacred Heart of Jesus. After giving it her best she could rest knowing that everything was in our Lord's hands:

> Regardless of how difficult a project is, I place it in the adorable Heart of Jesus. Then I can securely rest in peace, even when far away, knowing well that He knows what to do and brings to completion every work that I desire for His glory. In the field I shall work with all my might, but when obedience takes me away from one assignment to go to another where the harvest is ripe, I shall leave the

first. Loving my beloved Jesus, I shall trust Him to give sufficient help and enthusiasm to our dear sisters to succeed in accomplishing everything."[199]

In other words, she learned how to delegate authority in the most holy way, first to Jesus, and then to her sisters who were and still are the backbone of her missionary work.

St. John Paul ll, Letter to Mother Cabrini's Sisters

St. John Paul ll's message in part to the Superior General of the Sisters of the Sacred Heart of Jesus on June 24, 2002:

> This is what Frances Cabrini did courageously throughout her life, which she dedicated to bringing Christ's love to all those, far from their homeland and family, who risked drifting apart from God as well. She would often repeat to her daughters: "Let us imitate the charity of the adorable Heart of Jesus in the salvation of souls, let us make ourselves everything to everyone to win them all for Jesus, as he himself continues to do," and again: "O Jesus, if only I could open my arms wide and embrace the whole world to give it to you. Oh! How happy I should be!"[200]

Mother Cabrini Travels – Central and South America

As St. John Paul II so beautiful stated above, Mother Cabrini and her sisters traveled far from their homeland and families to bring Christ's love to the ends of the earth. It proved to be a difficult challenge in most cases but there were times when Mother Cabrini was treated like royalty, especially in Central America and countries like Panama, Nicaragua, and Costa Rica.

These countries suffered a lot of disparity with the majority being poor and the few, the rich elite. It was the minority that controlled the country and depending on their leadership in place, it could be quite brutal. Although Catholicism was the primary religion in these areas, those in power were careful to not let Catholic doctrine influence their own ideologies which were often contrary to the faith. Some of the leaders heavily monitored the churches and tried to sensor what the parish priest could say and do.

However, the leaders desperately needed quality education to help further advance their society which was lacking. This was particularly true in Nicaragua at the time with several factions competing against one another for power which led to mass corruption and violence in some cases. Control for power changed hands many times. Mother Cabrini's reputation for her excellence in administration and teaching spread quickly, even into these remote regions of the world.[201]

On the one hand, they knew that she would be teaching Catholic doctrine which might conflict with their ideologies, but on the other hand, they needed the schools which were in short supply so when Mother Cabrini steamed into their area, the leadership would literally roll the red carpet out hosting special dinners with dignitaries providing her with upscale accommodations which she often refused. They figured once she opened her schools and orphanages, they could tone down her Catholic dogma through bribes and the other means.

But they didn't know who Mother Cabrini was and greatly underestimated her. Mother Cabrini would never compromise on her values for any reason and because of this, her sisters were forced out of Nicaragua at one point because they would not comply with their corrupt agenda. This was unfortunate because it only hurt all the young children who were getting an excellent education, and more importantly, were learning about Jesus and their Catholic faith. This decision was very difficult for Mother Cabrini and her sisters. I'm sure they did everything possible to remain there but when the sisters' lives became endangered along with the children, it was time to leave. They didn't have a choice as they were being threatened by the local liberal leaders who did not want them preaching about Jesus. The local leaders were going around the President who invited Mother Cabrini to come in the first place. The city Prefect and Governor showed up with soldiers to escort them out to the awaiting steamship. They didn't want word to get out to the President so they hurried the operation to remove them, including two sick sisters who were not fit for travel.[202]

Andes Crossing By Mule

Despite the hardships and dangers, Mother Cabrini steamed throughout the coast of Central and South America tirelessly searching and responding to pleas for help. She even crossed the rugged snow-covered Andes by mule to reach her destination in Buenos Aires. Below is a small excerpt from her Andes adventure while attempting to jump across a narrow, deep ravine along their path:

> . . . We were at a height where one perceived an immense abyss on one side, whilst on the other there was a vast expanse of pure white snow, while further ahead there were heights awaiting us. But just in front of us was that large crevice, long and deep, which seemed ready to swallow us up and bury us. The muleteers, though not without fear, tried to make some of the mules jump the crevice, and seeing that it could be done, encouraged the passengers to do the same. I, as you have heard, was at the head of the line, and I was willing to be the first to go forward in order to encourage the others, for, to speak truth fully, I was not a bit afraid, feeling quite calm. My guide had his staff ready, as he thought he would have to carry me across, but I told him I could take longer jumps than the one across the crevice. He very respectfully showed me the danger, and then watched me attentively, knowing I would not fail to tell him or call him if I needed help.
>
> I jumped, or at least attempted to, but, probably owing to the cold and the keen air which deprived me of strength, I realized too late that I was like a feather, which, however much it is thrown forward, does not move unless carried by the wind; and so I should have buried myself alive had it not been for the muleteer, who, seeing the danger, dismounted and, stretching his feet across the crevice, held me back on one side of the chasm until he, with the help of his comrade, sprang across to the other side, where he drew me by the arm after him into safety. The shock produced such palpitation of the heart that I thought I should have died. The good muleteer

took me aside, and I fell fainting in the snow. I couldn't speak a word, and it was obvious from the frightened looks of the good man that he expected a tragedy. But this was not God's Will. As soon as I was able to speak, I told him to go and help the others; and I hadn't to tell him twice, as the need was urgent. I remained alone, stretched on that white bed of snow, and little by little, helped by the pure air, the palpitation ceased, and I was as lively as ever. I arose to find that all had crossed the dangerous pass and that the muleteer was waiting for me to mount my mule again. . . .[203]

Mother Cabrini gave it her all to serve Jesus the best she could and help bring others closer to Him and she thoroughly enjoyed doing it. There were times however when she and her sisters were persecuted by anti-Catholic Semitism in the US, and in Central and South America by atheist dictators, and even by some of the immigrants they were trying to serve – but she did not let that stop her pursuit to evangelize her beloved Jesus to the world.

She was fearless, even when she travelled into dangerous parts of the world, knowing full well that she could be harmed along with her sisters. Regardless, she was willing to take that risk placing her full trust in the Sacred Heart of Jesus to protect her, which He did on every account. At times she had to be cautious to whom she would talk to or trust. There were occasions when her guides became drunk at night where Mother Cabrini and her sisters were left on their own, in remote regions of the world, where they prayed steadfastly to our Lord Jesus for their protection.

Yes, Mother Cabrini saw it all, fancy banquets with the finest foods and accommodations, to run down motels and humble shelters that didn't have electricity, running water, or sewer.

St. Mother Cabrini and St. John Paul II have a lot in common, each with a different God given plan, but both lovers of God's creation in nature, and both helped change the world for the better by risking their lives to promote human dignity and foremost, the proclamation and evangelization of our Lord Jesus Christ as our Eternal Savior and Lord.

God in Everything

Mother Cabrini saw God in everything she did. She saw God in the young orphan girls who were left destitute and abandoned where their parents either died or left them on their own. She saw God in all her sisters who worked steadfast and obediently to help those they served in their ministry. She saw God in all of those she met during her fundraising efforts which varied from the poorest of the poor to the super rich. She saw God in all the clergy including deacons, priests, bishops, cardinals, and the pope.

Mother Cabrini saw God in all her business associates, landowners, and government officials she interacted with daily. She saw God in all the ordinary people she encountered, especially those who were suffering from poverty or other hardship. She saw God in the hard-working miners who risked their lives to help provide for their families. She saw God in her own family members, her dear mother and father, her brothers and sisters, and other family and friends.

Mother Cabrini saw God in the beautiful churches she encountered throughout the world, especially during holy Mass, and when she was praying in front of the Blessed Sacrament exposed. She saw God during all the mini retreats she attended to help renew her spiritual strength and to learn how to serve others with more love and compassion. She saw God through His wonderful creation during her many hours spent out in nature.

Mother Cabrini's Love for God's Creation in Nature

From her early childhood in the small town of Livagra, she would often visit her uncle who was the town priest to sail her little paper boats down the river pretending she was sending missionaries to help bring the good news of Jesus to China. When she was older, her long walks to and from her new teaching job along a beautiful, wooded area brought her great peace and serenity where she spent many hours praying under a tree. I believe it was there that she gained such a special appreciation for the outdoors sharing in God's beautiful creation. This is where she learned to refresh her mind, body, and soul in a peaceful setting that allowed her to come closer to God.

On her many voyages aboard a steamship headed for distant lands, she spent many hours on deck out in the open air, as she often said it was good for her lungs. She was always watching the sky to see what kind of message God was sending her that day whether it was a flock of ducks flying overhead, a seagull landing on the boat railing, the calmness of the sea or its turbulence, in it all she always took note and reflected on His creation.

Her love for God's handiwork in nature led to her to find the picturesque property she purchased on the Hudson River outside New York City, and the beautiful property in Seattle, Washington overlooking the lake, and the magnificent property in Mount Vernon Canyon, Colorado which overlooks the Front Range to the east with the stunning Rocky Mountains to the west, and the lovely property in Burbank, California sitting on top of a hill with its temperate climate and many birds that she greatly enjoyed feeding and taking care of. These are just a few of the places that Mother Cabrini and her ministry owned throughout the world that were surrounded by His nature.

Mother Cabrini through her own experiences, knew firsthand the healing power and restoration of spending time outdoors. This made it a high priority for her when selecting properties, especially for her orphanages where she knew it would be a great benefit to her young girls, many of whom were in desperate need of healing, peace, and solitude. Mother Cabrini would use whatever was within her means to help bring these little children and adult immigrants back to God.

Yes, Mother Cabrini did humanitarian work but that was not her primary goal and purpose but rather, it was to bring people to Jesus in any way she could, whether it was through an orphanage, a hospital, a school, or going down 900 feet into a mineshaft and traveling up to a mile or more underground in difficult and even dangerous conditions to seek out the miners who had drifted away from their Catholic faith. There was no place on earth that she wouldn't travel to seek out those who needed the good news of Jesus in their lives. . . .

Mother Cabrini was a missionary first to help bring souls to her beloved Jesus. From her small birth town in Italy, to bustling Rome, to the island of England, to the distant shores of the Americas where she encountered great coastal cities, lush rolling hills, The Great Plains, The beautiful Rocky Mountains, sprawling deserts, and in Central and South America where she set up her missions in the lush jungles, coastal deserts, and even traveled in the snow laden Andes Mountains on mules to reach her destination.

There was no place too far, difficult, or dangerous, despite her compromised health that included her lungs. I still can't figure out how she was able to go up to such a high altitude without passing out or even dying. I know firsthand how difficult it is to go up into these areas where breathing oxygen is difficult. There is no doubt in my mind that she had angels who carried her through these harsh environments. Regardless, she was human after all, and did succumb to malaria, exposed while traveling in Central America; but I guess in the end, this was her ticket into Heaven.

I feel so drawn to Mother Cabrini I think in part because we both share in our great love for God's beautiful creation in nature. I can only image how beautiful her images would have been if she were a photographer and had access to quality gear. But instead of a camera, she painted her experiences with her words which are more beautiful, allowing the imagination to depict a more surreal scene.

I also share in her Catholic Faith and special devotion and love for our Lord Jesus and our Blessed Mother Mary. She reached a level few ever experienced on earth and that is why she is a saint, something for us all to strive towards.

Her Devotion to Our Blessed Mother

Mother Cabrini understood that Mary was her teacher and the one who would draw her closer to Christ. She often said that the Sacred Heart of Jesus was her special director and Mary was her teacher. A priest once told her that saying that appeared to be out of excessive pride. Mother Cabrini out of obedience stopped expressing this for a while feeling unworthy until Jesus and Mary came to her in a vision on the same day at separate times, telling her it was ok to continue with her practice.[204]

Mother Cabrini writes that she entrusted her entire ministry to Mary:

> Mary, my Mother, you are the mysterious book of my destiny. In the beginning a new year of my existence, I kneel at your feet to beg all the graces I need to serve my Beloved Jesus better. You are beautiful and lovable, dearest mother – I love you. You are sublime and glorious – I praise you. You are kind and merciful – I trust you unreservedly. You are my mother, my teacher, my role model – I will obey and imitate you. . . .

> . . . I entrust the Institute to you. It is yours because you founded it, making use of this poor servant of yours as your instrument. You are our Foundress: be also our Mother – protect this inheritance of yours. Mary, we are your daughters. Direct us and guide us on the straight path, so that we may always fulfill the beautiful mission we have received on earth: to love Jesus, our Divine Spouse, with our whole heart and with all our strength. Beloved Mother, guide us so that everything we do may be always directed to the love of Him and the glory of His Divine Heart. . . .[205]

Ave Maris Stella (Hail Star of the Sea)

Mother Cabrini and her Sisters would pray and sing the Ave Maris Stella every day to honor Mary and was one of her favorite prayers. This beautiful song is a Latin hymn dating back to the Middle Ages:

> Hail, o star of the ocean,
> God's own Mother blest,
> ever sinless Virgin,
> gate of heav'nly rest.

> Taking that sweet Ave,
> which from Gabriel came,
> peace confirm within us,
> changing Eve's name.

Break the sinners' fetters,
make our blindness day,
Chase all evils from us,
for all blessings pray.

Show thyself a Mother,
may the Word divine
born for us thine Infant
hear our prayers through thine.

Virgin all excelling,
mildest of the mild,
free from guilt preserve us
meek and undefiled.

Keep our life all spotless,
make our way secure
till we find in Jesus,
joy for evermore.

Praise to God the Father,
honor to the Son,
in the Holy Spirit,
be the glory one. Amen.[206]

From her travels journal while crossing the Atlantic Ocean on her second voyage to New York she writes to her sisters:

> Oh, happy the soul that lives in the true love of Christ! My daughters, detach yourselves from all persons and all things, and you will have a foretaste of the Paradise of true, solid, and Heavenly love.
>
> Before we went to rest last night we were thinking of you making the Holy Hour perhaps for us. We united with you in spirit and tasted with you the Paradise of holy union with God. **Every day we invoke the Star of the Sea with the Ave Maris Stella, in honour of our loving Mother who truly protects us.** Only yesterday we escaped a collision

with those enormous masses of ice that were threatening our ruin. We owe this to our dear and powerful Mother. We are fairly happy. It seems that the passengers share our happiness, for first one and then another comes to stay and favour us with their company.[207]

I can only imagine the beautiful sound of music coming from Mother Cabrini and her sisters singing this beautiful hymn of praise out on the open deck of their ship. It must have been a great joy for the passengers to hear such comforting angelic voices on their long arduous journey. Below is a link to hear this beautiful song by the Daughters of Mary, Mother of Our Savior.[208]

https://www.youtube.com/watch?v=069OCfXLNgk

Mother Cabrini – a Gift From God

Mother Cabrini has been such a blessing and inspiration to me – she pushes me further in my faith and desire to overcome my weaknesses and shortcomings. I considered her my best friend and mentor.

There really is no secret to her success; it is out there for all to see, by doing the will of her beloved Jesus completely relying on Him for everything. Mother Cabrini did have one secret I found interesting that emboldened her ministry. She said, "I will never go anywhere without my powerful collection: My Patron saints and the 42 relics I carry."[209]

She did this by devoting a great deal of time in prayer and meditation to more fully understand and accept the will of her beloved Jesus who empowered and strengthen her to accomplish the smallest of things, and those that are not humanly possible.

Leading by example, she has helped motivate me to overcome the suffering in my life replacing it with hope and joy where I could have been feeling sorry for myself or embittered. Going to Mother Cabrini's Shrine in Denver has been instrumental in preparing me for life's unexpected challenges. It has been a place of spiritual and physical renewal necessary for healing. I am not alone as thousands of others have come closer to Jesus by visiting her beautiful shrines in our country and around the world.

Her childhood dream to become a missionary was realized in the most beautiful way, not the way she expected it, but isn't that how God usually works in us. Her missionary work to bring others to Christ lives on, even stronger today. Her sisters and lay people have continued her legacy in some of the most beautiful and important ways.

Fight Against Human Trafficking

Today, the need for orphanages is not the emphasis but rather, we have a lot of other problems and needs in our modern world. Mother Cabrini's international ministry doesn't just provide beautiful shrines or education through their schools and universities; they are also in the forefront fighting against human trafficking where often human traffickers prey especially on younger children and even adults where they are targeted for the sexual slave trade. This is a crime against humanity and great sin against God that needs to stop. I was thankful for the recent movie, *Sound of Freedom,* which did a good job exposing this barbaric trade unbeknown to many people. I knew this existed but not at the magnitude it was occurring which is shocking.

Mother Cabrini's ministry provides education and safe havens through their own existing ministries and community engagements, along with their partners, with many resources to help those who are victims or most vulnerable to avoid being exploited in this inhumane modern slave trade. Donating to the sisters' ministry is a great way to help support their good works in this important effort.[210]

https://www.mothercabrini.org/what-we-do/

Chapter 12

Signs From Heaven

Mother Cabrini Clouds

As this book began at the Shrine with the ominous but beautiful clouds over the Sacred Heart of Jesus statue back in August of 2019, history repeated itself but this time not at the Shrine, but instead, at my hometown of Durango. I haven't seen clouds like this since that time.

It was a beautiful day in April 2024 with hardly a cloud in the sky. Then towards the evening, the clouds started to quickly build coming out of nowhere. Less than a half an hour, the entire sky was covered in ominous black clouds that looked like something out of this world. When my wife looked up at the sky she instantly said, "Mother Cabrini clouds!"

I knew I had to get to a better vantage point to capture this rare moment. These were not the regular thunderhead clouds but were unique. I have taken thousands of pictures of stormy weather and this had a look all its own. I believed it was a sign from God, so I took it very seriously. When God gives a sign, I do my best to capture it to share with as many people as possible. The last thing I wanted was to let Him down, so I quickly gathered up my camera gear and drove to a spot overlooking the town with a beautiful view of the La Plata Mountains in the backdrop.

I was having a pretty rough health day making everything more difficult. I first took a video with my phone to capture its magnificence in motion.

It was beautiful yet eerie as the entire sky was engulfed by this amazing display of God's creation. It was emotional as well as I could feel God's love radiating through His nature. It reminded me of Mother Cabrini as she was constantly looking upwards not to miss any sign from God given to her each day. Her travel journals have many beautiful descriptions of ominous skies, especially sailing around the world. While writing this book I have come even closer to her, feeling a special bond, especially while out in nature.

Being a landscape photographer, I decided to place my emphasis on the beautiful La Plata Mountains off in the distance with the immense prophetic clouds above. It was now late in the evening well after sunset so it was a difficult shot to capture do to the darkness of both the mountains and the sky with spots of brightness making the exposure challenging to lock in. I did my best . . . .

In the clouds, I could see angels and other heavenly figures along with an element of darkness as if a spiritual battle were taking place above our town. Was this just some random anomaly or was it prophetic in nature where God was speaking to us. I know I was captivated by it and didn't want to leave. I waited until the clouds blended into darkness and lost their intensity and my wife and I drove home quietly thinking about what we had just witnessed. Later that evening, a strong wind came up and blew like crazy for about two hours and then suddenly stopped after midnight. Again, the last time we saw clouds like this was at the Mother Cabrini Shrine where after a few months, the world broke into chaos.

Total Solar Eclipse

The next morning it was clear as a bell without a cloud in sight. I have witnessed many storms over the years, but this one was unique and it occurred on Friday evening, only a few days after the total solar eclipse of April 08, 2024. This eclipse was unique as it darkened a heavily populated region of our country where millions of people were able to witness totality. Our area was forecasted to be only 70% eclipsed so I didn't take it too seriously at first.

On the morning of April 8, I awoke thinking about the much-anticipated eclipse that was pounded in the news for weeks. Imaginations were running high as many Christians were thinking something prophetic would happen and even the secular were coming out with their theories. Most were just looking forward to a rare event with many travelling from around the world to witness this unique event. One thing is for sure, God had millions of people looking up at the sky so anything could happen.

I got dressed and went out to see the sun just starting to rise but it was partially blocked by a thin layer of high clouds. Regardless, the sun was breaking through and I noticed a particular glow about it and took a quick phone picture out the window. The peak eclipse for our area was supposed to occur around 12:30 p.m. MST.

Solar Halo Surprise

While I was eating my breakfast, I looked out the window a few minutes later and something caught my attention. The partially obscured sun was now encircled by a heavenly globe with rainbow colors around its perimeter and the sun was looking like the Star of Bethlehem. I couldn't believe what I was seeing. . . . I went a bit crazy setting up all my camera gear, and with heart racing, I ran outside and started capturing God's beautiful creation. This was a complete surprise to me as I was expecting very little but wow, God had other plans.

This phenomenon can be explained by science which is called a sun halo or sun dog which can occur with the right atmospheric conditions and thin cloud cover. But this is a rare event that I haven't seen for nearly a decade and it was occurring on a special solar eclipse day. This was not just a coincidence, and I knew God was speaking again loud and clear. He was speaking to the entire world with various signs and wonders, and He had our full attention, including mine.[211]

It was about 8 a.m. in the morning when the picture above was taken. The sun halo was persistent and continued to surround the sun all morning. This sun halo reminded me of a protective bubble around Jesus the Son – a safe zone of Divine protection. When we follow Jesus closely, we share in this protected bubble from God.

I decided to move to another location to capture this anomaly during the peak eclipse near our local Animas River where I could try and get a nice landscape shot with the sun. I brought no special filters with me so I didn't capture the partial eclipse due to the brightness of the sun still getting through, but I did catch an amazing scene from God completely unexpected, the way He often works in our lives.

The above picture was taken during the peak of the partial eclipse where it became darker as the picture shows. Also, the temperature gradually became noticeably cooler along with the birds becoming more vocal during the peak hour. I wasn't witnessing totality like so many others were blessed to see, but I was being blessed just the same.

It was a beautiful moment which brought me to tears. There were a few other people down at the river watching with one woman close by with her dog. I felt this was something that should be shared with others so I yelled out to her and asked if she could see the sun halo? She came running up in excitement to show me her pictures taken. This woman was from the Canary Islands in Spain, which is a beautiful location itself, but she was completely overcome by God's beautiful gift to our area. It was a great moment especially to celebrate it with others.

The solar eclipse was such a beautiful gift from God as it brought together millions of people from different cultures and political affiliations where all were united in a rare moment, witnessing God's beautiful creation and awesome power and glory. It was so nice to see our divided country come together at least for a moment; thanks be to God. He got the world's attention in such a beautiful way. I do wonder if this solar eclipse could be a sign of things to come. God has used eclipses in the past to get the attention of His people who had fallen away, so the same is true for our times.

Rare Northern Lights

Then in early May about a month after the solar eclipse, the world experienced a beautiful display of the Northern Lights in places rarely, if ever seen. The world was looking up at the Heavens in awe of God's mighty power in His beautiful creation. The images and videos coming in from around the globe were breathtaking!

Space.com published an article with the following headline:

"We may have just witnessed some of the strongest auroras in 500 years."[212]

https://www.space.com/solar-storms-may-2024-strongest-auroras-500-years

Here in Durango, Colorado, the Northern Lights were barely visible to the naked eye and only in the higher elevations where I am not able to go now due to my condition. As a landscape photographer, I was so frustrated not being able to go up to 12,000 feet and capture this once in a lifetime event. In fact, I didn't even know it was occurring on the peak evening and was feeling extra terrible, especially from intense head pressure. The next day online I read the details regarding the event and learned that the extra electromagnetic frequency emitted from this solar storm was also affecting satellite communications and other sensitive electronic equipment, including my brain! I wish I were joking but this is my life now.

I wasn't able to witness the Northern Lights that evening, but God gave me this beautiful scene pictured below instead. This was taken at a lower elevation over the La Plata Mountains on my regular evening excursion. I named it *Heaven's Gate.*

After a few days I started feeling a bit better and traveled up to around 8,000 feet (my maximum) to try to get a picture over Haviland Lake, but no Northern Lights for me. Instead, I captured this:

I know this is a bit of a stretch, but I thought the top center resembled St. Michael the Archangel. After thinking about it, I wasn't disappointed not being able to capture the Northern Lights, after all, so many other people had already captured it for me.

There is no doubt that God is trying to get our attention, and He is doing a great job. It is good to admire His beautiful creation, but I think we need to think deeper; what exactly is God trying to tell us? If

God is speaking, we need to listen. I hear the secular world saying it's just a solar flare that science can explain. This is true but they forget to mention that God created it all and uses His creation to speak to us in many ways.

There is no need to worry about what may come . . . if God sends us something directly, or if He is just warning us about some kind of harm coming our way due to our own sinful nature, it will be for our own good, because He is merciful and loves us more than we can image. Instead of worrying, we need to spend more time getting closer to Jesus **now** while we still can. This is where Mother Cabrini's teachings can really help.

Do You Love Me?

Back in April 2024, the following Sunday after the ominous clouds appeared over the mountains, I awoke around 5 a.m. with a thought about Mother Cabrini I wanted to add to this book. I didn't want to forget about it so I kept going over it in my mind. While lying in bed my thoughts were suddenly interrupted by a strong voice deep in my heart that said, "Do you love me?" I knew it was Jesus, but I was still thinking about the Mother Cabrini content so for a brief moment, I actually tuned out what I heard in my heart. I must have been in some sort of a sleep state to be so foolish. But then His voice in my heart became even stronger, **"Do you love me?"** This time I dropped everything and replied, **"Not enough Lord, please teach me how to love you more."** Jesus replied, **"Come to My Table."**

Wow! . . . That pierced directly into my heart. I was so convicted at that point because I already knew what He was referring to. For more than 2 years I have not been going to Sunday Mass as it became too difficult to sit through because of my comprised health. There were times that I could hardly walk down the aisle to receive Holy Communion. I still wear a mask due to my compromised immune system which made it even harder. I asked two different priests if I could go instead during the week which was shorter with less people, and they gave me approval due to my health. It can be a mortal sin not going to Mass on Sunday or other holy day of obligation, unless there is a good reason for it.

Therefore, getting permission and absolution was very important to me. I was already going to Mass in person two days during the week and participating online the other days including Sunday. I would still go in person on Sundays during Easter and Christmas which proved to be very difficult but rewarding.

After Jesus asked me to come to His Table, I replied from my heart, "If I truly loved you Jesus with all my heart, I would crawl on my stomach to receive Your Precious Body and Blood whenever I had a chance." I felt convicted and had a strong desire to start going on Sunday again. The week before all this transpired was Divine Mercy Sunday which is very special to me, so I went on that day in person which was difficult to get through. Attending the previous Sunday helped open my heart to the Holy Spirit – a gift from our Lord's Divine Merciful Heart.

My wife was pleasantly surprised when I told her what had transpired, and that I planned on going to Sunday Mass again. Having this experience from our Lord gave me the strength and courage to do whatever I could to partake in our Lord's Table by overcoming the giant in my life. Working on Mother Cabrini's book really helped encourage me as well. She is a wonderful motivator filled with the Holy Spirit and by reading her journals, she showed me that it is not by my strength that I do anything, but it is only through our Lord. She really believed this and overcame her weakness in the most beautiful way setting the example.

Rejected in Our Suffering

Mother Cabrini spent a lifetime learning how to better trust Jesus and I'm sure she would vouch that it was not easy at times. When she was being abused by the Mother Superior at the House of Providence in Codogeno, Italy, she admitted that she did not yet understand the value of suffering. I think it is worth repeating her words again:

> I wept a great deal, and a missionary must never weep. Not to complain when I had to suffer and to bear it all with patience and fortitude would have been a virtue . . . But at that time I did not understand the value of the Cross and of suffering.[213]

It is not easy for anyone, especially while suffering. Being compromised in any way sets us up for pain, ridicule, gossip, isolation, bullying, loneliness, being ignored, avoided, and even despised by others. This is true whether we have some kind of physical ailment, character defect, or mental issue.

For most of my life I was blessed to be healthy and strong. It wasn't until I started losing my health, especially in the last couple years, that I started to have a better understanding and compassion for others who are suffering. I have always been one to look out for the underdog going all the way back to grade school where I used to stand up for the nerds and others who were being bullied. I was popular amongst the downtrodden crowd. I have also gone out of my way later in life to help those who were struggling, either through illness, loss of a spouse, or other hardships. It is just natural for me. But again, I really didn't understand how hard it was for them, and knowing what I know now, I would have gone about it a lot differently, with more compassion and understanding.

You really do find out who your friends are when trials come your way and you're not able to be the one giving most of the time. You find out those who were along for the ride as long as they were getting something out of you. It has been a learning experience, and even some surprises, as some of the people that remained loyal were those I least expected. In my case, it has been the truck drivers who have reached out the most in my time of need. One friend owns a fuel hauling business that I used to mentor through the Big Brothers Big Sisters program back when he was a teenager, and now he is mentoring me. Another truck driver is an old friend that goes back to my childhood years. We grew apart later in life and just recently started talking again. What is it about truck drivers anyways? . . .

Don't get me wrong, there are many out there who are struggling with their own issues and who don't have the strength or time to deal with other peoples' problems . . . I get that. It does not mean they don't care about you. And there are those who just don't know what to do so they stay away. There are a few who downright reject you if you don't have anything to offer them and will go someplace else to find what they're looking for.

Jesus knew about this all too well when some of His closest disciples bailed out on Him during His time of most need. So why would I expect anything different? But instead, Jesus used this as an opportunity to strengthen his friends, not ridicule them. We are all selfish in nature, something we have to battle against, and this includes those like me who are struggling with their health. I have found firsthand that God uses our weakness to help strengthen us. In my weakness I have had to rely more on God as others have distanced themselves from me. God is the only one who will never abandon us. People are weak and will let us down; but God never will – not in this life or the eternal one to come. This realization has never been stronger in my heart.

I'll be honest, having health issues has been a very difficult and humbling experience. I have taken great measures to hide my problems, too embarrassed to let others know. It is pride. After several years the pride starts to fade away with the realization that I am not superman and need help too. In some ways I have become a better, more compassionate person because of it.

So instead of looking at suffering as a curse, it can be a blessing from our Lord. That doesn't mean we can go up to someone who is suffering and tell them it is a gift and just offer it up. Yes, there is a time for that, but showing love and compassion must precede it. There is a time and a place for everything.

What about somebody like my dad who developed lung cancer from smoking too much? Our bodies are the temples of the Holy Spirit so we should do whatever we can to remain healthy. But even in our neglect, God can make all things good. I have seen this firsthand in my own life and family.

What about the young child stricken with cancer with no fault of their own? This is when it really gets difficult to understand. It all comes down to sin in our world which corrupts and causes disorder in everything, in our weather, and even our health. We all contribute to sin which has consequences; therefore, we become victims because of it. But even here, God uses our suffering for the good. . . .

One thing that has really helped me the past year is to start every morning off singing Psalm 118:24 regardless of how I feel. This simple but powerful Psalm has brought healing and great joy to my heart!

"This is the day the LORD has made; let us rejoice in it and be glad."

Venerable Archbishop Fulton Sheen

Reading books about the saints who suffered is also really helpful. The Venerable Archbishop Fulton Sheen, although not yet officially a saint, but well on his way towards canonization, has some brilliant insights on this subject. From his book, *Ex Libris, Fulton J. Sheen*, compiled by Alexis Walkenstein:

> Those who love God do not protest, whatever He may ask of them, nor doubt His kindness when He sends them difficult hours.

> . . . So the soul that has sufficient faith accepts all the events of life as gifts from God, in the serene assurance that He knows best.

> Every moment brings us more treasures than we can gather. The great value of the Now, spiritually viewed, is that it carries a message God has directed personally to us.[214]

Venerable Fulton Sheen is a brilliant theologian whose words of wisdom have really helped my wife and I out with our work as marriage preparation ministers. His book, *Three to Get Married,* is an excellent resource for our marriage preparation couples to further their relationship before and after marriage.

It is not easy being a steadfast Christian as there are many challenging areas that we face. God's main purpose for our lives is to bring us to Heaven. He will do whatever it takes, and it is up to us to trust Him in **all** things. The prayer of reading Holy Scripture is a beautiful remedy to help us overcome our trials as it provides many examples of the value of our suffering and how to not only endure it, but to thrive:

We know that all things work for good for those who love God, who are called according to his purpose. (Romans 8:28)

Not only that, but we even boast of our afflictions, knowing that affliction produces endurance, and endurance, proven character, and proven character, hope, and hope does not disappoint, because the love of God has been poured out into our hearts through the Holy Spirit that has been given to us. (Romans 5:3-5)

Rejoice in the Lord always. I shall say it again: rejoice! Your kindness should be known to all. The Lord is near. Have no anxiety at all, but in everything, by prayer and petition, with thanksgiving, make your requests known to God. Then the peace of God that surpasses all understanding will guard your hearts and minds in Christ Jesus. (Philippians 4:4-7)

Mother Cabrini understood this well. There were many people trying to take advantage of her especially when they saw her small stature and compromised health. Mother Cabrini didn't rely on her own strength; instead, she relied on Jesus. It didn't matter to her what others thought. What did matter was pleasing her beloved Lord and she had so much joy doing it! That is why she was so successful yet misunderstood by many, including her superiors, because she did not follow the wisdom of this world and often came up with ideas that were completely contrary. These ideas and dreams came to her from the Holy Spirit which is not of this world, and given enough time, she produced many fruits.

If Mother Cabrini had been strong and robust in her health, she might have let her pride take over instead of letting Jesus be the center of her life. This was true for so many saints of God. It would be better if we could have both but if given a choice, the soul is eternal which is far more important than the body. Whatever it takes for God's holy will to be done in us. The closer we come to our Lord, the more all this adversity in our lives will have purpose.

I already included this writing from Mother Cabrini in an earlier chapter, but I believe her words here are so powerful and true that it is worth repeating again:

> In all my trials in life, I should strive to the best of my ability to maintain a strong confidence and trust in the Sacred Heart of Jesus. The person with true faith will never be overcome. Loss of trust in God dishonors Him, since it implies He has failed us, which is impossible. It is always we who fail Him by placing obstacles to the work of grace. From now on, I will counteract mistrust with humble confidence in Him. The more I acknowledge my weakness, the greater will be His power to help me.[215]

Mother Cabrini – *"With God I Can Do Great Things!"*[216]

Mother Cabrini spent her whole life bringing people closer to Jesus. Her good works and fruits are hard to quantify but it would be safe to say that she and her sisters have helped millions come to Jesus and continue to do so. I know she has helped me personally and I am very grateful to her.

Her writings are thoughtful and convicting and bring comfort, peace, and joy drawing us closer to Jesus:

> . . . For me the name of Jesus is wisdom, justice, sanctification and redemption. He is my teacher, my guide, my pilot, my pastor. He is my doctor, my father, my judge and my advocate, my protector and defender.
>
> I have everything in my loving Jesus, my beloved Spouse, and he is everything to me. If I am ill, He is my health because he sustains me materially and spiritually. If I am hungry, He is my food which gently satisfies me. When I am weak, He fortifies me with His own strength. When I am poor, He enriches me. Ignorant that I am, He is my wisdom. Miserable sinner that I am, He purifies me every time I humble myself. He raises me up to His Divine Heart,

embraces me with His infinite goodness and makes me repeat: **"I can do all things in Him who strengthens me"** (Phil 4:13). **With God I can do great things!"**[217]

My Sister's MC Shrine Teaching Experience

March 22, 2024, on a beautiful Friday spring morning while sitting at my desk, feeling terrible with my head feeling like it was going to explode, and my whole body engulfed in weakness, I sat in front of my computer trying to salvage a real estate deal that was about to be terminated by the buyers. I suddenly heard a notification from my cell phone which I keep about 6 feet away and noticed a call coming in from my sister where she was trying to live chat with me. I quickly accepted her call and at first I didn't know where she was until she said with her excited voice, "Guess where I am?" She always says that while at Mother Cabrini's Shrine; an instant rush of joy overwhelmed me. . . .

Her call instilled confidence in me that the real estate deal was in God's hands. I had placed a Miraculous Medal along with Mother Cabrini's picture and relic card attached to my real estate sign entrusting the sale of this property to their intercession. Mother Cabrini had a special gift from God to negotiate fruitful real estate deals throughout her life and I feel confident God is still allowing her to help others in this sometimes-difficult task. The real estate deal I was struggling with went through a few weeks later. I thanked the Virgin Mary and Mother Cabrini and gave praise to Jesus.

At the time of my sister's call, I completely forgot about my real estate problems and entered the "Mother Cabrini" zone. My sister through live video so graciously showed me around the Mother Cabrini altar and the grounds which were heavily covered in snow. She purchased a Sacred Heart of Jesus candle, lit it, and we prayed for everyone in our family.

What a beautiful gift from God it was to be able to replace my fear and anxiety with prayer. My sister was following the Holy Spirit to break out of her busy day and go to the Shrine. She was on spring break but unfortunately was so buried with all her teaching responsibilities that she spent the whole time trying to catch up on her grading. She teaches college level writing and Middle School English. I reminded her that Mother Cabrini was an excellent teacher and she replied, "I know! I'm asking her to please help me! My workload is intense!!"

After she gave me the grand tour via face time, she had to call it short because of the tons of papers that needed to be graded. She planned to do this from the front seat of her car in the parking lot where she had a view of the Sacred Heart of Jesus statue located on top of the hill. She spent the next several hours working away, taking an occasional prayer break and stretching her eyes to look out her car window at the beautiful sites. Could there be a better place to grade papers? I think not. . . .

Then something funny happened. While grading in her car, one of the employees came up and knocked on her window to ask if she was all right as she had been parked there for several hours without leaving. She opened up the window and told the man what she was doing – he laughed and told her to enjoy the rest of her day!

Later, when I was doing an interview with Tommy Francis, I told him about my sister's experience and he quickly replied in laughter, "That was me who checked on her, I wish she would have told me you were her brother." Nothing gets past the sharp eyes of Tommy at the Shrine, always on the lookout to help those in need.

When she first arrived at the Shrine, there were only a few clouds around featuring a classic Colorado bluebird day. Later in the afternoon, beautiful angelic-like clouds appeared setting the stage for an incredible sunset. Before leaving, she was able to capture some incredible pictures. Below are two that really stood out.

In her generosity, she not only helped herself to renew her soul, but she also included me which I was very grateful as it has now been over four years since I've been able to visit the Shrine.

Mother Cabrini's Letter on Teaching to Her Sisters

Mother Cabrini's first mission in life was to help bring everyone she could to her beloved Jesus; everything else she did was secondary to this. And one of her most important instruments to help accomplish this was her exceptional teaching ability given to her from God. Back during the late 1800's and early 1900's, Mother Cabrini was fully aware of the impact education had on children. Below is an excerpt from her travels journal to her sisters:

> You, my good daughters, in your great mission of education, are the first co-operators in the Missionary works of the Sacred Heart, and for this reason you are especially dear to my heart in the great family which Jesus has given me. I expect much from you. Not only your native country and religion hope for great things from you, but all the world. To be a Missionary it is not necessary to go all over the world. The facility of transport and means of emigration today enable men to pass from one country to another with the same amount of ease as that with which they go out of their house into the garden. Every year we see thousands and thousands of our countrymen landing here. We see them in constant contact with irreligious and godless people. If every child that is entrusted to us in our schools is brought up in the fear of God, if we, moreover, train the little mind, we thereby educate the heart and instill into that child the principles of religion and honesty in such a manner that he will grow up a good Christian citizen. Is it not likely also that this pupil of ours may in turn become a teacher himself, and prove much more efficacious in his teaching, because familiar exhortations may often strike the mind more readily than sterile and academical instructions? The teacher who educates her pupils in the way I have indicated sows the mustard seed abundantly. This seed, according to the words of Our Divine Master Himself, will grow to a great height, and the Missionary will never know in this life how much fruit it will have produced unto Eternity.

My good daughters! May your school be not only a school of literature, science, mathematics and history, but also of virtue, solid Christian morality, and you will have rendered a great service not only to religion but also to your country. Moreover, you will greatly contribute to make our country honored and respected by all other nations.[218]

Unfortunately, today, most public schools do not honor our Lord; instead, they punish teachers or sometimes even the students if they mention the name of Jesus. Thank God for Catholic education and other charter schools where the Christian faith is not banned but rather encouraged. There are still many teachers who continue to live out Mother Cabrini's words and my sister is one of them. Both she and my mom, who is also a part-time teacher, have offered themselves up to the Sacred Heart of Jesus – fruits of Mother Cabrini alive and well in our family and the world.

Chapter 13

Return to the Shrine

After nearly five, long, arduous years it's hard to believe that I will be going back to Mother Cabrini's Shrine, Lord willing. At the time of this writing in late May 2024, we have booked our flight and our trip is about a week out. This will be the first time I have travelled by jet, with Denver being the final destination. Back when I was younger, my grandpa used to fly us back and forth from Denver to Durango in his Cessna 206 turbo single-engine plane on a number of occasions.

I don't feel ready to travel but at some point, I know I have to go. I feel in my heart . . . this is the time. I can't let my fear and illness control me. I have remedies that can help if worse case occurs but I am praying for the best outcome. I have travelled before in pretty bad shape with POTS, and yes, it was really difficult, but each time I was better for it. This time I won't have my trusted companion (Abbey our dog) with me for the first time in over four years while travelling. This time is different with many unknowns, but there is no way I can properly finish this book, or have such a good opportunity for healing unless I return. I have to quiet my mind and let Jesus calm my soul because in Him, I can do all things. . . .

Reading Mother Cabrini's writings bring peace to my heart and helps to get me in the mindset for the Front Range Mountains that, Lord willing, I will be visiting soon. Below is a beautiful descriptive letter she wrote to her students in 1906 while travelling near Colorado Springs and Trinidad, Colorado on her way to California where she writes about the beautiful landscapes of Colorado, and her beloved God:

> . . . While I am conversing with you, we have reached the Colorado Springs, the aristocratic city of Colorado, which rises out of the shadow of Pikes Peak, one of the highest summits of these mountains. The weak and consumptive are attracted here by the mildness of the climate, the salubrity of the surrounding mountains and the many and various mineral waters, which on every side spring up fresh, foaming and sparkling. The Indians, astonished at such a wealth of mineral waters, thought their god Manitou, an Indian word which means Great Spirit, lived in these mountains, and especially in the one called the "Garden of the Gods." On my return I will show you a view of this natural park, several hundred acres in extent, in which brightly-coloured rocks are scattered in thousands and sculptured by Nature in the most strange forms, now imposing, now grotesque, sometimes austere, sometimes frivolous, as it were, presenting the strangest appearances.

> . . . Having left the large manufacturing city of Trinidad, the train enters the heart of the mountain district. As the locomotive ascends slowly, we are able to admire the beauty of the landscape. Every minute the view changes. We behold austere mountains whose summits are whitened with shining snow, hills quite green with pine trees and reddened by the colours of the rock and soil, sharp peaks which seem to touch the sky and on which the eagle alone rests, plateaus where the hardy goat back from his mountain excursions comes to browse upon the green grass in which they are so rich, and where the slow ox and the proud buffalo pasture together quite unconscious that in the neighbouring glen the howl of the white bear resounds. Here and there silver streams descend among the rocks and soon become threatening torrents which, in rapids and waterfalls, follow their beds of many-coloured

rocks. The name Colorado was never better applied than to this enchanting country, to these most beautiful natural parks, where the hand of man could never add greater beauty than that with which Nature has enriched it.

In truth, here one exclaims spontaneously: How wonderful is God in His works! . . .[219]

It's hard to believe, Lord willing, that I'll be going back to the Shrine. I didn't make this decision to travel because I suddenly began to feel better, because I haven't. In some ways I have had improvements, but in others, I've become worse. The last thing I feel like doing right now is getting on a jet and traveling outside my home turf which has become my refuge the past three years. It's not that I don't want to travel because I love doing it. Before all this happened, we were always travelling somewhere, at least once a month. Then it all came to a screeching halt and it has been hard on everyone in my family, not just myself.

Whenever I step out of my comfort zone, I realize how bad my situation really is. As long as I do all the right things, eat the right foods, exercise just the right way, I can find ways to tolerate it, but going on a trip could easily throw all of this out the window. So I can expect to struggle a lot, and hope and pray that I can endure it. I have to expect the worst and hope for the best possible outcome.

Mother Cabrini was in this position most of her life. There were times she felt like she dying but she persevered and was better for it. Yes, it did catch up with her in the end, but by that time she had already accomplished more than a lifetime's worth of work. She followed the prompting of the Holy Spirit which isn't always easy to discern, but if you spend as many hours in prayer and meditation as she did, it becomes much easier.

There is no way I can properly finish this book without returning to the Shrine. I have pictures to take, videos to film, and most importantly, I need to experience the healing power and peace found at this Shrine. I've gone there before where I could hardly get out of the car and walk, but this time is different. I have several other conditions to deal with now on top of the ongoing problems, but nothing is too difficult for God.

It's easy to speak with confidence but it's another to put it into practice, especially when things become more difficult. On the Friday before our scheduled departure to Denver on Tuesday, my body completely fell apart with every condition I have been suffering with coming into full force. I was engaged in heavy prayer with my day starting off at 5:30 a.m. praying to God, precious Jesus, and the Holy Spirit, for about an hour. After finishing, I spent several hours on the computer working on this book and then went to Mass.

At first, I was feeling better than I have in several months and tolerated Mass really well. When I got home, my eye was feeling a bit itchy so I looked in the mirror and was shocked to see a bloody mass in the inside corner of my left eye. I've had a small eye capillary break in the past after taking too much aspirin, thinning my blood, or after coughing or sneezing too hard, but I couldn't remember doing anything that could have caused this. Then I remembered I blew my nose really hard in the morning and wondered if this could be the cause. After the eye bleed, my body went downhill the rest of the afternoon with heavy head pressure, heart palpitations, extreme leg weakness – I was a mess. I took my blood pressure and it was normal.

Regardless, we had Adoration coming up at 4:30 p.m. at our local parish and I wasn't about to miss it. It was so nice to just sit in the peaceful presence of our exposed Lord Jesus in the Eucharist. After an hour, I went home and my symptoms became worse. I felt like I was being attacked and kept saying, "The Body and Blood of Jesus, please protect me and my family, and the whole world." Regardless, my physical condition did not improve but my soul felt more at peace. In the evening like we always do, we said our Rosary, the Divine Mercy Chaplet, St. Padre Pio's prayer for healing, and went to bed. Thank God I slept pretty well and was thankful for a good night's rest.

The next morning I woke up saying my usual prayers to our Lord and after getting up, I noticed I was feeling a lot better – my heart was more calm, I had more strength in my legs and the rest of my body, but still had moderate head pressure. I was feeling so much better that I went a little crazy like I usually do when stronger. I started doing all kinds of work, blowing out the gutters up on the roof, blowing off our entire multi-hundred foot long driveway, and then I took a long walk after that. This was way more than I can usually tolerate at one time, but I felt pretty good while doing it. It is usually the next day that the repercussions come out from getting carried away. I tried to figure out what I did to feel so much better. Of course the previous day filled with prayer always helps. I also stopped eating blueberries for a day and a half thinking it was thinning my blood too much causing my eye to rupture. I usually eat at least a cup of blueberries per day. It helps chelate the extra iron from my foods and they taste great.

The rest of the day went pretty well and I was so thankful to God for it. The next day on Sunday, the Feast of the Body and Blood of Jesus, things went back to where they were before, I was struggling again in my body which effects everything else in my day. I was late to Mass which really upset me being a special feast day. I pushed it really hard the day before so it didn't surprise me how bad I was doing but it was still really disappointing. **"Jesus, I place all my trust in You."**

Spiritual Battle

Yes, the attacks are getting vicious. Sunday night I feel asleep on the couch just after finishing the St. Padre Pio prayer for healing. When I woke up and opened my eyes, I saw a terrible looking face and it moved quickly towards me and then disappeared. It was terrifying, causing a series of heavy heart palpitations and tachycardia. I then went into the kitchen to get our blessed Mother Cabrini holy water out of the fridge. After applying the holy water on my head and body, I drank some regular water and felt something hard in my mouth. I took it out and realized it was a sharp piece of glass that had broken off my cup! I believe Mother Cabrini through her intercession protected me from swallowing it. I have never had anything like this happen before. Precious Body and Blood of Jesus, please protect us from all evil.

The next day on Monday, my heart was in tachycardia along with more palpitations. My chest actually hurt, so whatever happened the night before was no illusion. Regardless, I wanted to get a pre-release of my book out on Facebook but kept running into problems. Just moments before going live, the power in our home suddenly went out erasing all the work I had written for my post. Thankfully, I had made a copy and sent it to my email. Why did the power go out just before I posted? Was God trying to tell me not to post it now, or was it another attack? I didn't think it was from God. In fact, it made me want to post even more and that's what I did. However, my website which was working fine earlier in the day suddenly crashed after going live. One more hurdle I had to cross but was able to find the problem rather quickly. But man, the fiery arrows kept coming. All this should be a sign that what I am doing will be fruitful, so I just have to keep on going, trusting in our Lord. . . .

Shrine Pilgrimage Begins

With heavy chest pressure and my POTS fully engaged, I struggled to get ready for my long-awaited trip to Mother Cabrini's Shrine and to see my family for the first time in nearly four-and-a-half years. I had forgotten about all the responsibilities necessary to leave our home – the watering of all the plants, and other items including packing for our trip. We chose to pack lightly so we wouldn't have to check any bags in with only one carry-on each. My back was too compromised at this point to manage the extra weight along with my other conditions. This would be a challenge trying to fit all my gear needed such as my camera, drone, and clothing, all in one small bag with wheels, a small miracle in itself. As the evening progressed the night before our departure, I was feeling terrible especially with all the added stress. I seriously wondered if I should even be going on this trip, but deep inside, I knew I had to go.

It was midnight after mostly finishing all the packing and saying our nightly prayers before we finally went to sleep, exhausted. Then about 3 a.m., a strong wind came up taking me out of a deep sleep. The wind was howling with heavy gusts and continued for about an hour. I wondered if a major storm had come upon us which would potentially delay our flight or even cancel it. But just as quickly as it started, the wind subsided and stillness was upon me. Unfortunately, I couldn't get back to sleep. My mind was running all over the place thinking about all the things I still needed to do before our flight which was scheduled to depart at 7:15 a.m. We had to get up at 5:15 a.m. in order to get ready and be on time.

Already awake as the alarm went off I jumped out of bed and finished the rest of my packing which took longer than I thought. This made my wife really nervous because she hates to be late, especially while travelling. Regardless, we made it there in plenty of time. A storm did move in with overcast skies but no rain. There was a time after my dad died that I became very nervous in a plane that lasted for about a year. I hoped that this fear did not return after going five years without flying. During takeoff our jet was hit with a gust of wind causing the landing gear and the rest of the plane to shutter but it didn't affect me one bit. I was more worried about the effects of altitude on my head pressure which was heavy before leaving. As the plane climbed to about 23,000 feet, I didn't feel any adverse effects. I praised Jesus and actually got better from that point forward.

Flight into the Heavens

The pilot took a different trajectory I was used to from previous flights veering further north. We were flying on the edge of the La Plata Mountains with a spectacular view. At this point I grabbed my camera out of the bag and started taking pictures as fast as I could. Our jet was flying directly over the heart of the San Juan Mountain range still loaded with beautiful snow. The storm that moved in the night before was now mostly gone but there where remnants of white fluffy clouds hugging the tops of the mountain ranges. It was so beautiful to behold.

It was truly Heaven for me to be high above the mountains again after nearly five years – it was a glorious reunion. I wasn't having any ill effects from the cabin pressure which was such a great relief. In fact, I felt a lot better than normal. Was it just adrenaline and the excitement of being free again, or was this the beginning of my healing process? After a beautiful flight with the exception of some turbulence coming into Denver (which didn't affect me at all), reality kicked in when we landed. Denver International Airport (DIA) had grown since the last time I was there and it was packed. Having to wheel around my heavy carry-on with my large camera bag attached flared up my lower back. The last thing I wanted to do was throw my back out, potentially jeopardizing my time at the Shrine, so I did something I've never done before. I requested a wheelchair to get me through the long corridors to the pickup area where my mom would be awaiting us.

I felt a bit guilty but I was definitely having back issues so I swallowed my pride, and let a very kind woman push me to our destination. Arriving at the passenger pick up area, Mom was nowhere to be found. We finally got a hold of her on the phone and we realized we were taken to the wrong area. Mom had to take a large loop around the airport which took around 15 minutes but then she drove to the wrong gate. After the third time circling the airport we finally met up. She said that was the most difficult time she's ever had picking someone up. Regardless, we were off to a place I haven't been in almost 5 years, home.

It was so nice to catch up with Mom and her husband even though they had just come to our house to visit a month prior. It felt like a lifetime since being back home. Mom has the most beautiful view of the Front Range Mountains out her window. The snow-capped peaks greeted me, glistening in the distant horizon with that fresh pure look that is so nice to behold. It helped to restore my mind, body, and soul.

Front Range Mountains, Colorado

It was hard to believe I was actually here. I was expecting the worst but was feeling better than I had anticipated which was a welcomed surprise. We took a break for a little while visiting but the thought of going up to the

Shrine overwhelmed me. After a few hours I couldn't wait any longer so in great anticipation, we set out on the 45-minute journey to the Shrine.

Heaven on Earth

When we arrived at the entrance, my wife and I were in awe at how beautiful and green it was with lupine wildflowers along the road and hillsides. I jumped out and started taking pictures just like the old days – it was as if I had never stopped and picked up right where I left off almost five years ago.

First sight at the MC Shrine

After I got my fix of nature, we headed up the road and it just kept getting more beautiful. Memories of past experiences began to flood my heart. I couldn't believe I was actually there – it was like a dream expecting to wake up – but it wasn't a dream, it was real, and I was taking it all in, thanking Jesus for allowing me to return to this beautiful paradise that Mother Cabrini gifted us all with, such a beautiful blessing, a place of refuge, a place of hope, prayer, and great beauty, and there I was right in the middle of it, taking it all in. I could feel my body, mind, and soul being rejuvenated by God's great glory, restoring me. . . .

When we reached the Shrine parking lot, I got out and expected my legs to be weak and my heart to be under a lot of stress, along with head pressure. After all, we had just climbed up in elevation to just over 7,000 feet, close to where I start feeling the effects of my condition, but it was just the opposite. Instead, I felt like I could take off running! I had to force myself to exercise self-control knowing full well how easily I could overdo it potentially ruining the rest of my trip.

I looked up and saw the statue of Jesus standing tall on the horizon, and everything in me wanted to run as fast as I could up the long staircase to my beloved Jesus, but somehow, I was able to show some restraint. Instead, I walked down the stairs to the springhouse and drank some of the pure water Mother Cabrini miraculously discovered. It tasted fresh and renewing. I then walked back up the stairs and looked into Mother Cabrini's small chapel where she was awaiting me with that holy look where her statue comes alive with her eyes piercing into my soul, greeting me with her silent hello. At this point I knew I was home, and reality started to kick in, I was really there, and I was being healed, and it already started once I got onto the plane, and it just became more real once I arrived at the Shrine.

Mother Cabrini Shrine Springhouse

Mother Cabrini – Altar Chapel

Jesus, Mary, and the Flower Bloom

As a volunteer Shrine photographer for their social media work, and due to my condition, I was given permission to access the top where the Sacred Heart of Jesus statue is located. I was not feeling well enough nor did I want to take the chance of blowing out walking up the stairs, just yet.

And there He was, standing before us, tall and wonderful, full of great love, the Sacred Heart of Jesus. There is no doubt that his presence flows through this man-made object because my soul was rejoicing and much better for it. It is so surreal up there. The views are spectacular and our Lord's presence can be felt in the most special way. Again, I couldn't believe I was there and gave praise and thanksgiving to our Lord for allowing it. I then peeked into the glass enclosure under Jesus where Mother Cabrini was patiently standing in prayer. Our eyes locked and I thanked her for all of her prayers for me and my family. I knelt and said a heartfelt prayer of thanksgiving to our dear Lord Jesus.

The lilacs surrounding the area were in full bloom and smelled wonderful, reminding me of Mary's presence. I don't remember a time I saw the Shrine so beautiful with all the wildflowers in bloom and fields so green and lush. I then went over and greeted the Virgin Mary who had been repainted mostly white since my last pilgrimage. I thanked her with all of my heart for her prayers. She was so beautiful standing in front of the blooming lilacs.

Virgin Mary with blooming lilacs at the Shrine

Just like the old days, it was now time to get to work as I wanted to get some pictures for the Shrine's use. I set up my gear behind some lilac bushed to use as foreground with Jesus the main feature of course. The lighting was perfect as the sun was setting, the golden hour, when everything becomes more saturated. Jesus was making all of this possible through His wonderful creation.

I was so excited to be back at it again that I didn't even think or notice my health condition. I was flying around as if I had angel wings feeling empowered by the Holy Spirit, and I knew Mother Cabrini was there praying for me with our Lord providing such a beautiful scene, something that I would be able to share with everyone. I was truly in heaven again and I was so thankful to be there doing what I love, it was such a wonderful gift.

While taking the picture I noticed a small cloud next to Jesus's outstretch right hand but I didn't notice how profound it was until I loaded it later that evening on my computer. There it was, a small cloud in the shape of a dove in flight with its wings gathered in. It looked like Jesus was releasing the Holy Spirit out to all of us. It was a delightful welcome back gift that I will always cherish. A minute after I took the first shot, I took another picture zoomed out more which showed the same dove, but this time in flight with its wings outstretched. This was just further confirmation for me. The main feature is Jesus and I was so happy how the pictures came out to share with others. The Shrine used this picture on their social media on the Feast Day of the Sacred Heart of Jesus. I was so grateful to contribute back to the Shrine again just like in the days past.

Sacred Heart of Jesus releasing dove

Sacred Heart of Jesus and dove

After it was time to leave, I was in a dream state on our drive home and yes, I was exhausted from our busy day but felt so peaceful and relaxed thanks to our Lord for such a beautiful day.

I shared our experiences with Mom and went to bed. Unfortunately, the pillow I was using keep me up most of the night with only a few hours' sleep. Regardless, the next morning I awoke feeling surprisingly refreshed and ready to go back to the Shrine. I didn't have anything lined up and would have to trust in our Lord to lead us.

Day Two at the Shrine with Sister Alice Zanon, MSC

We took it easy with a nice walk at my Mom's and relaxed a bit in the morning. We arrived at the Shrine midday and it was really hot, close to 90 degrees, completely different from the day before where we needed a jacket. After driving through the entrance, I received a call on my cell which I rarely have on and wondered how the call was getting through. When I answered, I was pleasantly surprised to hear it was Sister Alice asking if we were coming to the Shrine today. I had sent her a picture of Jesus and the dove last night so she knew we had made it there. I told her we had just entered the Shrine grounds and she said she would be available to meet in the next 5 minutes. The timing couldn't have been any better. I knew this was the Holy Spirit at work. Meeting her in person was such a wonderful experience; she is so kind, with a good knowledge of the Shrine. My wife and I could feel the Holy Spirit radiating from her soul.

Brother Jude Emmanuel Quinto, OFM Cap

We had a nice conversation catching up on things and then went outside to the Sacred Heart of Jesus statue (relocated from the Queen of Heaven orphanage) to take a few pictures of her and Jesus. We then went back inside to take a few more pictures at the newly remodel chapel which was beautiful. Sister introduced us to Brother Jude Emmanuel Quinto, OFM Cap, who is from the Capuchin Franciscan order. He has been working at the Shrine for many years with a great understanding of the spiritual aspects and is known by his brothers as the "Rescuer of Relics" due to his expertise in this area. He has a special devotion to Mother Cabrini and offered us some interesting insight about her life and mission. Brother Jude carries around a first class relic of Mother Cabrini and uses it often while praying, especially for others. He gave us a thought-provoking talk about Mother Cabrini and the origin of relics from the saints and why they are placed in a monstrance (a holy vessel) just as the Holy Eucharist is. He explained that just as the Body of Christ is broken up into pieces to consumed by the faithful, so to the bodies of saints are broken up into pieces, such as the hair or bone fragments, in order to be venerated by the faithful. His talk was brilliant and opened up a new level of thinking regarding this fascinating subject.[220]

https://catholicworldmission.org/what-is-a-monstrance/

I recorded his talk and added it to the website. After he finished, I asked if he would pray over me and he replied, "Yes, but wait here for just a moment, I'll be right back." He quickly returned with a beautiful Cross. He then pulled it apart and inside was a first class relic of the True Cross of Christ.[221]

https://truecrosschurch.org/relic-of-the-true-cross

I couldn't believe what was happening. Sister Alice and my wife were also present and we were all in awe and admiration of its presence. Brother Jude then asked my permission to place the Cross on my forehead and the first class relic of Mother Cabrini on my wrist. Of course I agreed and he prayed a beautiful prayer of healing over me. I was experiencing things deep within my body and soul that I have never felt before – it's hard to describe. I know it was healing, needed, and very appreciated. Brother Jude's kindness and passion for Jesus was refreshing – his wisdom and knowledge enlightening, his presence a gift to us all.

I had been taking pictures most of the afternoon and was pretty exhausted but I was at peace inside knowing that God was truly with us through his steadfast servants, Brother Jude and Sister Alice. I hadn't planned any of this and it came out better than I could've imagined, because God was in control, and He made His presence so evident. I could not believe how well I was tolerating all of the work taking pictures and running around most of the afternoon. Before I came to the Shrine, I could not have done that without completely collapsing. There is no doubt I was receiving supernatural strength while at the Shrine. I wondered if it would continue but that wasn't something to contemplate now as I needed to live in the moment and not worry about anything else. It was time to let God take over which was so freeing, something I haven't done very well in my life.

Sister Alice and Brother Jude Emmanuel Quinto, OFM Cap, with Mother Cabrini

Patrick Dillon, Sister Alice, and Mother Cabrini

Sister Alice with her beloved Jesus at the Shrine

Coming back home to my mom's, I was tired but very relaxed and content. I was getting away with activity that would have leveled me prior to coming to the Shrine. God was providing me with extra strength. It was so nice to be able to live like I used to, running around taking pictures, meeting people, and serving our Lord in a more hands-on manner. We had another good visit with my mom and her husband, and finally got to bed at a decent hour where I actually slept more than three hours, which was wonderful.

Day Three with John and Carol McEncroe

We woke up early in the morning in order to get to the Shrine before it got too hot. I had planned on getting pictures of the Stone House and nearby Holy Spirit Walk first thing. We arrived at the Shrine entrance mid-morning and as we crossed the gate, my cell phone rang again just like it did the previous day with Sister Alice. This time it was John McEncroe. He called to let me know that he and his wife would be coming to the Shrine in about an hour. This was excellent timing as I needed to get the pictures of the Stone House while the angle of the sun was still lower in the eastern horizon. Once again, God organized it all so perfectly.

The Stone House is such an integral part of the Shrine's history and continues to provide lodging for many pilgrims today. Upon arriving, the grounds were beautiful with the lilacs in full bloom giving off their sweat distinct fragrance that always reminds me of the Virgin Mary's presence. I photographed multiple angles of the Stone House (pictures included in Chapter 4) and decided to add this one from a different perspective.

Stone House with lupine wildflowers

We then drove down to the lower parking lot by the Bohannan Crucifix and as soon as we parked, John sent me a text saying they had arrived. Within minutes, we saw them pulling up next to our car. The timing was certainly a God thing. I believe He let Mother Cabrini take care of all the organizing. We hugged and said our hellos and then asked them where they wanted their picture taken for the book. He just looked up the stairs and said, "The 15th Station of the Cross, of course." After all, it was his inspiration and drive that enabled this beautiful project to be completed.

This would be the first time I had hiked up the stairs in nearly five years and was one of my goals coming to the Shrine. I was having some minor heart palpitations from the hard work earlier taking the pictures in the heat so I had some reservations, but I didn't let this stop me. The hike up these stairs halfway ended up being a special turning point in my life. I stumbled a little at first and took it slow. The further I walked, the better I felt. John and his wife easily made it up the stairs but were kind to me, giving me plenty of rest breaks. It was hot at the parking lot but as we walked up the stairs, a stiff cool breeze suddenly blew upon us making our journey very pleasant. Hot weather is definitely a trigger for

POTS so I was very thankful to God. I remarked that the Holy Spirit was upon us and John and Carol smiled and nodded in agreement.

Soon enough we reached the 15th Station. There's no doubt I was tired but I tolerated it better than expected. If I had tried something similar to this before coming to the Shrine, I would've crashed. I prayed it wouldn't happen this time placing my trust in Jesus to take care of me. I sat down on a bench by some shade and admired the 15th Station of the Cross which was so beautiful in person. John passionately retold his story about how it all came about which made more sense in person seeing it all firsthand. While telling his story, he welled up with tears, as this is a very special place for him. My wife decided to hike the rest of the way up to Jesus while John and Carol remained with me and continued with their fascinating stories.

One story was from John's wife Carol concerning the Holy Spirit Walk which we could see off in the distance. At first she was hesitant to talk about it but then she opened up. She humbly explained that while in deep prayer a few years back, the Holy Spirit spoke to her, revealing plans for this project. She was told in great detail how and where it should be built, on the Shrine grounds near the old barn. I mentioned her story earlier in chapter 6 of this book with pictures.

There are so many beautiful stories about this Shrine especially by those who have dedicated their lives to this place. Mother Cabrini is still at work keeping her ministries going, bringing people closer to Jesus through the hands of people like John and Carol.

The view from the 15th Station was so beautiful. I could imagine Mother Cabrini looking down from Heaven, seeing all the new poppies coming up with the gorgeous lilac bushes in full bloom along with the bright green grass and all the other wildflowers and plants flourishing around us. It was truly a piece of Heaven. I have noticed the people that work for Mother Cabrini are really in tune with nature. As we were sitting there, John and Carol pointed out a hummingbird sitting in a tree barely visible to the untrained eye. Soon afterwards, they noticed some turkey vultures circling in the heavy breeze above and below us. Later, they interrupted one of their stories when a butterfly soared by, and this kept going on as nature was all around us. I thought wow, they are really in tune with nature, it was beautiful to behold. Mother Cabrini was like this as well, as she was always pointing out nature around her and how it all related to her beloved Jesus. And there were her helpers doing the same thing nearly 100 years later.

John and Carol had another obligation so they had to leave but not until we all had a wonderful talk and experience up on the hill, in God's beautiful creation.

Poppy Bloom

After they had left, my wife and I stayed up at the 15th Station for a while longer to take some pictures of this beautiful Cross surrounded by blooming lilacs and nature all around it. I found a group of piercing red poppies in full bloom and just couldn't get enough of them taking pictures and videos.

On the way down I could feel the effects from all the activity with some minor leg weakness but I was holding up remarkably well considering how bad I was feeling before I came on this trip. I was able to do things I struggled with back home. There was definitely an extra level of energy and ability present at the Shrine. Other people have felt this as well because this place has a special connection to Heaven. It was no coincidence or placebo as my past and present experiences at the Shrine have confirmed this, and I was taking full advantage of it. The altitude at the Shrine is a little over 7,000 feet, which is higher than the 6,500 feet in Durango so the elevation wasn't a factor for me feeling better. If anything, it would make me feel worse being higher at the Shrine. For me, it was nothing short of miraculous. I was doing things I haven't done in several years and was so thankful to God for it.

Volunteers and Workers at the Shrine

After getting back to our car, we had a nice tailgate lunch. I noticed one of the volunteers busy cleaning the parking lot, trimming tree branches, and working like a busy bee in the near 90-degree weather. He had so much dedication taking care of the Shrine grounds as if it were his own. Then my wife and I saw something that really touched our hearts. Directly in front of us, there was a tow truck with a father and son team loading up a car. The son looked to be only 10 years old, but his dad had already trained him how to use the heavy winch. He was so professional at his job as his dad hooked the vehicle up with his son pulling the necessary tension when needed. Even though his dad was at a distance, he kept a watchful eye on his son but gave him his independence. It was inspiring to see his father pass his skills onto his son for his future career.

There were so many interesting things going on around us, people walking about with smiles on their face, children laughing and running around, and the look of anticipation in the pilgrims eyes when they were about to head up the stairs to see Jesus. And then while we were sitting there, I saw Tommy drive by escorting a septic truck to clean out the tanks from all the heavily used rest rooms in the area. I caught a quick glimpse of his face as he drove by with a look of determination, as he had many projects simultaneously going on throughout the Shrine. At the museum, I saw one of his workers repairing the roof despite the high temperature of the day. There were other workers scattered around with each knowing what their job was, and doing it well. Tommy's maintenance operation runs like a well-oiled machine in constant motion, and they all know how to do their job without disrupting the pilgrims. You could tell they have been doing this for a long time and it was fascinating to watch.

Holy Spirit Walk, the Old Wagon, and a Buck

After eating our lunch and taking in all the action, we headed up to the Holy Spirit Walk. I was able to get a nice shot of the entrance gate with the sun illuminating Jesus in the background (picture included in Chapter 6). The lighting was just right to capture Jesus in the background as you look through the gate. While doing this, my wife took advantage of the time to sit on the benches and pray to the Holy Spirit.

It was really hot so we decided to call it a day around midafternoon. Just down the road, I saw something that took me back in time. I could picture Mother Cabrini and her sisters riding in this old wagon checking out the grounds.

On the way down the hill about to the leave the Shrine grounds, Mother Cabrini had one more surprise for us. Just before the main entrance gate, I spotted a beautiful mule deer buck feeding in the brush with his beautiful growing antlers in full velvet.

It was such an unexpected gift, something that I live for to capture them in their native habitat. I was so thankful to God to be able to witness this and to be able to share this with all of you.

Family Reunion

Driving back to my mom's house was time to relax a bit before we had a big family get-together scheduled for 5:30 p.m. that evening. It was my sister's early birthday celebration and it would be the first time I had seen some of my family members in quite a while. It was so nice to finally talk with them all again, such a much-needed reunion. Everything had changed so much during the past five years with two of my nephews now married with children.

After the party, I worked on some pictures taken during the day, prayed the Rosary, and went to bed. I laid there before going to sleep in great anticipation of the next day as this was the Feast of the Sacred Heart of Jesus. I was so thankful for the opportunity to be at the Shrine in person to celebrate this great feast day with Sister Alice, Brother Jude, Father Lager, JoAnn, Tommy, John, and their families, along with all the other Shrine staff and visitors who would be present for Mass. This was truly a blessing.

Feast of the Sacred Heart of Jesus

After a good night's rest, the next morning I went for another walk with my mom and wife on the beautiful scenic path behind Mom's house with the spectacular views of the Front Range Mountains. After the walk feeling refreshed, my mom had scheduled a special appointment for me with her parish priest for Confession and wherever else the Holy Spirit led Father to do. I was running a bit late which made my mom nervous as he did her a favor squeezing me in his busy schedule at the last moment. When I arrived, Father was still finishing up some prayers with the faithful after his noon Mass was over. I came inside the beautiful Church, knelt down, and joined them in prayer. Before Confession, I told Father my mom was really concerned that I was late and he told me to tell her that because of the Feast of the Sacred Heart of Jesus, he added special prayers after Mass causing him to be late so all was well. Wow, the first time I was late where it didn't cost me – saved by Jesus's Sacred Heart.

Confession and the Anointing of the Sick

As usual, in Confession, Father was able to help me recall things I hadn't even thought about. He gave me a tool to manage certain problems when they occurred. Father told me, whenever an evil thought comes into my head, or I do something unholy, grab hold of it with both hands like you would with clay, and mold into a rose or other beautiful object and place it at the feet of Mary as a gift. He said pretty soon you'll have a whole garden before her and will have to find ways to expand it. I thought this was such a prudent and beautiful way to deal with this.

After putting this into practice, I find myself doing this a lot more than I thought, and yes, my garden at the feet of Mary is growing rapidly.

During Confession we were talking about the Holy Spirit and a heavy wind suddenly rattled the church walls and I said, "The Holy Spirit is with us," and Father smiled for a moment and put me back on topic. After Confession, he then asked if I wanted the Anointing of the Sick which I gratefully accepted. I felt so peaceful afterwards and told Father that I didn't want to leave. He just smiled again and said, "You can stay in the Church as long as you'd like but I have to get to another appointment." I thanked Father for his generous time and blessing. There is so much healing in the Anointing of the Sick and holy Confession – we are blessed as Catholics to receive such important Sacraments. I knelt down and prayed in Church for a while renewing my mind, body, and soul.

The Wind

Stepping outside, I was surprised to see a storm was upon us with the brisk wind providing relief from the 95-degree weather. I noticed the heavy gust that occurred while in Confession had caused some damage with broken tree branches laying on the ground and other debris scattered in the street. As I walked back to the car, I was feeling rejuvenated and raised my hands up to Heaven giving praise to our Lord Jesus for all He had done for me. Some by passers stared at me but I didn't care what they thought as I was free like an eagle in flight as another strong wind guest blew me towards my car. Dark ominous clouds with heavy wind and no rain or lightning was directly overhead only in our area, with the rest of the Front Range looking mostly clear. I took this as a sign from God, and I could feel His mighty power over me.

Back at Mom's, my sister had arrived and the first thing she mentioned to me was the sudden heavy wind gust that occurred earlier. She was getting coffee at a local shop and said it rattled the doors with dust blowing everywhere outside. She waited until it calmed down before leaving. It made a real impression on her and the other people in the coffee shop. I told her that it happened while I was in Confession and she started laughing saying, "I knew it was something from God." I believe it was the Holy Spirit talking to us, just as I heard the wind howling the night before our trip to the Shrine – this seems to be the theme now, the wind.

Sacred Heart of Jesus Mass

It was now about three o'clock in the afternoon and the special Mass for the Sacred Heart of Jesus at the Shrine was about to begin at 5:30 p.m. My mom and sister were planning on going with us to celebrate Mass. While visiting, we lost track of time and realized that Friday rush-hour in Denver starts early so we would be caught right in the middle of it. This jeopardized our chances to get to Mass on time. We quickly got ready to go and headed down the road to the interstate which was already backed up upon entering it. We were only able to go 30 miles per hour for a short distance and then we came to a complete stop. If this continued, there is no way we would make it to Mass on time which caused some panic, especially since I told Sister Alice I would be taking pictures of her renewing her vows. This quickly became a spiritual exercise trusting in Jesus to take care of everything.

The trip to the Shrine is about 45 minutes in light traffic and it was already 4:15 p.m., and we had made little progress. We said a prayer to God and asked Mother Cabrini for her intercession that the freeway would open up. Soon afterwards, the traffic started to pick up to over 40 miles per hour. Rush-hour usually gets worse the closer you get into Denver but on this occasion, it actually became lighter. From that point onward, we made really good time and arrived at the Shrine at 5 p.m., half an hour early. Thank you Jesus!

Angel Cloud

This was the first time I was at the Shrine with my family for nearly five years. I can't tell you how grateful I was to be living out this dream again. Getting out of the car, I loaded up all my camera gear and headed for the chapel. As I came up to the Sacred Heart of Jesus statue located in front by the base of stairs, I felt an extra sense of holiness and looked up into the sky and couldn't believe my eyes. The sky was mostly clear with the exception of high cirrus clouds in the shape of a dove or an angel to west of the chapel. I instantly knew this was a special gift from God meant for Sister Alice and Sister Antonia who would both be renewing their vows as Missionary Sisters of the Sacred Heart of Jesus on His feast day during Mass. I did my best to capture this moment for them and our Lord did not disappoint.

Sacred Heart of Jesus with Angel Dove

Upon entering the chapel I instantly just saw Sister Alice sitting in the pews with her face beaming with a beautiful light. The sun was coming through the stained glass windows highlighting every detail of the Mother Cabrini collection – there was no doubt that I was truly in Heaven. . . . It was a beautiful Mass celebrated by Father John Lager, OFM Cap, along with Brother Jude Emmanuel Quinto, OFM Cap. I was able to take pictures of the Sisters renewing their vows and afterwards, I had the privilege of taking pictures of all involved. This was the first time I had the privilege of briefly meeting Sister Antonia who currently does part-time ministry for her local parish undertaking home visitations for those in need. She also helps out at the Shrine at times. This special Mass was such a beautiful celebration and blessing for all. Sacred Heart of Jesus, we place all our trust in You.

Sister Antonia Plata, MSC, and Sister Alice Zanon, MSC, renewing their vows, and Brother Jude Emmanuel Quinto, OFM Cap, in the background.

Sister Alice, Sister Antonia, and Father John Lager, OFM Cap

Sister Antonia, JoAnn Seaman – Shrine Executive Director, and Sister Alice

Grand Finale at the Shrine

After taking the pictures I headed outside and noticed Tommy was already running around in his truck taking care of business. He did an excellent job with the Readings at Mass and as soon as it was over, he went right to work. There was a potluck dinner afterwards so I hoped he would take time off to join the others which he finally did. But not before I took some pictures of him for the book along with him helping me out to go up and see Jesus. I felt bad about him being late to the dinner but of course, Tommy told me not to worry about it. I was able to track him down and get some nice shots dressed up for Mass. The picture below was one of my favorites as it really tells the story – Tommy is Mother Cabrini's trusted right-hand man.

Tommy Francis with Mother Cabrini

Tommy reminds me of a combination of my late dad, Clint Eastwood, and my grandpa who had a heart so tender at times he could woo anyone out of their darkest moment.

This was the last day I would be at the Shrine so I wanted to take full advantage of it. Spending time with Jesus was the best way to end this wonderful pilgrimage which had already exceeded all my expectations. Little did I know that Mother Cabrini, through her intercession to our Lord, had something special planned. After all the pictures where taken and the work was finished, my mom and sister joined me and my wife on an epic adventure to see Jesus one last time.

Upon arriving at the foot of the Sacred Heart of Jesus, the weather was calm with white puffy clouds mostly behind and above Jesus with beautiful patches of aqua blue sky in-between. It was beautiful and something I haven't seen here before.

Sacred Heart of Jesus at the Shrine

I was hoping to get some nice shots for my book and for the Shrine's social media projects just like the old days, and my wish was granted immediately upon our arrival. It felt so nice to be a volunteer again working for the Shrine on this holy evening of the Sacred Heart of Jesus.

While standing there admiring the beautiful scenery, off to the west sunbeams suddenly came down from the Heavens and lit up the distant horizon and mountain peaks in a golden glow of our Lord's Divine rays of Mercy.

Rainbow Surprise

A few minutes later out east towards Denver, there were some dark clouds with a bit of virga streaking out of the bottom of them. And then it happened; a small unique rainbow abruptly appeared as if God had just painted it in the sky. It was located directly above the Holy Spirit Walk with the tip of the small rainbow pointing down towards it. I instantly took this as a sign from God meant for John's wife Carol who was inspired by the Holy Spirit for its creation.

Everything was happening so quickly that I could hardly keep up with all the action. I didn't have the right lens on but started snapping off pictures regardless. I then switched to my telephoto lens but by that time, the rainbow had mostly disappeared. I was thankful to have captured it. My mom, sister, and wife were all in awe and keep saying it was the Holy Spirit. I agreed.

Rainbow over Holy Spirit Walk

Just seeing one of these marvels of God's creation is a good night for any landscape photographer but our Lord, on His special feast day of His Most Sacred Heart, was just getting started.

The Wind and Tongues of Fire

Unexpectedly, dark clouds began to form above us and the wind began to howl, replacing the soft gentle clouds with dark ominous formations that were very similar to the ones seen back in August of 2019. But this time there was no rain or lightning, just dark clouds and heavy wind. It started gusting so hard that my wife, mom, and sister went back to the car to seek shelter. But for me, this was why I came, to experience God's power and great glory, and Jesus was there watching over me, blessing me, through his awesome nature.

There I was, alone with Jesus and Mary, with Mother Cabrini standing under her beloved Jesus in a fierce windstorm, and I was thoroughly taking in every moment of it. I could feel the power of the Holy Spirit as the wind pushed hard against my body. I have never experienced winds like this before. It was my turn and knew God had something special planned, and I was loving every minute of it. It was so uplifting standing on top of the world with Jesus, with the wind whipping my hair about, with my arms outstretched towards the Heavens yelling out praises of thanksgiving to our Lord for allowing me to return to the Shrine, and providing such a beautiful experience – this was far beyond anything I could've ever dreamed about. There I was living out this dream in one of the most beautiful places on earth, with the power of the Holy Spirit, and our beloved Jesus standing before me, healing me, loving me, blessing me in such a beautiful way.

I was crying tears of joy celebrating life more than I have in years with all of my pent up emotions, frustrations, and hardships from my illness being blown right out of me. I was standing next to Jesus and peaked inside to say hello to Mother Cabrini and thanked her for all she was doing for me. I then lowered my head to avoid the heavy wind and made my way over to the Virgin Mary. While I was thanking her for all her prayers for me, my family, and the world, with the lilac bushes in full bloom whipping back-and-forth in the heavy winds, it happened. . . .

As I was videoing Mary, I started seeing streaks of light coming from all directions similar to a strobe light. At first I thought it was dust from the wind but there was nothing hitting my face. I was then overwhelmed by the presence of the Holy Spirit as if Tongues of Fire were being cast down from Heaven upon me – I couldn't believe what was happening but my soul knew and was rejoicing, and soon my body followed. I kept praising Jesus and the Holy Spirit for this beautiful gift upon me – my whole body was being rejuvenated, I felt so much peace and joy like never before. I raised my hands up to Heaven and continued to praise our mighty God for his great power and glory. I felt the presence of our holy Mother Mary and felt as if she were about to appear. But instead, it was all about the heavy wind and the luminous beams of flashing light. Through it all I was recording everything via video on my phone.

Although the flashing beams of light may draw more attention, it was the wind that made the biggest impact on me. Others who see this may come up with various explanations on how the flashes of light could've happened, the camera sensor, or some other technical reason which may very well be the case, but that doesn't matter to me, because I was experiencing something incredible, and there will never be an explanation that will take any of this away from me. What I do know, there was no lightning involved or lights on at this time. This whole experience went on for over a half an hour where Heaven was opened up to me, and it was so beautiful, healing, and life changing. I took it all in and never wanted it to end.

Pushed around by the wind, I again walked over to the glass enclosure under of the statue of Jesus and looked in on our Mother Cabrini who was standing there with her hands in prayer. I thanked her again for her powerful intercession, allowing all of this to happen. I could really feel her presence as I know how much she loves nature, experiencing this in spirit with me, God's holy angels, our Blessed Mother Mary, the power of the Holy Spirit, and our beloved Jesus with God the Father.

The wind started blowing even harder so I knew it was time to go. I walked back down to the car where my family was waiting. I was so struck with emotion that I completely lost it upon entering the car, crying like a baby. I apologized and my mom told me to "let it all out, just let it all out." It was embarrassing but there was nothing I could do to hold back the floodgates – God had touched me in a special way and this was part of my healing, and my mom was fully aware of it. After I calmed down a bit, I wondered if the video I had taken had truly captured what I was witnessing, so I played it back for their review. Immediately, my sister yelled out, "Oh my, it's a miracle!" My camera had captured it all, and they were mesmerized by the footage and said it was meant for my healing. I told them "No, this was meant for all of us, for all of our healings, for everyone who sees this."

There was a lot to contemplate on the way back to my mom's house as we talked the whole thing over with great joy. It was so nice to be together with my family again to experience such a beautiful event, on the Feast of the Sacred Heart of Jesus. As I prayed on the way home, I felt God telling me that this wonder received was not about me. Instead, it was about Him. And it was a sign for those who need encouragement, who do not believe, who are struggling, especially in their faith. For this reason I decided to include this in my book and trailer to share with others. There were other events that I did not feel called to include here.

It was about 10:00 p.m. when we arrived home and my wife and I would have to wake up at 5 a.m. the next morning to catch our flight. But I had work to do, pictures to edit from the beautiful Mass. I stayed up until after midnight editing pictures for Sister Alice and the others that were taken after Mass. While editing, I looked back at my phone video of the night's events and did a screen shot of one of the light flashes and was shocked to see a golden beam of light over Mary. Later I did this with several other areas of the video and found several other golden beams all around her.

Beam of golden light over the Virgin Mary

Beam of golden light near the Virgin Mary

Return Home

5 a.m. the next morning came awful quick with little sleep, but we were able to make it to the airport in time to catch our flight. The Tuesday prior I had arrived at Denver International Airport needing a wheelchair to get around. Now on our trip home, I was walking on my own strength through all the security checks and long corridors to our gate and tolerated it well. There is no doubt that I received some type of healing. I could still feel underlying symptoms but was much better than I was before I came, both physically and spiritually. I'm so thankful to Jesus for this.

I was prayed over by two holy priests, and experienced the healing power and grace that only Mother Cabrini's Shrine can offer. I was reunited with family after a 5-year absence and I met and prayed with wonderful people at the Shrine. I couldn't have asked for anything else. If all of that didn't give me a healing it is God's holy will for me as He knows what is best.

I was able to do things at the Shrine I haven't been able to for several years. This was not just a placebo or adrenaline as I have MRIs showing how serious my condition is concerning my lower back and cervical spine. I know what I was capable of doing before I came to the Shrine and what I am able to do now after going. All my expectations have been exceeded. The whole trip was like a dream where everything was planned by God and Mother Cabrini was my travel agent. This gift continued into our flight home. As we sat down in our plane, I was disappointed to see that we were directly over the back of the wings obscuring our views of the mountain peaks on our way back to Durango. Then I noticed my seat was broken, wobbling back-and-forth. At first I was a bit irritated then I realized it was a blessing. Our plane was only half full which provided seats further up that were vacant. I showed the stewardess the broken seat and she let us move up towards first class ahead of the wings with an excellent view of the ground below. I ended up getting a great picture of Pigeon and Turret Peaks with a rare look at the northeast side that's only visible to extreme hikers and by air. This was such a beautiful gift where God took care of it all. It made me wonder how many times in my life I didn't fully surrender myself to Jesus and trust Him, especially when things didn't appear to be working out. Praise you Heavenly Father, Praise you dear Son, Praise you Holy Spirit, all in One.

Turret and Pigeon Peaks (center), San Juan Mountains of SW Colorado, aerial shot

Update After My Return

Coming home from the Shrine was bittersweet. I was feeling so much better in every way and this continued for the first few days upon our return. I had responsibilities to take care of with this book my highest priority so I was anxious to get back to work finishing the last chapter among other things I was behind on. God had given me everything I needed to finish this book while at the Shrine. I was feeling so much better that I took on a commercial project that required me to work out in the hot sun which would've been off-limits before. I also went right to work editing the rest of my book and writing the final chapter. This proved to be a major undertaking. It meant spending many hours working on the computer which is the worst thing possible for my condition. After a few days of pounding away, day and night, my left eye started to bleed out again from the same capillary as before. I knew the strain from looking at the screen so intently was causing this so I put a patch on my left eye to help reduce the stress. This proved to be very helpful as my eye started to rapidly heal.

Unfortunately, all the extra work caused my body to crash again. It was pretty demoralizing to go back to where I was prior to the trip. But, I had gained a lot of hope and trust in Jesus that everything would work out according to His will. Regardless, I kept getting worse as the days progressed with my POTS in full force along with heavy weakness, and major head pressure. But I just kept fighting through it. The healing I received at the Shrine appeared to be a mixture of the first time where I was healed instantly after drinking the spring water. My second healing at the Shrine took several months after I returned home before I felt better. This time my condition definitely improved while at the Shrine, but I've suffered a setback after my return. I just need to be patient and place all my trust in our Lord, knowing full well that He is healing me according to His will.

Father John Lager, OFM Cap, Phone Interview

After hearing so many good things about him, I was able to meet Father John Lager for the first time after the Feast of the Sacred Heart of Jesus Mass. I talked with him for a few minutes and asked if we could do a phone interview and he agreed. A week after I returned, I was able to catch up with him where we had a nice discussion about the Shrine and his role over the years. As mentioned before, he has been instrumental in helping out with the fundraising and has been the spiritual advisor and visiting priest for many working at the Shrine, including the sisters based there.

Both JoAnn Seaman, the Shrine's Executive Director, and Father John were originally from Kansas where he was the associate pastor at JoAnn's parish where he taught her Junior and Senior High School. His relationship with JoAnn's family goes way back. Father John has been at the Shrine for nearly 40 years where he has blessed the many faithful with the Sacraments of the Church including Confession and Holy Mass throughout the years.

I asked Father John what the Shrine means to him and he replied:

> Mother Cabrini's Shrine is always such an important place, where a saint walked first, where her spirit and charism of her order continues to flourish, and it is such a great place, an oasis of prayer and opportunities to contemplate the life of the saint who walked these grounds. She had such a great love for God and especially the poor emigrant. This is the place where she wanted to provide the orphan girls in Denver a place of rest, comfort, and communion, with the gift of beauty and nature. I think those type of things are

most important for us today to continue to celebrate. This is a place of pilgrimage, a place of hospitality, it's a place of prayer, and I do believe today it is a place of hope for people who find life really burdensome . . . it's a place of hope."[222]

Father's response was so beautiful and spot on to Mother Cabrini's purpose in her ministry which continues today. Due to the recent increase in the number of pilgrims coming to the Shrine, I asked Father, "So Mother Cabrini and all of your prayers are going to provide, right?" Father quickly responded, "Yes, always, just trust that, trust that!" Father ended our call with a beautiful Scriptural prayer from St. Francis and he was then off to administer Confession to the faithful.

Shrine to the Rescue

On Friday, two weeks after I returned, I was having a tough morning with my health and organizing my book. I decided to call the Shrine and see if I could talk with Sister Alice to get some needed information. She is usually really difficult to get a hold of, but by the grace of God, I was able to get through and we had a wonderful talk. I also had some questions for Brother Jude regarding an audiotape that I recorded of him, and was blessed to be able to get him on the phone, especially since he was leaving for Italy the next day. Again, like with Sister Alice, he is full of wisdom and the Holy Spirit, and he put me at ease during our call. Before getting off the phone, he prayed for me and the success of the book, that it will help others come to Jesus. It was a short, beautiful prayer and I really appreciated it.

Double Rainbow

Feeling invigorated, I went back to work on the book and noticed I didn't have any pictures of Tommy's dad, Carl. He said he was going to send some pictures via email the previous week but I never saw it come in. I decided to search the junk file and there it was, waiting for me. They were great pictures, but the file sizes were too small for print so I texted Tommy and I asked if he could send them in a larger format. He said he would get back to me later that evening which he did, sending the larger files that should work out fine. As I was cleaning them up on my photo-editing program, I looked out the window and saw a rainbow forming. I dropped everything and ran outside to witness a big, beautiful, double rainbow that was positioned right over the front of our house. It appeared to be in multi dimensions, as if the gates of heaven had been opened up. I have witnessed hundreds of double rainbows and this one stood out uniquely. I believe this one was a special sign for Tommy from his dad and Mother Cabrini.

Double Rainbow over Durango, Colorado

After taking the pictures and video, I sent a copy to Tommy and told him his dad's ears must've been burning. He agreed.

I think this type of thing happens more often than we think where our loved ones have the special grace to gift us like this on certain occasions. It was a special blessing for me to reconnect with those at the Shrine, this time by phone. I can't tell you how much better I was feeling after all of this transpired, it was healing for my body and soul.

At this point I had written most of the last chapter, had turned in chapters 1 through 12 for final formatting, and was anxious to get this book out. But I knew it was all up to our Lord, the timing, and everything else involved. I just have to keep doing my part and rely on Him for everything else. This message really hit home at our local parish Mass during Father John's homily the following Sunday. Father brought up a prayer with an unknown author that went something like this: **Lord,**

help me to remember that nothing is going to happen to me today that you and I together can't handle. This sounds like something Mother Cabrini would pray. This is how she lived her life, doing her part, and letting our Lord handle the rest. This is good advice for all of us and something I will add to my daily prayers.

My time at the Shrine was not just about me. It was for all of you to help in your journey of faith. God asked me to write this book to reach those who need encouragement, are brokenhearted, in pain, rejected, struggling in their faith, lonely, in want and need of hope. We are living in challenging times but God always provides a way, because He loves and cares about us more than we could ever imagine. . . .

Mother Cabrini's life work has proved to be timeless, and the fruits of her love and labor are alive and well today. It is my prayer that by reading this book, you have come closer to Jesus which was the whole purpose of her ministry which continues today through her sisters and all of us.

Words of wisdom from Mother Cabrini to her sisters:

> We can do nothing because we are poor and weak, but let us have a lively faith and trust in Him who strengthens us. Let us expand our hearts to help so many souls lying under the yoke of the king of darkness. With the fire of our love, let us break the heavy chains keeping them bound in this terrible service of the devil. When we see our efforts unsuccessful, let us throw ourselves at the feet of Jesus. Groaning over the world's inequity, let us beg His Divine Heart to lay bare His infinite treasures of mercy. Hardships must never discourage the spouse of Christ; rather, they should make her stronger and more determined. Do not be dismayed by rejection and mockery. Go forward always, with the serenity and fortitude of angels, because you are the angels of the earth and so must continue on your way in the midst of so many contrary influences. Everyone can be serene when things run smoothly; it is in difficult situations that fidelity and constancy are proven.[223]

. . . The Road to heaven is narrow, laden with stones and thorns. No one can walk on it, but only fly with the wings of the spirit. In order to fly, the spirit must detach itself from the physical demands and earthly pleasures. Through detachment from itself and stripping away of pride, the spirit will be able to fly freely over the stony road in happiness and joy, without feeling pain. This expected benefit is so great that my every pain becomes my delight. In my sufferings, joy abounds. . . .[224]

Mother Cabrini's Cross

Mother Cabrini – Circa 1900

Above Photos Courtesy of The Missionary Sisters of the Sacred Heart of
Jesus and the St. Frances Cabrini Collection, Holy Spirit Library,
Cabrini University, Radnor, PA 19087

About the Author

Patrick Dillon was born in the small mountain town of Durango, Colorado. He loves the outdoors and spends as much time as possible enjoying God's beautiful creation.

He is an internationally published landscape photographer focusing his efforts in the beautiful San Juan Mountains of Southwest Colorado, the Desert Southwest, Malibu, California, and the Lower Mainland of British Columbia, Canada. His works can be found online at https:// patrickdillonphoto.com/.

Patrick has also published the award-winning book, Steadfast Christian – A Higher Call To Faith, Family, and Hope and Crosses, Sunsets, and Sinners – A Brother and Sister's Medjugorje Journey.

He graduated from Metropolitan State University with a combined bachelor's degree in environmental science and real estate finance. He followed his dad and grandpa's footsteps with a career in general contracting and real estate. He continues with his studies in science through his recent company, Team 3 Health, LLC, as a Board Certified Environmental Wellness Specialist. https://team3health.com/

Patrick and his wife are certified Catholic marriage preparation ministers for their local parish and abroad.

He is passionate about his Catholic faith and the wellbeing of his family, local community, and country. Patrick and his family currently reside in the beautiful Rocky Mountains of Southwest Colorado.

For more information, view pictures, speaking requests, suggestions, contact info, and updates, please visit his website at:

https://stmothercabrini.com/

Endnotes

1   National Gallery of Art. "Mountain of the Holy Cross." Accessed April 10, 2023. https://www.nga.gov/collection/art-object-page.103590.html.

2   Cabrini, Frances Xavier, and Patricia Spillane. "My Retreat according to the Spiritual Exercises with the Sisters in New York Christmas, 1894 to January 1, 1895," *Journals of a Trusting Heart – Retreat Notes of St. Frances Xavier Cabrini (1876-1911)*, 129. Claretian Communications Foundation, Inc., 2014.

3   Frances Xavier, *Travels of Mother FRANCES XAVIER CABRINI, 93*

4   Dillon, Patrick. "Patrick Dillon Photography | Landscape Photography in the San Juan Mountains of SW Colorado." Patrick Dillon Photo, n.d. https://patrickdillonphoto.com/.

5   Frances Xavier, Cabrini. "Genoa to New York— September, 1894." PDF. In *Travels of Mother Frances Xavier Cabrini: Foundress of the Missionary Sisters of the Sacred Heart of Jesus*, 71. Chicago, United States of America: Missionary Sisters of the Sacred Heart of Jesus, 1944. https://archive.org/details/travelsofmotherfrancesxaviercabrini

6   Frances Xavier, *Travels of Mother FRANCES XAVIER CABRINI,* 108

7   Maynard, *Too Small a World,* 18

8   Maynard, Theodore. "Chapter One – a Child at Play." Internet Archive. In *Too Small a World; the Life of Francesca Cabrini*, 17. Bruce Publishing Company, 1945. https://archive.org/details/toosmallworldlif0000mayn/.

9   Maynard, *Too Small a World,* 18

10 Maynard, *Too Small a World*, 18

11 Maynard, *Too Small a World*, 19

12 Maynard, *Too Small a World*, 19

13 Maynard, *Too Small a World*, 21

14 Maynard, *Too Small a World*, 22

15 Maynard, *Too Small a World*, 22

16 Maynard, *Too Small a World*, 24

17 Maynard, *Too Small a World*, 24

18 Maynard, *Too Small a World*, 25

19 Maynard, *Too Small a World*, 25

20 Maynard, *Too Small a World*, 29

21 Maynard, *Too Small a World*, 25

22 Maynard, *Too Small a World*, 29

23 Maynard, *Too Small a World*, 30

24 Maynard, *Too Small a World*, 21

25 Maynard, *Too Small a World*, 20

26 Maynard, *Too Small a World*, 30

27 Maynard, *Too Small a World*, 31

28 Maynard, *Too Small a World*, 33

29 Maynard, *Too Small a World*, 34

30 Maynard, *Too Small a World*, 35

31 Maynard, *Too Small a World*, 36

32 Maynard, *Too Small a World*, 36

33 Maynard, *Too Small a World*, 41

34 Maynard, *Too Small a World*, 42

35 "The Founding of the Institute." *Missionary Sisters of the Sacred Heart of Jesus*, www.mothercabrini.org/who-we-are/our-history/the-founding-of-the-institute. Accessed 24 Mar. 2024.

36 Cabrini, Frances Xavier, and Patricia Spillane. "My Retreat in the Spiritual Exercises 1878, House of Providence, Codogno." In *Journals of a Trusting Heart – Retreat Notes of St. Frances Xavier Cabrini (1876-1911)*, 49. Claretian Communications Foundation, Inc., 2014.

37 Cabrini and Spillane, *Journals of a Trusting Heart, 50*

38 Maynard, Theodore. "Light Over Lombardy." Internet Archive. In *Too Small a World; the Life of Francesca Cabrini*, 43. Bruce Publishing Company, 1945. https://archive.org/details/toosmallworldlif0000mayn/.

39 Maynard, *Too Small a World, 43*

40 Maynard, *Too Small a World, 44*

41 Maynard, *Too Small a World, 44*

42 Maynard, *Too Small a World, 47*

43 Maynard, *Too Small a World, 50*

44 Maynard, *Too Small a World, 4*

45 Galilea, Segundo. "A Decisive Encounter (1887-1888)." In *Weakness, Strength - The Life and Missionary Work of Saint Frances Xavier Cabrini*, 59. 1996. Reprint, Claretian Publications, 2004.

46 Segundo, In *Weakness, Strength, 59*

47 Maynard, Theodore. "Under Obedience to Leo." Internet Archive. In *Too Small a World; the Life of Francesca Cabrini*, 106. Bruce Publishing Company, 1945. https://archive.org/details/toosmallworldlif0000mayn/.

48 Maynard, *Too Small a World, 4*

49 Galilea, Segundo. "A Decisive Encounter (1887-1888)." In *Weakness, Strength - The Life and Missionary Work of Saint Frances Xavier Cabrini*, 60. 1996. Reprint, Claretian Publications, 2004.

50 Cabrini, Frances Xavier, and Patricia Spillane. "My Retreat According to the Spiritual Exercises Our Lady of Grace, Codongo, September 24, 1885." In *Journals of a Trusting Heart – Retreat Notes of St. Frances Xavier Cabrini (1876-1911)*, 69. Claretian Communications Foundation, Inc., 2014.

51 Sullivan, Mary Louise. "We Saw the Beautiful Statue of Liberty." *Mother Cabrini: Italian Immigrant of the Century*, 62. New York, Center for Migration Studies, 1992.

52 Sullivan, *Mother Cabrini*, 62

53 Sullivan, *Mother Cabrini*, 63

54 Sullivan, *Mother Cabrini*, 79

55 Maynard, Theodore. "Under Obedience to Leo." Internet Archive. In *Too Small a World; the Life of Francesca Cabrini*, 120. Bruce Publishing Company, 1945. https://archive.org/details/toosmallworldlif0000mayn/.

56 Maynard, *Too Small a World, 123*

57 Maynard, *Too Small a World, 124*

58 Maynard, *Too Small a World, 120*

59 Maynard, *Too Small a World, 124*

60 Maynard, *Too Small a World, 132*

61 Maynard, *Too Small a World, 133*

62 "Mother Cabrini, the First American Saint of the Catholic Church." *The National Endowment for the Humanities*, www.neh.gov/article/mother-cabrini-first-american-saint-catholic-church. Accessed 10 Mar. 2024.

63 Sullivan, Mary Louise. "For This I Brought You to the United States." *Mother Cabrini: Italian Immigrant of the Century*, 225. New York, Center for Migration Studies, 1992.

64 Sullivan, *Mother Cabrini*, 225

65 Sullivan, *Mother Cabrini*, 226

66 Frances Xavier, Cabrini. "Letter to the Students of the Teachers' College in Rome, February, 1906." PDF. *Travels of Mother Frances Xavier Cabrini: Foundress of the Missionary Sisters of the Sacred Heart of Jesus*, 230-31. Chicago, United States of America: Missionary Sisters of the Sacred Heart of Jesus, 1944. https://archive.org/details/travelsofmotherfrancesxaviercabrini.

67 Galilea, Segundo. "The Faith That Conquers the World (1914-1916)." 1996. In *Weakness, Strength – The Life and Missionary Work of Saint Frances Xavier Cabrini*, 152-53. Claretian Publications, 2004.

68 Sullivan, Mary Louise. "For This I Brought You to the United States." *Mother Cabrini: Italian Immigrant of the Century*, 226. New York, Center for Migration Studies, 1992.

69 Sullivan, *Mother Cabrini*, 227

70 Attaway, Julia. "A Bullet on a Train." Cabrini Shrine NYC, March 5, 2024. https://cabrinishrinenyc.org/a-bullet-on-a-train/.

71 Sullivan, Mary Louise. "For This I Brought You to the United States." *Mother Cabrini: Italian Immigrant of the Century*, 227. New York, Center for Migration Studies, 1992.

72 Maynard, Theodore. "Francesca Rides West." Internet Archive. In *Too Small a World; the Life of Francesca Cabrini*, 264-65. Bruce Publishing Company, 1945. https://archive.org/details/toosmallworldlif0000mayn/.

73 Sullivan, Mary Louise. "For This I Brought You to the United States." *Mother Cabrini: Italian Immigrant of the Century*, 227. New York, Center for Migration Studies, 1992.

74 "Queen of Heaven Orphanage, 4825 Federal Boulevard, Denver. History Colorado." Accessed November 20, 2024. https://www.historycolorado.org/media/10733.

75 Sullivan, Mary Louise. "For This I Brought You to the United States." *Mother Cabrini: Italian Immigrant of the Century*, 228. New York, Center for Migration Studies, 1992.

76 Cabrini, Frances Xavier. "Letter to the Students of the Teachers' College in Rome, February, 1906." *Travels of Mother Frances Xavier Cabrini: Foundress of the Missionary Sisters of the Sacred Heart of Jesus*, 259-60. Chicago, United States of America, The Missionary Sisters of the Sacred Heart of Jesus, https://archive.org/details/travelsofmotherfrancesxaviercabrini.

77 Staff, Denver Catholic. "Letter: The 'Ol' Gully Ranch Homestead,' Mother Cabrini, And." *Denver Catholic*, March 10, 2021. https://denvercatholic.org/letter-the-ol-gully-ranch-homestead-mother-cabrini-and-the-miracle-at-toll-gate-creek/.

78 Sullivan, Mary Louise. "For This I Brought You to the United States." *Mother Cabrini: Italian Immigrant of the Century*, 228. New York, Center for Migration Studies, 1992.

79 Sullivan, *Mother Cabrini*, 229

80   Maynard, Theodore. "Francesca Rides West." Internet Archive. In *Too Small a World; the Life of Francesca Cabrini*, 266. Bruce Publishing Company, 1945. https://archive.org/details/toosmallworldlif0000mayn/.

81   Maynard, *Too Small a World*, 263-64

82   Di Donato, Pietro. "Immigrant Saint: The Life of Mother Cabrini." *Immigrant Saint: The Life of Mother Cabrini*, 154-55. New York, Mcgraw-Hill, 1960. https://archive.org/details/immigrantsaintli00dido/page/136/mode/2up.

83   Cabrini, Frances Xavier. "On the Occasion of the Inauguration of the House in Denver November, 1902." Internet Archive. *Travels of Mother Frances Xavier Cabrini: Foundress of the Missionary Sisters of the Sacred Heart of Jesus*, 234-35. Chicago, United States of America: The Missionary Sisters of the Sacred Heart of Jesus, 1944. https://archive.org/details/travelsofmotherfrancesxaviercabrini/.

84   National Gallery of Art. "Mountain of the Holy Cross." Accessed April 10, 2023. https://www.nga.gov/collection/art-object-page.103590.html.

85   Sullivan, Mary Louise. "Before the Mine Yields Anything." *Mother Cabrini: Italian Immigrant of the Century*, 133. New York, Center for Migration Studies, 1992.

86   Sullivan, *Mother Cabrini, 133*

87   Spuhler, Jaci. "Holy Cross City: The Gold Camp Built on Hope." Eagle County Historical Society, January 30, 2023. https://eaglecountyhistoricalsociety.com/holy-cross-city/.

88   Sullivan, Mary Louise. "Before the Mine Yields Anything." *Mother Cabrini: Italian Immigrant of the Century*, 133. New York, Center for Migration Studies.

89   Cabrini, Frances Xavier. "Cabrini to Dossena, 1710–1711, Mia Figlia Carissima, [Sr. Ignazia Dossena]." In *Cabrini to Dossena*, 95–96. Cabrini University, 1909. Typescript, CRCC

90   Mother Cabrini Shrine org. "The Shrine - Mother Cabrini Shrine." Accessed February 28, 2024. https://mothercabrinishrine.org/the-shrine.

91   Mother Cabrini Shrine org. "The Shrine - Mother Cabrini Shrine." Accessed February 28, 2024. https://mothercabrinishrine.org/the-shrine.

92   Francis, Tommy. Mother Cabrini Shrine, Golden, Colorado, Head of Maintenance, *Historical Shrine Information Interview*. 25 Jan. 2024.

93   Ripatrazone, Nick. "Mother Cabrini, the First American Saint of the Catholic Church." The National Endowment for the Humanities. Accessed March 10, 2024. https://www.neh.gov/article/mother-cabrini-first-american-saint-catholic-church.

94 Mother Cabrini Shrine org. "The Shrine - Mother Cabrini Shrine." Accessed March 12, 2024. https://mothercabrinishrine.org/the-shrine.

95 Mother Cabrini Shrine org. "The Shrine - Mother Cabrini Shrine." Accessed March 12, 2024. https://mothercabrinishrine.org/the-shrine.

96 Sullivan, Mary Louise. "These Past Twenty-five Years, All Is the Work of God." *Mother Cabrini: Italian Immigrant of the Century*, 235-36. New York, Center for Migration Studies, 1992.

97 Ripatrazone, Nick. "Mother Cabrini, the First American Saint of the Catholic Church." The National Endowment for the Humanities. Accessed March 22, 2024. https://www.neh.gov/article/mother-cabrini-first-american-saint-catholic-church.

98 Mother Cabrini Shrine. "Instagram." Accessed March 16, 2024. https://www.instagram.com/p/Czlk47tpwqe/.

99 Francis, Tommy. Mother Cabrini Shrine, Golden, Colorado, Head of Maintenance, *Historical Shrine Information Interview*. 25 Jan. 2024.

100 Francis, Tommy. Mother Cabrini Shrine, Golden, Colorado, Head of Maintenance, *Historical Shrine Information Interview*. January 25, 2024.

101 Francis, Tommy. Mother Cabrini Shrine, Golden, Colorado, Head of Maintenance, *Historical Shrine Information Interview*. January 25, 2024.

102 Mother Cabrini Shrine. "The Shrine – Mother Cabrini Shrine." Accessed February 28, 2024. https://mothercabrinishrine.org/the-shrine.

103 Barbagallo, Sr. Maria. "Free Yourselves And Put On Wings." *Free Yourselves and Put On Wings: A Journey of Cabrinian Spirituality*, 3rd ed., 47, 48, 56. Segraf sri - Secugnago (LO) Italy, 2019.

104 Barbagallo, *Free Yourselves And Put On Wings*, 48

105 Barbagallo, *Free Yourselves And Put On Wings*, 48

106 Barbagallo, *Free Yourselves And Put On Wings*, 56

107 Mother Cabrini Shrine. "The Shrine – Mother Cabrini Shrine." Accessed February 28, 2024. https://mothercabrinishrine.org/the-shrine.

108 Mother Cabrini Shrine org. "The Shrine - Mother Cabrini Shrine." Accessed February 28, 2024. https://mothercabrinishrine.org/the-shrine.

109 Mother Cabrini Shrine. "The Shrine – Mother Cabrini Shrine." Accessed February 28, 2024. https://mothercabrinishrine.org/the-shrine.

110 Francis, Tommy. Mother Cabrini Shrine, Golden, Colorado, Head of Maintenance, *Historical Shrine Information Interview*. May 8, 2024.

111 Francis, Tommy. Mother Cabrini Shrine, Golden, Colorado, Head of Maintenance, *Historical Shrine Information Interview*. May 8, 2024.

112 Mother Cabrini Shrine. "The Shrine – Mother Cabrini Shrine." Accessed February 28, 2024. https://mothercabrinishrine.org/the-shrine.

113 Mother Cabrini Shrine. "The Shrine – Mother Cabrini Shrine." Accessed February 28, 2024. https://mothercabrinishrine.org/the-shrine.

114 Francis, Tommy. Mother Cabrini Shrine, Golden, Colorado, Head of Maintenance, *Historical Shrine Information Interview*. January 25, 2024.

115 Mother Cabrini Shrine. "The Shrine – Mother Cabrini Shrine." Accessed February 28, 2024. https://mothercabrinishrine.org/the-shrine.

116 McEncroe, John. "Mother Cabrini Shrine, Golden, Colorado, Retired Maintenance Worker, Historical Shrine Information Interview." *Historical Information Concerning the Mother Cabrini Shrine, Golden, Colorado*, December 20, 2023.

117 Francis, Tommy. Mother Cabrini Shrine, Golden, Colorado, Head of Maintenance, *Historical Shrine Information Interview*. February 02, 2024.

118 Miceli, Mother Ignatius. "With Faith and Prayer." *Cabrinian Colorado Missions*, 66,76. Boulder, Colorado: D & K Printing, 1996.

119 Miceli, *Cabrinian Colorado Missions*, 76

120 Miceli, *Cabrinian Colorado Missions*, 76

121 Maynard, Theodore. "Francesca Rides West." Internet Archive. *Too Small a World; The Life of Francesca Cabrini*, 302. Bruce Publishing Company, 1945. https://archive.org/details/toosmallworldlif0000mayn/.

122 Maynard, Theodore. "Francesca Rides West." Internet Archive. *Too Small a World; The Life of Francesca Cabrini*, 302-3. Bruce Publishing Company, 1945. https://archive.org/details/toosmallworldlif0000mayn/.

123 Maynard, *Too Small a World*, 303

124 Sullivan, Mary Louise. "We Saw the Beautiful Statue of Liberty." *Mother Cabrini: Italian Immigrant of the Century*, 62. New York: Center for Migration Studies, 1992.

125 Sullivan, *Mother Cabrini*, 62

126 Maynard, Theodore. "The Hope of Retirement." Internet Archive. *Too Small a World; The Life of Francesca Cabrini*, 309. Bruce Publishing Company, 1945. https://archive.org/details/toosmallworldlif0000mayn/.

127 Maynard, *Too Small a World,* 309

128 Sullivan, Mary Louise. "For This I Brought You to the United States." *Mother Cabrini: Italian Immigrant of the Century*, 230. New York: Center for Migration Studies, 1992.

129 Maynard, Theodore. "The Hope of Retirement." Internet Archive. *Too Small a World; The Life of Francesca Cabrini*, 311. Bruce Publishing Company, 1945. https://archive.org/details/toosmallworldlif0000mayn/.

130 Maynard, *Too Small a World,* 311

131 Maynard, *Too Small a World,* 311-312

132 Maynard, *Too Small a World,* 312-313

133 Maynard, *Too Small a World,* 314-317

134 Maynard, Theodore. "Death In Chicago." Internet Archive. *Too Small a World; The Life of Francesca Cabrini*, 318,19. Bruce Publishing Company, 1945. https://archive.org/details/toosmallworldlif0000mayn/.

135 Sabatella, Carmelo. "Mother Cabrini Shrine, Burbank, California, President of the Italian Catholic Federation (ICF), Mother Cabrini Chapel Committee, Historical Shrine Information Interview." *Historical Information Concerning the Mother Cabrini Shrine, Burbank, California,* August 8, 2024.

136 Maynard, *Too Small a World,* 318

137 Maynard, *Too Small a World,* 319

138 Maynard, *Too Small a World,* 320

139 Maynard, *Too Small a World,* 320

140 Maynard, *Too Small a World,* 320-321

141 Maynard, *Too Small a World,* 322

142 Maynard, *Too Small a World,* 323

143 Maynard, *Too Small a World,* 324

144 Maynard, *Too Small a World,* 325

145 Maynard, *Too Small a World,* 325-326

146 Barbagallo, Sr. Maria. "Free Yourselves and Put on Wings." *Free Yourselves and Put On Wings: A Journey of Cabrinian Spirituality,* 3rd ed., 57. Segraf sri - Secugnago (LO) Italy, 2019.

147 Missionary Sisters of the Sacred Heart of Jesus. "Our History." Accessed March 13, 2024. https://www.mothercabrini.org/who-we-are/our-history/.

148 Cabrini University. "01SM_Infant Peter Smith Saved from Blindness by Mother Cabrini's Miracle." Cabrini University. Accessed February 28, 2024. https://cdm17305.contentdm.oclc.org/digital/collection/p17305coll9/id/0/rec/1.

149 Cabrini University. "07SM_Ordination Card and Remembrance of First Solemn Mass of Reverend Peter J. Smith, June 2-3, 1951 (Verso)." Cabrini University. Accessed February 29, 2024. https://cdm17305.contentdm.oclc.org/digital/collection/p17305coll9/id/6/rec/7.

150 Cabrini University. "02SM_Sister Delfina Grazioli Saved from Illness by Mother Cabrini's Miracle." Cabrini University. Accessed February 29, 2024. https://cdm17305.contentdm.oclc.org/digital/collection/p17305coll9/id/3/rec/2.

151 Missionary Sisters of the Sacred Heart of Jesus. "The World Was Too Small." Accessed March 18, 2024. https://www.mothercabrini.org/who-we-are/our-history/the-world-was-too-small/.

152 Francis, Tommy. Mother Cabrini Shrine, Golden, Colorado, Head of Maintenance, *Historical Shrine and Queen of Heaven Information Interview.* February 2, 2024.

Note – I will only be adding one endnote from my interview with Tommy Francis on February 2, 2024, unless a direct quote is used. This will be the case for the remaining interviews I conducted with Tommy. All information received and used here from Tommy Francis is from his recollection and may or may not be accurate. I have also interjected my thoughts and opinion throughout which may not represent Tommy's values, opinions, or beliefs.

153 Francis, Tommy. Mother Cabrini Shrine, Golden, Colorado, Head of Maintenance, *Historical Shrine and Queen of Heaven Information Interview.* February 02, 2024.

154 Miceli, Mother Ignatius. "My Queen of Heaven Girls at the Summer Home." *Cabrinian Colorado Missions,* 128-9. Boulder, Colorado: D & K Printing, 1996.

155 Miceli, *Cabrinian Colorado Missions,* 129-30

156 Miceli, *Cabrinian Colorado Missions,* 130

157 Francis, Tommy. Mother Cabrini Shrine, Golden, Colorado, Head of Maintenance, *Historical Shrine and Queen of Heaven Information Interview.* March 27, 2024.

158 Francis, Tommy. Mother Cabrini Shrine, Golden, Colorado, Head of Maintenance, *Historical Shrine and Queen of Heaven Information Interview.* March 27, 2024.

159 Francis, Tommy. Mother Cabrini Shrine, Golden, Colorado, Head of Maintenance, *Historical Shrine and Queen of Heaven Information Interview.* March 27, 2024.

160 Francis, Tommy. Mother Cabrini Shrine, Golden, Colorado, Head of Maintenance, *Historical Shrine and Queen of Heaven Information Interview.* March 27, 2024.

161 Francis, Tommy. Mother Cabrini Shrine, Golden, Colorado, Head of Maintenance, *Historical Shrine and Queen of Heaven Information Interview.* March 27, 2024.

162 Francis, Tommy. Mother Cabrini Shrine, Golden, Colorado, Head of Maintenance, *Historical Shrine and Queen of Heaven Information Interview.* March 27, 2024.

163 Miceli, Mother Ignatius. "With Faith and Prayer." *Cabrinian Colorado Missions,* 66,76. Boulder, Colorado: D & K Printing, 1996.

164 Francis, Tommy. Mother Cabrini Shrine, Golden, Colorado, Head of Maintenance, *Historical Shrine and Queen of Heaven Information Interview.* March 27, 2024.

165 Francis, Tommy. Mother Cabrini Shrine, Golden, Colorado, Head of Maintenance, *Historical Shrine and Queen of Heaven Information Interview.* March 27, 2024.

166 Mother Cabrini Shrine Staff. "Mother Cabrini Shrine Happy Shrine Staff Saturday." Facebook, March 16, 2024. https://www.facebook.com/photo?fbid=817842657058253&set=a.229905089185349.

167 Francis, Tommy. Mother Cabrini Shrine, Golden, Colorado, Head of Maintenance, *Historical Shrine and Queen of Heaven Information Interview.* March 27, 2024.

168 Francis, Tommy. Mother Cabrini Shrine, Golden, Colorado, Head of Maintenance, *Historical Shrine and Queen of Heaven Information Interview.* May 08, 2024.

169 McEncroe, John. "Mother Cabrini Shrine, Golden, Colorado, Retired Maintenance Worker, Historical Shrine Information Interview." *Historical Information Concerning the Mother Cabrini Shrine, Golden, Colorado*, December 20, 2023.

Note – I will only be adding one endnote from my interview with John McEncroe on December 20, 2023, unless a direct quote is used. All information received and used here from John McEncroe is from his recollection and may or may not be accurate. I have also interjected my thoughts and opinion throughout which may not represent John's values, opinions, or beliefs.

170 Sabatella, Carmelo. "Mother Cabrini Shrine, Burbank, California, President of the Italian Catholic Federation (ICF), Mother Cabrini Chapel Committee, Historical Shrine Information Interview." *Historical Information Concerning the Mother Cabrini Shrine, Burbank, California*, August 8, 2024.

171 Merelli, Tony. "Mother Cabrini Shrine, Golden, Colorado, Mother Cabrini Shrine Volunteer, Retired Denver Water Board Engineer, Historical Denver and Shrine Information Interview." *Historical Information Concerning the City of Denver, Colorado, and the Mother Cabrini Shrine, Golden, Colorado*, December 20, 2023.

Note – I will only be adding one endnote from my interview with Tony Merelli on April 4, 2024, unless a direct quote is used. All information received and used here from Tony Merelli is from his recollection and may or may not be accurate. I have also interjected my thoughts and opinion throughout which may not represent Tony's values, opinions, or beliefs.

172 Merelli, Tony. "Mother Cabrini Shrine, Golden, Colorado, Mother Cabrini Shrine Volunteer, Retired Denver Water Board Engineer, Historical Denver and Shrine Information Interview." *Historical Information Concerning the City of Denver, Colorado, and the Mother Cabrini Shrine, Golden, Colorado*, December 20, 2023.

173 Merelli, Tony. "Mother Cabrini Shrine, Golden, Colorado, Mother Cabrini Shrine Volunteer, Retired Denver Water Board Engineer, Historical Denver and Shrine Information Interview." *Historical Information Concerning the City of Denver, Colorado, and the Mother Cabrini Shrine, Golden, Colorado*, December 20, 2023.

174 Merelli, Tony. "Mother Cabrini Shrine, Golden, Colorado, Mother Cabrini Shrine Volunteer, Retired Denver Water Board Engineer, Historical Denver and Shrine Information Interview." *Historical Information Concerning the City of Denver, Colorado, and the Mother Cabrini Shrine, Golden, Colorado*, December 20, 2023.

175 Zanon, Sr Alice. "Mother Cabrini Shrine, Golden, Colorado, Mother Cabrini Shrine, Missionary Sister of the Sacred Heart of Jesus, Personal life and Shrine Information Interview." *Historical and present Shrine Information,* May 22, 2024.

Note – I will only be adding one endnote from my interview with Sister Alice conducted on May 22, 2024, unless a direct quote is used. All information received and used here from Sister Alice Zanon is from her recollection and may or may not be accurate. I have also interjected my thoughts and opinion throughout which may not represent Sister Alice's values, opinions, or beliefs.

176 Zanon, Sr Alice. "Mother Cabrini Shrine, Golden, Colorado, Mother Cabrini Shrine, Missionary Sister of the Sacred Heart of Jesus, Personal life and Shrine Information Interview." *Historical and present Shrine Information,* May 22, 2024.

177 Zanon, Sr Alice. "Mother Cabrini Shrine, Golden, Colorado, Mother Cabrini Shrine, Missionary Sister of the Sacred Heart of Jesus, Personal life and Shrine Information Interview." *Historical and present Shrine Information,* May 22, 2024.

178 Zanon, Sr Alice. "Mother Cabrini Shrine, Golden, Colorado, Mother Cabrini Shrine, Missionary Sister of the Sacred Heart of Jesus, Personal life and Shrine Information Interview." *Historical and present Shrine Information,* May 22, 2024.

179 Barbagallo, Sr. Maria. ""I Can Do All Things In Him Who Strengthens Me": Losing yourself To Find Yourself In God." *Free Yourselves and Put On Wings: A Journey of Cabrinian Spirituality,* 3rd ed., 140. Segraf sri - Secugnago (LO) Italy, 2019.

180 EWTN Global Catholic Television Network. "Lorica of Saint Patrick | EWTN." Accessed May 24, 2024. https://www.ewtn.com/catholicism/devotions/lorica-of-saint-patrick-349.

181 The National Endowment for the Humanities. "Mother Cabrini, the First American Saint of the Catholic Church." Accessed March 26, 2024. https://www.neh.gov/article/mother-cabrini-first-american-saint-catholic-church.

182 Fenton, Francesca. "Why Is June the Month of the Sacred Heart of Jesus? – EWTN Global Catholic Television Network." Ewtn - Great Britian, June 19, 2022. https://ewtn.co.uk/article-why-is-june-the-month-of-the-sacred-heart-of-jesus/.

183 Fenton, Francesca. "Why Is June the Month of the Sacred Heart of Jesus? – EWTN Global Catholic Television Network." Ewtn - Great Britian, June 19, 2022. https://ewtn.co.uk/article-why-is-june-the-month-of-the-sacred-heart-of-jesus/.

184 Dysautonomia International. "Dysautonomia International: Postural Orthostatic Tachycardia Syndrome (POTS)." Accessed January 4, 2023. http://dysautonomiainternational.org/conditions.php?ID=1.

185 Andersen, Gaby, Patrick Marcinek, Nicole Sulzinger, Peter Schieberle, and Dietmar Krautwurst. "Food Sources and Biomolecular Targets of Tyramine." Nutrition reviews, August 27, 2018. Accessed April 9, 2024. https://doi.org/10.1093/nutrit/nuy036.

186 Cabrini, Frances Xavier, and Patricia Spillane. "A Mysterious Book of Inspirations." *Journals of a Trusting Heart – Retreat Notes of St. Frances Xavier Cabrini (1876-1911)*, 14-15. Claretian Communications Foundation, Inc., 2014.

187 Segal, Dayva. "Vagus Nerve: What to Know." WebMD, October 6, 2022. Accessed April 4, 2024. https://www.webmd.com/brain/vagus-nerve-what-to-know.

188 Nhgri. "About Hemochromatosis." National Human Genome Research Institute.gov, March 9, 2019. https://www.genome.gov/Genetic-Disorders/Hereditary-Hemochromatosis.

189 US EPA. "Health Effects of Exposures to Mercury | US EPA," March 15, 2024. Accessed April 12, 2024. https://www.epa.gov/mercury/health-effects-exposures-mercury.

190 Stony Brook University. "How Does Mercury Get into Fish? | The Gelfond Fund for Mercury Research and Outreach." Accessed April 13, 2024. https://www.stonybrook.edu/commcms/gelfond/mercury_and_fish/mercury_in_fish.php.

191 Dillon, Patrick. "Team 3 Health | Healthcare, Environmental Wellness, Heavy Metals, Nutrition, Outdoors, Exercise." Accessed April 14, 2024. https://team3health.com/.

192 e-Catholic 2000. "The Secret of Mary by Saint Louis de Montfort." Accessed October 23, 2023. https://www.ecatholic2000.com/montfort/secret/secret.shtml.

193 insight856. "Mysteries of Holy Rosary 4 of 4 (FREE Audiobook)." Video. *YouTube*, September 5, 2015. Accessed October 29, 2023. https://www.youtube.com/watch?v=9JJFxDohpsU.

194 V-Catholic. "St. Faustina, Our Lady's Prophecy, and the 'Great Sign' of Mercy - Vcatholic." Vcatholic, March 26, 2021. Accessed January 5, 2023. https://v-catholic.com/marian-messages/st-faustina-our-ladys-prophecy-and-the-great-sign-of-mercy/.

195 Sabatella, Carmelo. "Mother Cabrini Shrine, Burbank, California, President of the Italian Catholic Federation (ICF), Mother Cabrini Chapel Committee, Historical Shrine Information Interview." *Historical Information Concerning the Mother Cabrini Shrine, Burbank, California*, August 8, 2024.

196 Dillon, Patrick. "Patrick Dillon." Facebook. Accessed May 10, 2024. https://www.facebook.com/profile.php?id=100017309984734.

197 Cabrini, Frances Xavier, and Patricia Spillane. "A Mysterious Book of Inspirations." *Journals of a Trusting Heart – Retreat Notes of St. Frances Xavier Cabrini (1876-1911),* 9-10. Claretian Communications Foundation, Inc., 2014.

198 Cabrini and Spillane, *Journals of a Trusting Heart,* 11

199 Barbagallo, Sr. Maria. "Ardently, Swiftly." *Free Yourselves and Put On Wings: A Journey of Cabrinian Spirituality,* 3rd ed., 101. Segraf sri - Secugnago (LO) Italy, 2019.

200 Vatican.va. "To the Missionaries of the Sacred Heart of Jesus (July 4, 2002) | John Paul II," June 23, 2002. Accessed March 6, 2024. https://www.vatican.va/content/john-paul-ii/en/speeches/2002/july/documents/hf_jp-ii_spe_20020704_missionarie-sacro-cuore.html.

201 Frances Xavier, Cabrini. "Panama to Buenos Aires – October, 1895." PDF. In *Travels of Mother Frances Xavier Cabrini: Foundress of the Missionary Sisters of the Sacred Heart of Jesus,* 138–39. Chicago, United States of America: Missionary Sisters of the Sacred Heart of Jesus, 1944. https://archive.org/details/travelsofmotherfrancesxaviercabrini.

202 Cabrini, *Travels of Mother Frances Xavier Cabrini,* 99-100

203 Frances Xavier, Cabrini. "Panama to Buenos Aires – October, 1895." PDF. In *Travels of Mother Frances Xavier Cabrini: Foundress of the Missionary Sisters of the Sacred Heart of Jesus,* 138–39. Chicago, United States of America: Missionary Sisters of the Sacred Heart of Jesus, 1944. https://archive.org/details/travelsofmotherfrancesxaviercabrini..

204 Cabrini, Frances Xavier, and Patricia Spillane. "A Mysterious Book of Inspirations." In *Journals of a Trusting Heart – Retreat Notes of St. Frances Xavier Cabrini (1876-1911),* 15–16. Claretian Communications Foundation, Inc., 2014.

205 Cabrini, Frances Xavier, and Patricia Spillane. "My Retreat for my birthday, July, 1901, Buenos Aires." *Journals of a Trusting Heart – Retreat Notes of St. Frances Xavier Cabrini (1876-1911),* 168-69. Claretian Communications Foundation, Inc., 2014.

206 Catholic Culture. "Liturgical Year : Prayers : Ave Maris Stella (Hail Star of the Sea)." Accessed April 15, 2024. https://www.catholicculture.org/culture/liturgicalyear/prayers/view.cfm?id=882.

207 Frances Xavier, Cabrini. "Second Voyage to New York–April, 1890." PDF. *Travels of Mother Frances Xavier Cabrini: Foundress of the Missionary Sisters of the Sacred Heart of Jesus,* 10. Chicago, United States of America, Missionary Sisters of the Sacred Heart of Jesus, 1944, https://archive.org/details/travelsofmotherfrancesxaviercabrini.

208 DaughtersofMaryPress. "Ave Maris Stella - Daughters of Mary, Mother of Our Savior." Video. *YouTube*, January 1, 2023. https://www.youtube.com/watch?v=069OCfXLNgk.

209 Cabrini, Frances Xavier, and Patricia Spillane. "My Retreat according to the Spiritual Exercises with the Sisters in New York Christmas, 1894 to January 1, 1895." *Journals of a Trusting Heart – Retreat Notes of St. Frances Xavier Cabrini (1876-1911)*, 129. Claretian Communications Foundation, Inc., 2014.

210 Missionary Sisters of the Sacred Heart of Jesus. "What We Do." Accessed April 24, 2024. https://www.mothercabrini.org/what-we-do/.

211 NOAA's National Weather Service. "What Causes Halos, Sundogs and Sun Pillars?" Accessed April 10, 2024. https://www.weather.gov/arx/why_halos_sundogs_pillars.

212 Kuthunur, Sharmila. "We May Have Just Witnessed Some of the Strongest Auroras in 500 Years." *Space.Com*, May 20, 2024. https://www.space.com/solar-storms-may-2024-strongest-auroras-500-years.

213 Maynard, Theodore. "Chapter One – a Child at Play." Internet Archive. In *Too Small a World; the Life of Francesca Cabrini*, 42. Bruce Publishing Company, 1945. https://archive.org/details/toosmallworldlif0000mayn/.

214 Sheen, Fulton J. "Sanctifying the Moment." In *Ex Libris: Fulton J. Sheen*, edited by Alexis Walkenstein, 33. 2018. Boston, United States of America: Pauline Books & Media, n.d.

215 Cabrini, Frances Xavier, and Patricia Spillane. "My Retreat according to the Spiritual Exercises Our Lady of Grace, Codogno, September 24, 1885." *Journals of a Trusting Heart – Retreat Notes of St. Frances Xavier Cabrini (1876-1911)*, 69. Claretian Communications Foundation, Inc., 2014.

216 Cabrini, Frances Xavier, and Patricia Spillane. "My Retreat according to the Spiritual Exercises with the Sisters in New York Christmas, 1894 to January 1, 1895," *Journals of a Trusting Heart – Retreat Notes of St. Frances Xavier Cabrini (1876-1911)*,128-29. Claretian Communications Foundation, Inc., 2014.

217 Cabrini and Spillane, *Journals of a Trusting*, 128-29

218 Frances Xavier, Cabrini. "Letter to the Students of the Teachers College in Rome, February, 1906." PDF. *Travels of Mother Frances Xavier Cabrini: Foundress of the Missionary Sisters of the Sacred Heart of Jesus*, 267-268. Chicago, United States of America: Missionary Sisters of the Sacred Heart of Jesus, 1944. https://archive.org/details/travelsofmotherfrancesxaviercabrini

219 Frances Xavier, Cabrini. "Letter to the Students of the Teachers College in Rome, February, 1906." PDF. *Travels of Mother Frances Xavier Cabrini: Foundress of the Missionary Sisters of the Sacred Heart of Jesus*, 263-65. Chicago, United States of America: Missionary Sisters of the Sacred Heart of Jesus, 1944. https://archive.org/details/travelsofmotherfrancesxaviercabrini.

220 Nassar, Angie. "What Is a Monstrance? - Catholic World Mission." Catholic World Mission, December 7, 2023. https://catholicworldmission.org/what-is-a-monstrance/.

221 Shrine of the True Cross. "Precious Relic of the True Cross." Accessed June 15, 2024. https://truecrosschurch.org/relic-of-the-true-cross.

222 Lager, Fr. John. "Mother Cabrini Shrine, Golden, Colorado, Mother Cabrini Shrine, OFM Cap, Personal life and Shrine Information phone interview." *Historical and present Shrine Information*, June 19, 2024.

Note – I added one endnote from my interview with Father John Lager conducted on June 19, 2024, to cover all contents of the interview. All information received and used here from Father John is from his recollection and may or may not be accurate. I have also interjected my thoughts and opinion throughout which may not represent Father John's values, opinions, or beliefs.

223 Barbagallo, Sr. Maria. "'Ardently, Swiftly." *Free Yourselves and Put On Wings: A Journey of Cabrinian Spirituality*, 3rd ed., 108-9. Segraf sri - Secugnago (LO) Italy, 2019.

224 Cabrini, Frances Xavier, and Patricia Spillane. "My Retreat According to the Spiritual Exercises Beginning on the Feast of the Assumption of my dear Mother Mary August 15, 1893, Codogno." *Journals of a Trusting Heart – Retreat Notes of St. Frances Xavier Cabrini (1876-1911)*, 116. Claretian Communications Foundation, Inc., 2014.

Made in the USA
Las Vegas, NV
23 September 2024

95687449R00193